WORLDS OF PRINT

PRINT NETWORKS
PREVIOUS TITLES IN THE SERIES

WORLDS OF PRINT

DIVERSITY IN THE BOOK TRADE

Edited by
John Hinks
and Catherine Armstrong

OAK KNOLL PRESS
&
THE BRITISH LIBRARY
2006

© The Contributors 2006

First published in 2006 by
Oak Knoll Press
310 Delaware Street
New Castle
DE 19720
and
The British Library
96 Euston Road
London NW1 2DB

Cataloguing in Publication Data
A CIP Record for this book is available
from both the British Library and
the Library of Congress

ISBN 1-58456-191-2 (Oak Knoll)
ISBN 0-7123-4937-5 (BL)

Typeset by Ella Whitehead
Jacket design by Wil Reiner
Printed in England by St Edmundsbury Press, Bury St Edmunds

Contents

Book Trade People

Methodology of Book History

Introduction

THIS VOLUME EMERGES out of the British Book Trade History Conference of 2004, which was held at the University of Edinburgh and generously supported by their Centre for the History of the Book. It is the eighth in the successful *Print Networks* series, originally founded by Peter Isaac, celebrating the research of scholars, book trade practitioners and enthusiasts in the field of the history of the book trade. This volume represents a new departure for the series, in that it is showcasing for the first time papers in significant numbers concerning printing, publishing and bookselling in the former British colonies. However, the hallmark of the series has been retained too, with several papers reflecting interests in regions close to that in which the conference was held. It is the geographical focus, ranging from the local to the international, that became the overarching theme of this volume's papers, and hence the title: *Worlds of Print*.

This series has always attempted to avoid too strong a focus on the trade in London, preferring to bring the trade in and to the provinces to centre stage. The current volume represents a natural progression, developing that aim and expanding its remit to explore the book trade between metropolis and colony. The people who created, distributed and consumed books are naturally the concern of this volume, but the aim of the editors was not to examine these men and women in isolation but rather as part of the local, regional, national and international networks to which they belonged at various points in their careers. Of course these connections were sometimes fraught with tensions, as Sondra Miley Cooney shows in her piece on the relationship between the Chambers firm and their London contact W. S. Orr. But other papers reveal fruitful partnerships built between book traders producing all sorts of printed artefacts, from newspapers to novels, from pamphlets to encyclopaedias.

The papers presented to the conference were of such a high standard that the editors have chosen to include sixteen in this volume. Because of this number, for the first time in this series the papers are presented in thematic sections: firstly, four papers on Colonial Connections; secondly, four papers on the Scottish Book Trade; thirdly, seven papers on Book Trade People. The last section contains David Gants's paper on new approaches to the methodology of book history. These papers present a wide chronological range from the late fifteenth to the late twentieth centuries, each revealing a snapshot of the diverse and fluid worlds of print. The first paper, by Catherine Armstrong, examines the contrasting responses of printers and booksellers in Edinburgh and London to the disastrous Darien expeditions of the late 1690s. These journeys, an attempt by Scotland to rival England's colonial success, ended in financial and human tragedy, and printers and booksellers used pamphlets and newspapers to spread the word to eager readers. However, these were dangerous times for printers caught up in the political rows fermenting in both capital cities linking the failure of the Darien expedition to the Jacobite cause. The other three papers in this section focus on the connections between book trade practitioners in Britain and in her antipodean colonies. Noel Waite describes how the most significant printing and bookselling firm in New Zealand, Whitcombe and Tombs, should be seen as a window into the philosophies of education and religious conversion that drove the Empire in the nineteenth century. Waite explores how the partners established their business and then interprets the significance of their choice of books for publication and their commercial and philanthropic practices.

Staying in the nineteenth century, but migrating to Melbourne for the next paper, again focusing on the importance of 'location' for book trade historians. Wallace Kirsop highlights a unique and fascinating bookshop, Cole's Arcade, a distinctly popular bookshop, reflecting the development of the city of Melbourne itself (known as the 'Chicago of the south') in that readers were encouraged to browse for as long as they wanted. The act of reading and the enjoyment of this act in an unusual building is central to understanding E. W. Cole's significance, as was his eccentric nature. For Nicole Matthews, also examining the Australian market, books themselves form the object of investigation, as opposed to the people who created them or the places in which they were made or sold. Her paper describes the popular fiction sold by Collins in the mid-twentieth century and the complex marketing strategies employed by the company when selling material to a specifically Australian readership. Matthews believes that the different book jackets used from those sold in Europe show that Collins thought there was a uniquely Australian taste for books. This marketing practice was ahead of its time and shows us the direction in which many other companies would follow in the later decades of the century.

The second group of essays discuss different aspects of the Scottish book trade, starting with Scotland's earliest printers, Chepman and Myllar, whose work and significance in the context of the broader history of fifteenth-century printing is explored by Lucy Lewis. Moving from a period hitherto neglected by historians, the next paper examines the printing activities of another shadowy group, the Scottish freemasons. Although the connection between freemasonry and the book trade has long been acknowledged by academics in this field, Stephen Brown's work is ground-breaking because it reveals the lack of Scottish eighteenth-century printed texts about freemasonry. He offers explanations for this, based on the intentions of the personnel in the book trade at that time. The remote north of Scotland is the next geographical location to be put under the microscope in Jane Thomas's paper on the circulating libraries of Elgin. The history of libraries, both public and private, has always been a central part of book history in general and these volumes in particular. Thomas surveys the lives of several of Elgin's booksellers in the late eighteenth and nineteenth centuries, showing how influential these men were in creating a taste among the local populace for printed literature. Simultaneously, in Edinburgh, David Steuart was collecting, writing, printing and selling books, many of which he had acquired through his travels and business connections in Europe. Brian Hillyard examines Steuart's relationship with the Italian typographer Giambattista Bodoni through the archive of their letters to each other, seventeen in all, written between 1791 and 1799. Hillyard shows that, although Steuart was a lover of fine books, and always looking out for opportunities to make money, in the end he was not able to capitalize on his relationship with Bodoni and sell his work successfully in Scotland. Finally in this section, turning again to Australia, Caroline Viera Jones's paper explores the relationship between Scottish publisher George Robertson and the colonial book trade, with special reference to Robertson's *The Australian Encyclopaedia* of 1925–26. His editing of the encyclopaedia reflected not only a nascent Australian nationalism, but also Robertson's Scottish roots and Jones argues that this combination was significant in determining how the readers of the encyclopaedia saw themselves and their country.

The theme of libraries is revisited in the first essay of the third section: Jane Francis's work on schoolmasters' libraries of the seventeenth and eighteenth centuries. Her work on these private collections is made all the more fascinating by the fact that the libraries themselves are still housed in their original venues today, thus giving Francis's analysis of the means and motives for collection an added dimension of understanding the space within which these books were displayed and used. Giles Bergel focuses not on the consumers of eighteenth-century print culture, but the producers of it, and one company in particular, the Dicey Press of Northampton and London. As with many book trade practitioners, the firm had a sideline in patent medicines, and these two trades encouraged each other. Bergel's paper exemplifies the sorts of trade links between metropolis and province that were emerging during this period as the means of communication improved and literacy increased. David Shaw's work also illuminates book trade practices in a British locality, namely East Kent. His bookseller, James Abree, also sold patent medicines, and distributed newspapers, in fact the most profitable arm of his business. From surviving records it has been possible for Shaw to trace the networks of communication and distribution through which the *Kentish Gazette* and the *Kentish Post* reached their readership. Surprisingly these local newspapers had a very lucrative London readership as well. The connections between publishers and their agents are not always productive or friendly, as shown in Sondra Miley Cooney's paper on William Somerville Orr and the Chambers firm. From the 1830s onwards Orr was instructed to sell reprints of Chambers's *Journal* from his shop in the city of London. But by the 1850s, Orr was facing bankruptcy, unable to repay the substantial debts he had incurred with Chambers, with a great deal of bitterness on both sides. Frederick Nesta describes another book trading relationship that could often be stormy, that between publisher and novelist. He surveys the business connection between author George Gissing and his publisher Smith, Elder & Co. Nesta examines the negotiations that took place over the format of the novels, the number to be printed and, of course, the financial arrangements between the two parties. This paper shows how difficult it was during the later nineteenth century for an author to make any sort of profit at all from his published works. Finally, Michael Powell's work on the early twentieth-century Daisy Bank Press of Gorton near Manchester – in Powell's words 'a minor provincial publisher' – not only reveals a great deal about the lives of founder Jesse Pemberton and his heirs, but also illuminates the world of the consumer of Victorian and Edwardian cheap print. The books produced by Daisy Bank, a combination of escapism and 'how to' tracts with fancy colourful covers, had a direct appeal for the better-educated working classes of Lancashire. It is this combination of concern for the motives and experiences of book traders with the contextual and geographical locations in which they operated that epitomizes this *Print Networks* volume.

Catherine Armstrong

Contributors

Catherine Armstrong was awarded her PhD from the University of Warwick in July 2004 on the topic of Representations of 'Place' and 'Potential' in North American Travel Literature 1607–1660. She is currently working as a seminar tutor at the University of Warwick.

Giles Bergel was one of the *Print Networks* conference fellows for 2004 and is Visiting Lecturer and Research Assistant at Royal Holloway, University of London.

Stephen Brown is the Master of Champlain College at Trent University in Ontario and the 3M Fellow in the Department of English. The author of over fifty articles and book chapters and editor of the manuscripts of the Scottish eighteenth-century printer, William Smellie, he is currently engaged as co-editor of volume two of the Edinburgh History of the Book in Scotland.

Jane Francis spent almost her entire career in industrial librarianship, following postgraduate training in America. Parental influence (her father spent a lifetime in the British Museum, in the Department of Printed Books, before becoming Director and Principal Librarian) ensured an interest and involvement in historical bibliography.

David Gants is Associate Professor of English and Canada Research Chair in Humanities Computing at the University of New Brunswick. He publishes on bibliographical, textual, and technological matters, and is the Electronic Editor of the Cambridge Edition of the Works of Ben Jonson. He is also director of the Early English Booktrade Database project, which seeks to describe, quantify, and classify every book in the STC period.

Brian Hillyard joined the staff of the National Library of Scotland as a rare books curator in 1977 and is now Rare Book Collections Manager. His research into David Steuart's book-trade activities dates backs to the early 1980s when he investigated the provenance of the National Library's copy of the Gutenberg Bible, which had been purchased from Steuart.

John Hinks is an Honorary Fellow at the Centre for Urban History, University of Leicester, where he is researching networks and communities in the British book trade. At the University of Birmingham he is an Honorary Research Fellow in the Department of English, where he edits the British Book Trade Index (www.bbti.bham.ac.uk) and teaches on the MA Text and Book, and a Visiting Lecturer in the Department of Modern History, where he teaches early modern cultural history.

Caroline Viera Jones is Honorary Fellow in the Department of English, University of Melbourne. She is editor of the *Journal of the Sydney Society for Scottish History* and a book, loosely based on her article, is forthcoming.

Wallace Kirsop is Honorary Professorial Fellow in French Studies at Monash University and General Editor of *A History of the Book in Australia*.

Lucy Lewis completed her doctoral thesis in 2000 at London University on 'British Boethianism 1380–1486'. She is now based at Cambridge University Library.

Nicole Matthews teaches media and cultural studies at Liverpool John Moores University. In addition to her book *Comic Politics* (Manchester University Press), she has published on autobiography in the media and popular genres of film, television and literature.

Sondra Miley Cooney is Associate Professor Emerita of English at Kent State University. Her research is concerned with the W. & R. Chambers publishing firm from its founding in 1832 to the publication of *Chambers's Encyclopaedia* during the years 1860–1868. She is currently working on a biography of Robert Chambers, one of the firm's founders.

Frederick Nesta is University Librarian and Chief Information Officer, Lingnan University, Hong Kong, China, and a postgraduate student in the Department of Information Studies, University of Wales, Aberystwyth.

Michael Powell is Librarian of Chetham's Library Manchester. He has published a number of papers in previous *Print Networks* volumes on aspects of the book trade in Manchester.

David Shaw is Secretary of the Consortium of European Research Libraries and was President of the Bibliographical Society (2002–2004). His main area of research is European printing in the fifteenth and sixteenth centuries but he has had a long interest in the provincial book trade in eighteenth-century England, particularly in Kent. He was the Editor-in-Chief of the *Cathedral Libraries Catalogue* (union catalogue of books printed to 1700) and is currently preparing a typographical catalogue of the British Library's books printed in France between 1510 and 1520.

Jane Thomas was one of the *Print Networks* conference fellows for 2004. She has degrees in history, Scottish history and information and library studies. She works as an independent scholar and as a librarian, in Elgin, Moray.

Noel Waite is a Lecturer in Design Studies at the University of Otago. He has been involved with the History of Print Culture in New Zealand project since its inception in 1995 and has contributed to *Book & Print in New Zealand* (1997) and *A Book in the Hand: Essays on the History of the Book in New Zealand* (2000).

'A Just and Modest Vindication': Comparing the Responses of the Scottish and English Book Trades to the Darien Scheme, 1698–1700

CATHERINE ARMSTRONG

THE DARIEN SCHEME of the late seventeenth century has variously been described as the most ambitious and the most disastrous of the early colonial enterprises. By attempting to boost Scotland's finances and bring her economic success in trade comparable to that of her neighbour to the south, the Company of Scotland Trading to Africa and the Indies not only lost many people their fortunes and two thousand others their lives but, some historians say, led to the weakening of Scotland and finally the Act of Union itself.[1] The fateful expeditions to Darien, a small area in Central America in what is now Panama, took place in the atmosphere of Jacobite unrest following the arrival of William III in London. Several of the authors who wrote about the effect of the failed expedition on the Scottish people had been involved first in Monmouth's failed rebellion of the mid-1680s and then in helping to bring William to the throne a few years later. The voyages must also be placed in the context of the growing English ambition in North America and the Caribbean. In the early years of the seventeenth century England had hoped to emulate her more successful rival, Spain, in acquiring colonies in the New World that would provide both wealth and luxury commodities. This drove the English to settle first Virginia and then New England which, although not bringing in the treasures of gold and silver acquired by the Spanish, had by the end of the century provided the nation with the basis of substantial mercantile empire. The desire was also present in Scotland to settle an overseas trade colony and emphasize her independence, both political and financial.

Turning to the expeditions, the story of these is well known and has been explored fully by historians from the mid-nineteenth century onwards. In July 1698 five ships sailed from Leith carrying over one thousand migrants many of

---

1 For example, recent historical analyses have included D. Armitage, 'Making the Empire British', *Past and Present*, vol. 155 (May 1997), pp. 34–63; M. Ibeji, 'The Darien Venture', BBC History Online Website:
<www.bbc.co.uk/history/state/nations/scotland_darien_print.html> [10 July 2004].

whom were starving highlanders, the organizer of the enterprise, William Paterson, and an unopened package revealing their destination. Paterson had raised a huge amount of money to support the voyage with many investors each putting in thousands of pounds; with £500,000 his company's coffers contained around half of Scotland's available national capital. He had chosen Darien because of the stories of William Dampier and Lionel Wafer who were what Victorian commentators grandly called 'buccaneers' – explorers and raiders flying the English flag around the globe and taking the opportunity to out-sail and out-trade the Spanish and French whenever they could. Paterson, the organizer of the Scots venture, had met Lionel Wafer who told him of the fertile lands, the friendly Indians and most significantly the unclaimed territory that would await settlers in Darien. The area was also thought to be the key to navigation to China and Japan and the riches that awaited there; this was true but would not be fully realized until the completion of the Panama canal in the twentieth century.

Of course, the reality of Darien was far from this fabled land of plenty. While the natives did give the settlers some support, bringing them food when they were most desperate, the hot and wet climate brought crippling disease to the settlement before there had barely been chance to fortify it. Paterson's wife died and after that he lost faith in the venture. It did not help that in Spring of 1699 the English ordered colonists in Jamaica and North America not to provide the Scottish settlers with any provisions, thus cutting off an important source of food and of commodities for trade with the natives. By March 1699 settlers were dying at the rate of ten per day, and the survivors abandoned New Edinburgh and Fort St Andrews limping home via Jamaica, still more dying on the way.

The second wave of settlers had no idea of this tragic turn of events and three more ships, carrying 1300 more migrants left in August 1699, soon to be followed by five more relief ships from Leith. Arriving in Darien to find it abandoned and battered by storms, they set out to try to rebuild the shattered colony but once again disease led to a breakdown in law and order and many lucky colonists escaped to Jamaica and the North American mainland rather than stay in Darien. Tension broke out in the colony as the pious Presbyterian ministers accused the demoralized settlers of immorality and depravity, even as they lay dying. This second colony was tormented by attacks from the Spaniards at nearby Porto Bello, who claimed the area as their own, and Darien was finally surrendered to the Spanish in April 1700. Two hundred and fifty of the Scottish survivors, weakened by hunger and disease, died on the final voyage home.

This unmitigated disaster in the history of empire building has surprisingly caught the imagination of very few historians over the years, despite a wealth of documentary evidence illuminating the period. In the mid-nineteenth century the idea emerged of the possibility of a canal in Panama which traders to the East might traverse with their valuable wares, although the canal itself was not completed until 1914. In his 1853 book *The Isthmus of Darien Ship Canal*, Dr Cullen held a romantic view of the Scots enterprise, that they were defeated not by incompetence and natural causes but by the jealousy of William III who, influenced by 'Spanish and Dutch intrigues', starved the Scottish colonists out of Darien by refusing to trade with them.[2] Cullen also referred to the historical novel written about the expedition the previous year by Bartholomew Elliott Warburton, the Irish novelist who himself tragically died on his way to Panama. Subsequently Darien received some attention from scholars of both Scottish history and the history of the Caribbean, including Francis Hart Russell in the 1930s who edited and published many of the most significant letters relating to the enterprise.[3] John Prebble has written many books about the Darien Scheme, bringing it to the attention of a new generation of readers, but his own historical scholarship has been criticized by others who claim that it once again overly romanticizes the enterprise. In recent years David Armitage has used the Darien story as part of his attempt to write a history of the entire Atlantic world, placing the Scots' ambitions to build an American empire in the context of the power relations between England and Scotland as well as the transatlantic trading networks.[4]

I believe these various authors have neglected a very significant aspect of the Darien story. The way that contemporary commentators in England and Scotland tried to understand and interpret the unfolding tragedy in print has largely been ignored, in favour of analyses of the vast archive of company papers and manuscript letters and diaries. The nightmare of the failed enterprise was broadcast to the literate public in London, Edinburgh, Glasgow and Dublin using seven different genres of print. Unlike today the authors were not the most significant contributors to the output of information; booksellers and printers were also incredibly important, as shown when the King attempted to censor some of this material. Both booksellers and printers in this period could also act as publishers: funding and promoting the distribution of the pamphlet or newspaper.

The first genre of printed material to emerge carrying information about Darien was the descriptions of the country by explorers and early settlers. These were usually based on the format of the promotional literature and travel narratives that had emanated from English pens following, first, the exploration, and

---

2   Dr Cullen, *Isthmus of Darien Ship Canal with a Full History of the Scotch Colony of Darien* (London, 1853), p. 48.

3   F. Russell Hart, *The Disaster at Darien* (London, 1930).

4   Armitage, 'Making the Empire British'.

then the settlement of Virginia, nearly one hundred years previously. These works were often large and expensive, seeming to be the sort of book displayed in a library to enhance the prestige of the owner. Once the Scottish settlement had been established, newspapers eagerly took up the exciting story and they form the second printed genre. News often reached the paper's offices by word of mouth or from a manuscript letter and the information was hurriedly included in the latest edition. The amount of information and analysis was very limited. Even the *Edinburgh Gazette* was usually more concerned with political news from Europe than the comings and goings of the Darien Company, although there was a brief mention of Darien in over half of the issues published during the duration of the settlement. The *Gazette* appears to have been used by the Company on a regular basis to place advertisements for interested migrants to join the expedition, or to inform sailors when the ships in the harbour would leave and of their rates of pay. Once news had reached Scotland of the successful arrival of the first fleet at Darien (it appeared in the *Gazette* on 6 March 1699), poems began to appear praising the heroism and bravery of those first Scottish pioneers. Poems were written by both ladies and gentlemen, in English and Latin, and printed during those first early months of settlement. Not all poetry written about Darien sang the praises of those migrants risking their lives to make Scotland's fortune. A satirical poem, possibly a ballad intended to be sung, appeared early in 1700 in London ridiculing the Scots for having ambitions beyond their capability. The song characterized the nation as greedy 'pedlars' who were trying to become 'merchants'.[5]

The fifth and sixth categories of print culture are the pamphlets that formed the central part of the debate over the causes of the failure of the Darien scheme. The plethora of polemical leaflets is separated into two very broad groups, those that were pro-Scottish and those that were pro-English. As explained more fully below, the pro-Scottish offerings expressed the opinion that the Scots were justified in settling Darien because the natives were friendly and independent, that is that the land had not previously been settled by the Spanish. These pamphlets also claimed that the English, and even William III himself, had been wrong to prevent the English Caribbean and North American settlements from trading with the Scottish colony. Many authors wrote in direct opposition to these arguments, forming a genre of print that I refer to as the pro-English pamphlets. These were not always written by Englishmen opposed to the entire scheme but they argued that Scotland had been wrong to settle Darien in particular because it was possessed by the Spanish. These pamphlets also claimed that the Scottish settlement had failed because of the

---

5 *Caledonia, or the Pedlar Turn'd Merchant: A Tragi-Comedy as was Acted by His Majesties Subjects in Scotland in the King of Spain's Province at Darien* (London, 1700).

incompetence and over-ambition of the Company's leaders. Finally the last category of print culture that permeated the Scottish and English bookshops was of memoirs of the settlers published a few years after the collapse of the colony. The most famous of these were the memoirs of Francis Borland, a minister who sailed with the second wave of migrants and whose memoirs were written in manuscript form immediately after his return and then published in 1715.[6] This genre of print encompassed all the previous categories, as men such as Borland were able to respond to the early descriptive promotional material, to the romanticising or satirical poetry and to the vitriolic pamphlet debates of 1699–1700. After Borland's memoirs were reprinted in the 1770s in Glasgow, possibly in response to the British North American colonies' bid for independence, little was heard of the history of the Darien scheme until the middle of the nineteenth century.

So, how can we relate these various styles of print and the different stories that they told to the history of the printing and bookselling trades in both England and Scotland, and indeed Dublin, where printers also became embroiled in the controversy over books about Darien? This flurry of printing activity took place a few decades before the world of print culture was really opened up because of the rapidly expanding book production industry and the growth in literacy that accompanied it in the mid to late eighteenth century. By the time of the Darien disaster, printing and bookselling had flourished in both London and Edinburgh for almost two centuries and in Glasgow for over fifty years.[7] In 1695, the same year that the Scottish Company received its charter to trade and settle overseas, the printing trade was revolutionized by a change in the licensing laws that allowed the proliferation of the print medium outside London. Local newspapers such as the *Edinburgh Gazette* quickly began printing, just in time to report the exciting and then tragic news from Darien. These newspapers worked alongside existing forms of print such as the pamphlet and the broadside to keep an eager public informed; many authors such as George Ridpath, the Whig journalist vehemently opposed to union with England, worked on newspapers, his notorious *Flying Post*, and pamphlet literature. Printers too became involved in the production of newspapers and other material about Darien, the prime example being James Watson, the first printer of the *Edinburgh Gazette*, who also infamously printed *Scotlands Grievances Relating to Darien* in 1700. As can be expected, booksellers not only took advantage of the public's interest in pamphlet news about the colony but also distributed the newspapers as well. John Vallange was the main seller of the

---

6   F. Borland, *The History of Darien by the Rev. Mr. Francis Borland ... written mostly while the author was in the American Regions* (Glasgow, 1779).

7   See the Scottish Print Archival Trust website for more information: <www.scottishprintarchive.org/history.html>.

Gazette when, after the first few months of production, it stopped being hawked on street corners. He proudly held a complete run of back issues for customers to browse through and make purchases from, so obviously at this stage the *Gazette* was not considered ephemeral. Vallange also sold elaborate maps of the Darien region at the considerable price of eighteen shillings apiece, although the standard price for one of his smaller pamphlets seems to have been seven pence.[8] In fact the price of one of Vallange's earliest pamphlets, *A Short Account from and Description of Darien*, justified its price of seven pence by arguing that much of the material contained within had been distilled from accounts of the journey of William Dampier and Lionel Wafer that had already been published. However, those books were very large and expensive so presumably the anonymous author of *A Short Account* and Vallange himself thought that a cheaper version would sell very well to a different audience especially in the light of renewed interest in the region.[9] Vallange was able to place an advertisement in the *Gazette,* not only for the back issues of that newspaper but also for his pamphlet stock relating to Darien, thus showing the value of newspaper advertising at this time in bringing more custom to his shop 'on the north side of the street, a little above the cross'.[10]

As mentioned previously, the *Gazette* acquired much of its news of Darien through word of mouth, from letters sent to correspondents and from other newspapers in London. For example the first mention of Darien, in the paper's third issue, contained information from a Glasgow merchant's son living in Jamaica who claimed that the Scots had arrived safely and were being well treated by the natives. A few weeks later when news filtered through of the death toll of seventy on the voyage to Darien the newspaper paid one hundred guineas in gold to the gentleman who brought them news of the tragedy.[11] Perhaps even in those early days the promoters of the newspaper realised that the market for bad news often outstrips that for positive information. In spite of the windfall that a perceptive author, printer or bookseller might expect to make from the unfolding events in Darien, there was a darker side to the experience of printers during this period. This is alluded to in the 'errata' section of *Scotlands Grievances,* a notorious pro-Scottish pamphlet printed in Edinburgh in 1700 in which it was written that 'it should not be wondered at that many faults should escape the press in those few sheets when all must be

---

8   *The Edinburgh Gazette,* 11 (3–6 April 1699).

9   *A Short Account from and Description of Darien* ... (Edinburgh, 1699), p. 1.

10   *The Edinburgh Gazette,* no. 11. Advertisements were also placed at the back of certain books promoting other items of similar polemical persuasion. For example, *Scotlands Right to Caledonia* (Edinburgh, 1700) advertised six other books about Darien that readers might find interesting.

11   *The Edinburgh Gazette,* 10 (30 March–3 April 1699).

done in hurry and fear'.[12] This climate of 'hurry and fear' will now be thoroughly explored.

The Darien printing controversy involves seven pamphlets written by four different authors several of whom, along with the printers and sellers of their texts, were put at risk of arrest and imprisonment. Books were burned by the hangman and proclamations issued offering large rewards for the capture of the pamphleteers who were seen in the words of one of William III's earliest proclamations on the subject to be 'stirring up sedition and rebellion between English and Scots'.[13] The first author to enter the fray was Andrew Fletcher, under the pseudonym 'Philo-Caledon', lauded by Scottish nationalists to the present day for his patriotic spirit. He wrote the pamphlet *A Defence of the Scots Settlement at Darien*, which was advertised in the *Gazette* as being sold at eight pence apiece by William Dickie in Glasgow and John Vallange in Edinburgh.[14] Fletcher had been one of those who supported Monmouth's rebellion and then lived in exile in Holland until 1688. He was a key figure in the early history of the Scottish Company introducing William Paterson to wealthy Scottish investors and contributing a thousand pounds himself. His pamphlet was a response to the rumours in the summer of 1699 that England had ordered her colonies not to trade with New Edinburgh. Fletcher pleaded with his readers, and presumably the English government, not to starve the colony out of existence and to work with the Scots for the greater good of both nations. He also attempted to prove that the Spanish had no claim on the land at Darien, a factor that was crucial in the decision of the English not to support their neighbour's colonial efforts. Fletcher also wrote a second pamphlet on the subject, *A Short and Impartial View of the Manner and Occasion of the Scots Colony Coming Away from Darien*, once news of the abandonment of the first colony became public knowledge.

The main respondent to Fletcher was Walter Harris, or Herries, who had been a surgeon on board the first voyage and had absconded and somehow made his way back to England. He may well have been an undercover English agent but the King was so concerned that one of his pamphlets would provoke hostilities between the English and Scots that he issued a reward for the capture of Harris and the printer of his text, *A Defence of the Scots Abdicating Darien*. King William was probably right: in November 1699 Lord Galway sent a letter from Dublin Castle claiming that 'the Jacobites base great hopes on the annoyance caused by the Darien affair. We shall be watchful in that quarter and

---

12 G. Ridpath, *Scotlands Grievances Relating to Darien Humbly Offered to the Consideration of the Parliament* (Edinburgh, 1700), errata.

13 *By the King. A Proclamation. William R.* (London, 1699).

14 *The Edinburgh Gazette*, 98 (28 Jan–1 Feb 1700).

report what happens'.[15] *A Defence of the Scots Abdicating Darien,* along with another book written by Harris, that directly answered, point by point, the issues raised in Fletcher's work, argued that the Company organizers were corrupt and had sent the settlers (of whom Harris was one) to almost certain death in an environment for which they were totally unprepared. Harris also claimed that the natives were working for the Spanish, who were in effect their liege-lords, and therefore that the ground settled by the Scots was in the possession of the Spanish.[16] The King's Proclamation of late 1699 showed his displeasure at the provocative nature of this work and he ordered the books to be burned and offered a £500 reward for the capture of Harris and a £200 reward for the capture of the printer who, as might be expected, had not put his name on the colophon![17] However, on 7 January 1700, Harris was in contact with the English Secretary of State, James Vernon, an ardent opponent of the Scottish Company who had given the order to English colonies not to provide New Edinburgh with supplies. Harris wrote of his intention to answer 'the last scurrilous and rebellious pamphlet' while looking after his wife who was unwell.[18] The letter seemed to suggest that Harris felt he had nothing to fear from Vernon at any rate. The effort to capture Harris was obviously not successful because, on 1 January 1701 the King had issued a second proclamation, this time in Edinburgh, offering six thousand Scottish pounds for Harris.[19]

In response to Harris's work, a third author wielded his pen, this time it was George Ridpath whose two books *An Enquiry into the Causes of the Miscarriage at Darien* and *Scotlands Grievances Relating to Darien* were both suppressed by the authorities at the time of their publication. Ridpath accused Harris of being a Catholic and issued a forthright defence of the Scottish settlement, causing William to issue a proclamation for his arrest and that of his printer too, offering £500 for the author and £200 for the printer. Once again copies of both texts were publicly burned.[20] According to the *Calendar of State Papers,* Andrew Bell the printer of *An Enquiry* was caught because he was betrayed by one of his fellow printers. Bell was a Scotsman working in London as a bookseller, publisher, map seller and pharmacist.[21] On 30 January 1700 a letter was received from Lord Galway saying that the Dublin printer Patrick

15 *Calendar of State Papers Domestic,* vol. 10 ed. Edward Bateson, 11 Nov 1699 (Liechtenstein, 1969), p. 287.

16 *A Defence of the Scots Abdicating Darien* (London, 1699), p. 48.

17 *By the King. A Proclamation. William R.* (London, 1699).

18 *Calendar of State Papers Domestic,* p. 345.

19 F. Russell Hart, *The Disaster of Darien* (London, 1930), appendix.

20 *The Edinburgh Gazette,* 101 (8–12 Feb 1700).

21 British Book Trade Index website, <www.bbti.bham.ac.uk>, [10 July 2004].

Campbell had received a copy of *An Enquiry* from Bell with directions to print it. Campbell was willing to be a witness against Bell in order to save his own skin. By 11 March a warrant had been issued for Bell's arrest 'for publishing a false and traitorous libel', and two weeks later Bell was prosecuted. He cannot have been too severely punished as he was working in the London book trade until 1711.

Ridpath's second work, *Scotlands Grievances*, the book that contained many errors because the printer was working in a climate of fear, was so disliked by the authorities that they arrested its printer, James Watson, and imprisoned him in the Tolbooth in Edinburgh. Interestingly, Watson was released on 1 June 1700 when a mob started a fire at the gaol and battered down the doors.[22] It is unclear whether the crowd was incensed at the arrest of Watson and intended to free him or whether his escape was a by-product of the mob action directed towards some other end. Another author, Robert Ferguson, who had also been a supporter of Monmouth and William of Orange before changing sides to the Jacobite cause, wrote a tract in response to Harris's *Defence of the Scots Abdicating Darien*. Although Ferguson was constantly in and out of London gaols for his part in various conspiracies there is no evidence that his pamphlet *A Just and Modest Vindication of the Scots Design for Having Established a Colony at Darien* ever aroused the suspicion of the authorities in the same way that Ridpath's work had done.

The *Calendar of State Papers Domestic* reveals a fascinating case of mistaken identity in the midst of this pamphlet war that adds further confusion to this already tangled web of prosecutions. James Hodges a pamphleteer allegedly in the employ of the Duke of Hamilton, one of Darien's biggest investors, was supposedly employed to write a reply to Harris's *Defence of the Scots Abdicating Darien*.[23] It seems that he failed to do so as no copies of the pamphlet survive, if indeed it was ever written. He was accused in February 1700 of being the author of *An Enquiry into the Miscarriage at Darien* actually written by George Ridpath. The records reveal that evidence was taken from three witnesses who argued that Hodges was the author of the book which at that time was being publicly burned in London. Anne Dunbar was a servant to Hodges in Drury Lane and she claimed that Hodges intended to take the book to 'Duke Hamilton' for distribution in Scotland, although at no point does she claim that Hodges was the author. Elizabeth Clark, who found Hodges his lodgings in Drury Lane confirmed this statement. She became fearful when the book was ordered to be burned and would have no more to do with him. Finally the most damning evidence came from James Cuff, a watchmaker of Ship's Court

---

22 *Oxford Dictionary of National Biography*.
23 See Kinnaird Family Website, <www.kinnaird.net/darien.htm>, [10 July 2004].

in London, who claimed that he had met Hodges near the chocolate house in Charles Street. Hodges showed him some papers, which Cuff remembered as the book in question. Cuff told him that he knew someone who might print the book but Hodges allegedly replied that he already had a printer. Once the proclamation was issued for apprehending the author Cuff began to receive anonymous threatening letters referring to the potential £500 reward. One said 'If you discover [i.e. reveal] that business in relation to the Scots papers which you saw, it shall be a dear £500 to you'.[24] There was insufficient evidence against Hodges and he was not charged.

The confusion clearly felt by the authorities at the time as to what was written by whom is reflected in the difficulties that present-day historians and bibliographers have in matching author with printer and bookseller, and even author with text. To add to the difficulties of studying so many pamphlets with similar titles, and many that have no reference to printers' or booksellers' names on the colophons, one of the central pamphlets in the debate: *A Defence of the Scots Abdicating Darien*, actually written by Walter Harris, is wrongly attributed in the Bodleian Library catalogue to one James Hodges! This was an easy mistake to make because in *An Enquiry into the Causes of the Miscarriage*, his reply to the pamphlet in question, George Ridpath constantly refers to its author, whom he is violently attacking, as 'H----s', into which the surnames of both Hodges and Harris could fit. However, evidence from the *Calendar of State Papers* shows that James Hodges was suspected of being a pro-Scottish pamphleteer, that is on the same side as Ridpath, and therefore could not be the 'H----s' mentioned by Ridpath. Walter Harris has been proved to be the author of several other pro-English pamphlets discussed here and so it seems logical also to fit Harris into 'H----s' as the author of *A Defence of the Scots Abdicating Darien*.

What did contemporaries make of this aggressive pamphleteering? Many who did not have a strong view in support of either side, or who had an interest in seeing the truth about the Darien scheme emerging, found the whole printed exchange rather distasteful. As early as December 1699 Archibald Stobo, a Presbyterian minister who had been to Darien on the second expedition, wrote to the directors of the Company in Scotland. He believed that all authors, printers and booksellers were spreading 'nothing ... but meer lies' about Darien and that this meant that the wrong sort of people were learning about the colony and thus it was bound to fail.[25] Obviously, Stobo did not feel that he was the right sort of colonist either, because he left Darien at the first

---

24 *Calendar of State Papers Domestic*, William III, vol. 10 (6 February 1700).
25 'Letter from Archibald Stobo, Dec 25 1699', Darien Letters from the Spencer Collection, Glasgow University Library (Glasgow, 1971).

opportunity and settled in Charleston, South Carolina, never returning to his native Scotland.

In conclusion, what is the significance of the Darien disaster in relation to the history of print in both England and Scotland? First, it shows how politicized the print industry had become by this period; the industry worked within a passionate political context in which censorship was a tool used not only to suppress the views of one's political opponents, but also to suppress the entire debate with authors on both sides being prosecuted. The story also shows the importance of the newspapers in spreading information to the eager public about the fate of the expedition. The connections between those writing for and printing newspapers and those involved in the pamphlet debate are also significant. By this period most practitioners of the print trade had realized the importance of the integrated print medium, the inter-textuality that worked between twice-weekly newspapers such as the *Gazette* and printed pamphlets, and also the links between newspapers and the oral transmission of news. Finally, the story of the vulnerability of printers and booksellers to prosecution and imprisonment shows that, during this period, being a member of the English or Scottish book trade could be a rather dangerous profession!

The Octopus and its Silent Teachers:
A New Zealand Response to the British Book Trade

NOEL WAITE

N EW ZEALAND'S most significant publishing house was founded in 1882, bringing together its namesakes' modest bookselling and printing businesses. However, Whitcombe & Tombs soon came to be characterized, from both within and without, as 'The Octopus' because of its encompassing embrace of the multiple activities that go to make up the bewildering array of business that is the book trade. Its bookshops became gateways to New Zealand print culture – both providing and limiting access – and their rapid spread was indicative of the emergence of a national market for printing and publishing. Education was the touchstone for all its activities and the company rapidly established itself as an independent player within New Zealand and in its relations with the British book trade.

The missionary zeal with which printing was established in the new colony of New Zealand was both literal, as regards Maori translations of the Bible, and metaphorical in the planned settlements like Christchurch. Within three weeks of the arrival of settlers the first issue of *The Lyttelton Times* appeared on 11 January 1851. One year later seventeen-year-old George Tombs, newly arrived with his parents from England, was apprenticed in the printing department to the same newspaper. His experience there convinced him of the need for a good jobbing printing concern and bindery in the city.

The earliest known publication by these future partners is *On the Sale of Bullion at the Bank of England*, which appeared in 1864 from G. Tombs & Co. A number of publications appeared under a joint imprint with partner George Jones from 1868. These ranged from practical guides such as almanacs and the *New Zealand Garden Calendar for All the Year Round* (1878) to the unique literary efforts of the likes of George Willmer, whose *The Lowing Herd and Zealandia* (1869) Hocken described as 'two lamentable efforts at versification' on the subject of wild cattle hunting, and *Reign of Pain and Plaguy Drain* (1876), a verse series on local drains by 'Hydrology'.[1] Perhaps of more consequence from the pen of the bovine bard was the thirty-page *Elementary Geography of New Zealand* (1871), an early effort to provide for the specific

---

1 T. M. Hocken, *A Bibliography of the Literature Relating to New Zealand* (Wellington, 1909), p. 264.

13

educational needs of the new colony. An association with Canterbury University College was also developed with the publication of inaugural professorial addresses from the likes of Professor Bickerton (1881),[2] mentor of Sir Ernest Rutherford.

Described as having 'a merry eye for merry occasions' George Tombs was by all accounts a congenial employer, and his involvement as referee in on-site staff cricket matches certainly suggests a flexible managerial style.[3] While possessed of a relaxed manner, he took considerable pride in the quality of his work. He won a Bronze Medal for Excellence in Printing and Binding at the Sydney Exhibition in 1879 (as Tombs & Davies) and then carried off the First Award of Merit and Silver Medal in Canterbury at the New Zealand International Exhibition in 1882.[4] His display of binding and letterpress was described in the *New Zealand International Exhibition Record* as the 'best all-round one of the class [Stationery, Printing & Publications] in the New Zealand Court' and later as 'the best exhibitor'.[5] It included the *Canterbury College Calendar* which contained examination papers in Greek and algebra. The judge on this occasion was George Whitcombe, who clearly recognized the value of Tombs's skill and the potential of a partnership.

George Hawkes Whitcombe was born on 14 November 1855 in Brittany. He arrived in New Zealand, at Auckland, working his way south to Christchurch in 1874. After a short period teaching, he entered into partnership in a small book and stationery business, with E. S. Bowden. He soon bought out Bowden, taking over his agency for the New Zealand Educational Book Depository in the Canterbury province. From 1878 to 1881, Crerar, Whitcombe & Co. traded from the same premises as a bookselling and stationery business, specializing in educational textbooks, until Crerar terminated the partnership. With a shrewder appreciation of the hard-headed requirements of a sound business, Whitcombe sought to combine his sales and Tombs's production experience of educational resources into a successful venture.

The official partnership notice in the *Press* on 2 November 1882 stated that the two firms 'will be carried on as one concern, at 202 Cashel Street

---

2   A. W. Bickerton, *University Reform: The Inaugural Address for 1881* (Christchurch, G. Tombs, 1881).

3   Arnold Shrimpton, *c.*1933. 'Whitcombe & Tombs Jubilee History' (unpublished manuscript, no pagination), Whitcombe & Tombs Collection, Auckland War Memorial Museum (hereafter referred to as AWMM/WT).

4   *International Exhibition Official Catalogues Sydney 1879* (Sydney, 1879) and *New Zealand International Exhibition Record 1882, Wellington* (Christchurch, James Caygill, 1882).

5   New Zealand International Exhibition Record 1882, Wellington (Christchurch, James Caygill), pp. xxiv–xxv, 62.

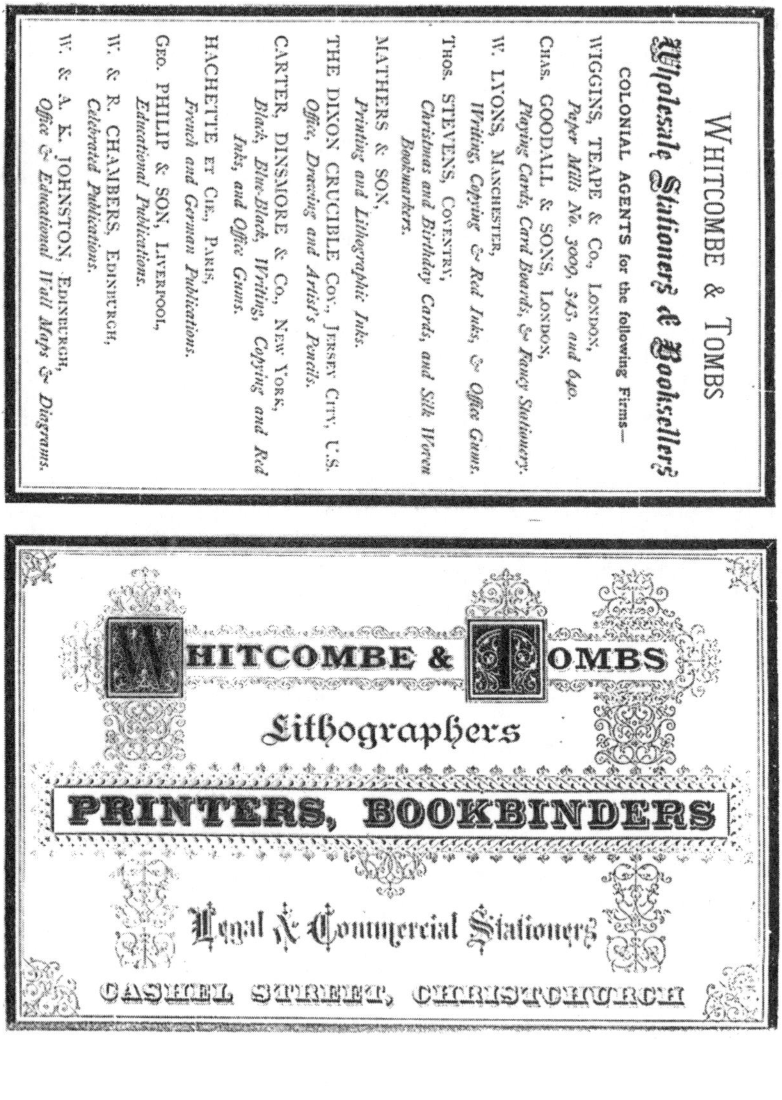

Fig. 1. Promotional card for Whitcombe & Tombs, c.1882. Collection of Auckland War Memorial Museum, New Zealand

under the style of Whitcombe & Tombs'.[6] Handwritten balance sheets dated 1 November show G. Tombs & Co. had assets of £4000.5s.9d., and an admirable balance of assets over liabilities of £3356.10s.1d.; Whitcombe & Co. brought more substantial assets of £8672.8s.6d., but with higher total liabilities of £3855.13s.0d.[7] George Whitcombe has usually been credited with recognizing that many English schoolbooks were misfits and there was a need for textbooks more suited for New Zealand conditions but it would seem more likely that his acumen extended more towards realizing the potential profit to be made from combining printing production and retail. His experience with the Book Depository had made him closely attuned to the demand for such books, and the possibility of supplying all school requirements, including his own manufactured stationery, was particularly alluring.

The ornately decorated card (Fig. 1) from this period details the extensive range of the new firm's services which included printing (including copperplate), the production of commercial and legal stationery, lithography, diesinking, illuminated testimonials and bookbinding. They also operated as wholesale stationers and booksellers, being the agents for the companies listed. At the beginning of 1883 they issued an extensive 51-page *Classified Catalogue of Educational Works and School Stationery.*[8] Manufactured stationery was especially prominent. By importing materials in their raw state, ruling and making them up in their new factory and buying in bulk, they were able to achieve considerable price reductions. As well as school stationery and furniture, forty pages were devoted to books on subjects from Algebra to Spanish and Spelling. It also announced that in conjunction with their London publishers they had opened a Teachers' Specimen Library that housed sample copies of the latest publications. The booklet represented a considerable effort to cater for the needs of teachers and clearly indicated the centrality of education to the operation of the firm.

From these modest beginnings, it soon became apparent that further capital would be required in order to sustain the growth of the business. A balance sheet for the first nine months of the new partnership's operation showed a profit of £3755 in goods sold, which was equal to approximately twenty per cent of capital on a twelve-month basis. They had also managed to spend nearly £2000 upgrading plant and machinery while reducing liabilities. The partners' share of this was £564 each, although George Tombs was

---

6   Whitcombe & Tombs (WT). 1882. Partnership notice, Christchurch *Press*, no pagination.

7   Whitcombe & Tombs (WT). 1882. Balance sheet, 1 November 1882. AWMM/WT -- 2 November 1882.

8   *Classified Catalogue of Educational Works and School Stationery* (Christchurch, Whitcombe & Tombs, 1883).

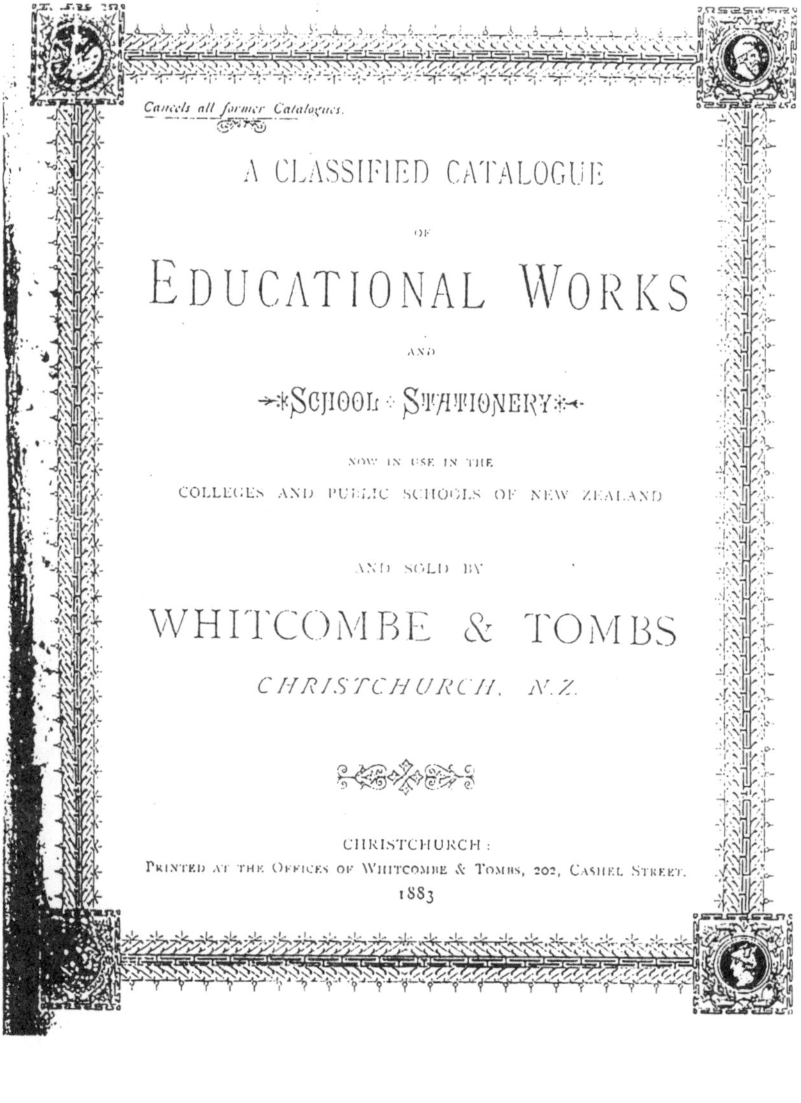

Cancels all former Catalogues.

A CLASSIFIED CATALOGUE

OF

EDUCATIONAL WORKS

AND

✦SCHOOL · STATIONERY✦

NOW IN USE IN THE

COLLEGES AND PUBLIC SCHOOLS OF NEW ZEALAND

AND SOLD BY

WHITCOMBE & TOMBS

CHRISTCHURCH, N.Z.

CHRISTCHURCH:
PRINTED AT THE OFFICES OF WHITCOMBE & TOMBS, 202, CASHEL STREET.
1883

Fig. 2. Educational catalogue, 1883. Collection of Macmillan Brown Library, University of Canterbury, New Zealand. Z4103 W581ce

required by their initial deed of partnership to pay his partner the sum of £500 for goodwill.[9]

An offer of capital from Alex Cowan was rejected by Whitcombe, presumably because of his past experience with Crerar when such capital was withdrawn. Instead, he sought public share capital, the prospectus stating that '[t]his Company is formed for the purpose of purchasing and extending the well-known and rapidly-increasing business of Messrs Whitcombe & Tombs, Manufacturing Stationers, Booksellers, Lithographers, Printers and Bookbinders, of Cashel Street, Christchurch'. The prospectus also drew attention to the upgrading of facilities that had resulted in plant and machinery that was 'of a capacity sufficient to cope with a large increase in trade'.[10] Whitcombe & Tombs became a public limited liability company on 30 October 1883. Initial nominal share capital was £40,000 in 8000 shares of £5 each, of which the original partners were to retain 2000. George Whitcombe purchased a further 800 shares and assumed the position of Managing Director while George Tombs was to be General Manager of the Manufacturing Department.

With a firmer financial base in place, Whitcombe & Tombs now turned its attention to books, specifically educational ones. Aware of the success of Thomas Bowden's geography textbooks of the late 1860s (published in London by George Philip), George Whitcombe chose to commission new ones. *Geography of New Zealand and Australia* by I. I. Patterson was the first published in July 1884. George Whitcombe even had a hand in compiling this text and the four-colour illustrations. This was soon followed by a number of other titles featuring local content.

One of their popular textbook authors, Henry Hill, who was a teacher and inspector, had also begun a monthly magazine, *The New Zealand Schoolmaster*, in 1881. It was designed to supply teachers with educational news, and included teaching aids and contributions from leading educationists. Through direct daily contact with teachers at his bookshop, George Whitcombe understood the value of keeping informed about educational requirements, and so the decision to purchase *The New Zealand Schoolmaster* in 1883 was an astute one. It was to serve as an excellent advertising medium for Whitcombe & Tombs until severe competition from a rival paper, *The New Zealand Journal of Education*, the official journal of the New Zealand Educational Institute, caused it to cease publication in 1908.

However, publishing was not confined to educational topics and their first significant general book, Alfred Cox's *Recollections*, was published in 1884.

---

9   Balance sheet, 1 November 1882–31 August 1883, AWMM/WT. Although the word 'crap' pencilled into the margin would suggest that one partner was not altogether satisfied that this unequal division was entirely justified.

10   1883 Prospectus, AWMM/WT.

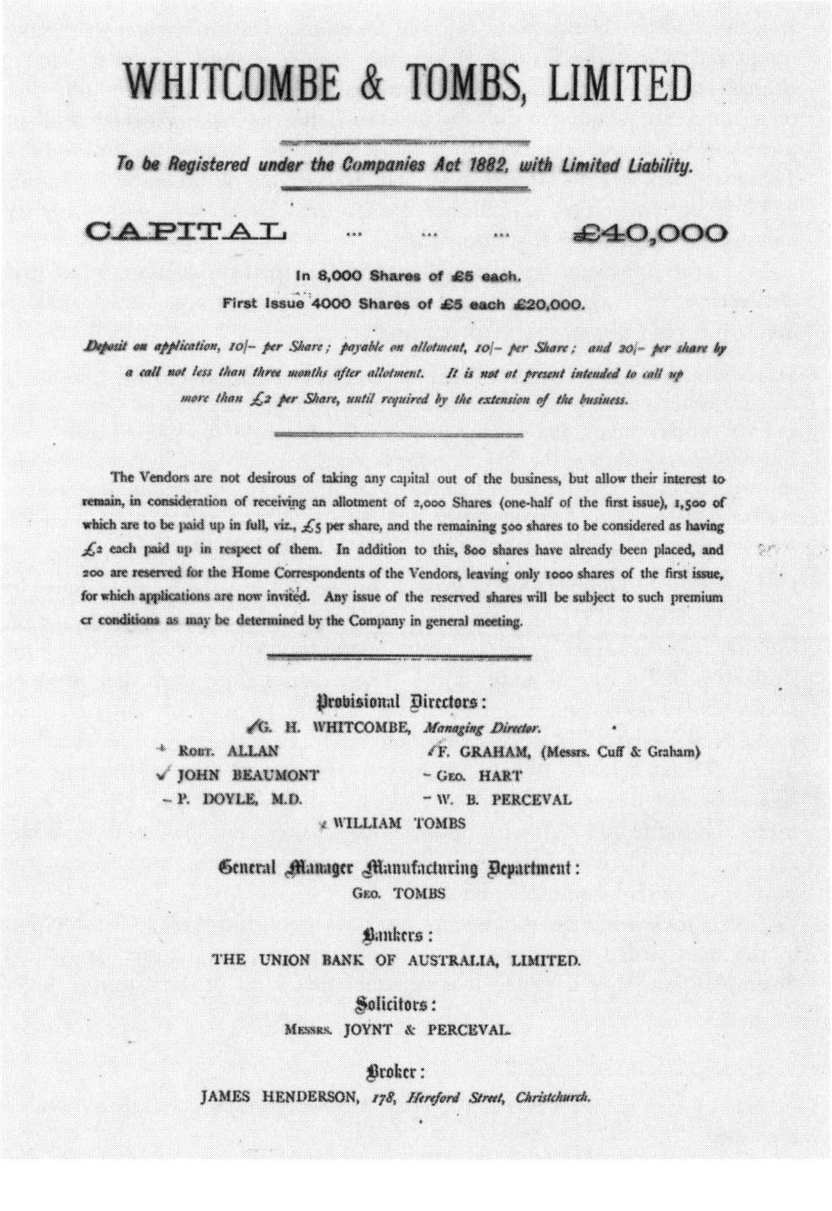

WHITCOMBE & TOMBS, LIMITED

To be Registered under the Companies Act 1882, with Limited Liability.

CAPITAL £40,000

In 8,000 Shares of £5 each.
First Issue 4000 Shares of £5 each £20,000.

Deposit on application, 10/- per Share; payable on allotment, 10/- per Share; and 20/- per share by a call not less than three months after allotment. It is not at present intended to call up more than £2 per Share, until required by the extension of the business.

The Vendors are not desirous of taking any capital out of the business, but allow their interest to remain, in consideration of receiving an allotment of 2,000 Shares (one-half of the first issue), 1,500 of which are to be paid up in full, viz., £5 per share, and the remaining 500 shares to be considered as having £2 each paid up in respect of them. In addition to this, 800 shares have already been placed, and 200 are reserved for the Home Correspondents of the Vendors, leaving only 1000 shares of the first issue, for which applications are now invited. Any issue of the reserved shares will be subject to such premium or conditions as may be determined by the Company in general meeting.

Provisional Directors:
G. H. WHITCOMBE, *Managing Director.*

Robt. ALLAN
JOHN BEAUMONT
P. DOYLE, M.D.
WILLIAM TOMBS

F. GRAHAM, (Messrs. Cuff & Graham)
Geo. HART
W. B. PERCEVAL

General Manager Manufacturing Department:
Geo. TOMBS

Bankers:
THE UNION BANK OF AUSTRALIA, LIMITED.

Solicitors:
Messrs. JOYNT & PERCEVAL.

Broker:
JAMES HENDERSON, *178, Hereford Street, Christchurch.*

Fig. 3. Original prospectus, 1883. Auckland War Memorial Museum, New Zealand

Generally, these books were warmly received. The *Marlborough Express* recognized that '[t]he firm of Whitcomb [*sic*] & Tombs, Limited, Christchurch, are beginning to occupy a prominent place as publishers', noting that their books 'are valuable in showing that the Colony is making a great stride in providing for its own wants in such subjects as these little works deal with'.[11] This may seem a modest assessment, but considering Whitcombe & Tombs had only been operating as publishers for less than a year, it suggests that they had made a considerable first impression.

A significant factor was the high standard of their production, a fact that was, even at this stage, being recognized in international trade journals such as the *British and Colonial Printer & Stationer*:

Messrs Whitcombe and Tombs of Cashel-street, Christchurch, New Zealand, send us a selection of their work, which is exceedingly praiseworthy. They evidently have a large and well-stocked office, and employ printers who thoroughly understand their craft. The folding trade card of the firm, forming 6 pages, is a really fine specimen of work, and would not be excelled in this country. The type used is evidently of American origin. Very few persons unacquainted with the resources of this prosperous colony would imagine that printing of such a high class was being done there.[12]

Perhaps their best-known publication in this regard was the humble diary. In terms of production quality, these compared well with the best English diaries, but they had the advantage of containing useful local information, such as New Zealand postal rates and stamp duties. These diaries along with their account books, school books and examples of their binding were prominently featured at the New Zealand Industrial Exhibition 1885 and favourably commented on in the *Official Record*.[13] Arnold Shrimpton commented that 'leading business houses prided themselves on their Ledgers – huge Royal and Double-royal tomes, bound in full calf, with double Russia bands' and that in 1933 Whitcombe & Tombs were 'even then doing magnificent work, especially in the binding of Letterpress for connoisseurs'.[14]

After their initial burst of energy, the book publishing tailed off somewhat as the firm settled on books of a general and practical nature. As Arnold Shrimpton was later to note: 'It is apparent that most of these [early] books

---

11 Anon. Review of *First Lessons in Geography*, *Marlborough Express*, 2 October 1884, no pagination.
12 Anon. *British & Colonial Printer and Stationer and Newspaper Press Record*, 23 September 1884.
13 New Zealand Industrial Exhibition 1886, Wellington: The Official Record (Wellington, 1886), pp. 94–5.
14 Shrimpton, 'Whitcombe & Tombs Jubilee History'.

Fig. 4. Educational journal, 1887. Hocken Collections, Uare Taoka o Hakena, University of Otago, New Zealand

were useful rather than beautiful'.[15] It is difficult to say whether this was due to their increasing retail trade or competition from local newspapers which, as Jim Traue has described, played a more dominant role than their English counterparts.[16] Nevertheless, their Annual Report for 1885 declared: 'During the past year, your Directors have endeavoured to secure an increase of local and interprovincial trade, and extend operations generally'.[17] Their consolidation and growth in a time of depression was remarkable, but it was this development of a national distribution network that set the stage for their later publishing.

Whitcombe & Tombs's well equipped printery was increasingly employed to fulfil the demands of the educational field which it had made its speciality, in particular the printing of school stationery. George Whitcombe's name appeared on their *Public School Copy Books* in 1886 and the more wide-ranging series of *Southern Cross Copy Books* in 1889. He had definitely assisted in compiling the latter series and the result, as editor Arnold Shrimpton pointed out, reflected Whitcombe's own simple philosophy in that they 'preached the gospel of honesty and independence & those who followed the advice in full would most surely become excellent business men and women'.[18] Anne Crighton's less partial assessment of George Whitcombe seems closer to the mark when she describes him as having 'all the hallmarks of a self-made man. He was stubborn, autocratic and idealistic', and his success was 'the result of hard work and a harder head. In each move he demonstrated a ruthlessness and a single-minded determination which, while far from admirable, was assuredly successful in his case because of the soundness of his judgement and his enterprise'.[19]

Shrimpton's and Crighton's comments are interesting in light of the adoption of *Southern Cross Readers* by the Otago Education Board in 1889. As Don McKay outlines, this was a first step towards the development of a national reader, in which Whitcombe & Tombs were to play a significant, and murky part.[20] Inspectors required additional readers for teachers and the Otago

---

15 Ibid.

16 See J. E. Traue, 'The Two Histories of the Book in New Zealand', *Bibliographical Society of Australia and New Zealand (BSANZ) Bulletin*, 25.1&2 (2001), 8–16; 'But Why Mulgan, Marris and Schroder?: The Mutation of the Local Newspaper in New Zealand's Colonial Print Culture', *BSANZ Bulletin*, 21.2 (1996), 107–15.

17 Annual report, 31 August 1885, AWMM/WT.

18 Shrimpton, 'Whitcombe & Tombs Jubilee History'.

19 Anne Crighton, 'The Whitcombe & Tombs Dispute, 1890, Causes, Course and Consequences' (unpublished History 615 Honours paper, Canterbury University, 1983), p. 4.

20 D. McKay, 'The School Text-Book Controversy and the Development of the National School Reader: An Otago Perspective', *New Zealand Journal of Educational Studies*, 10.2 (November 1975) 140–50.

Educational Institute recommended the Royal Star series produced by Thomas Nelson & Sons of Edinburgh. The Southern Cross series were acknowledged to be better adapted to the requirements of New Zealand, but they were initially rejected. According to Mark Cohen, the President of the Dunedin and Suburban Schools Conference, they were too biased toward natural history and contained words 'beyond the intelligence of the children to be taught'. These reservations were overcome after Whitcombe & Tombs sent a letter to the Board urging that their books should be adopted in State schools because they were the product of local industry 'in which a large amount of capital had been embarked [sic]' and because they had been developed in association with New Zealand school teachers and Inspectors.[21]

Educationist Hugh Price offers an interesting contemporary assessment of these readers in '"Lo! It is my Ox": Reading Books and Reading in New Zealand Schools 1877–1900'. He concluded that 'Nelson's reading books promoted a sense of duty and non-questioning obedience to authority, with habits of diligence and industry' and 'were a lively and potent part of the British class system'. By comparison, 'the readers published in New Zealand were less class-structured than the books imported from Britain' although they did follow the familiar pattern of Nelson's successful series in terms of their educational method. Whitcombe & Tombs's 'carefully planned readers' were 'success-oriented, and played an important part in the drive for universal literacy', but their apparent egalitarianism seems an unintended consequence of George Whitcombe's competitive enterprise.[22]

At the beginning of 1889 George Tombs was involved in the establishment of the Canterbury Master Printers' Association in response to cut-throat competition. George Tombs was elected their first president and instituted a stabilizing printing tariff. Another initiative in 1890 was to lobby the Minister of Education to legislate that all school books and stationery be printed in New Zealand, a move with obvious benefits for Whitcombe & Tombs.[23] I have argued elsewhere for the importance of industrial relations in understanding the development of a national infrastructure for book publishing in New Zealand.[24] Similarly, Whitcombe & Tombs's role as a regional focal point in

---

21 M. Cohen, Letter to editor, *Otago Daily Times*, 10 February 1891, p. 4.
22 Hugh Price, '"Lo, It Is My Ox!": Reading Books and Reading in New Zealand Schools 1877–1900', *Paradigm*, 12 (1993) 2, 3, 8.
23 A. E. J. Arts, *A History of the Canterbury Master Printers' Association 1889–1989* (Christchurch, 1989), p. 11.
24 See N. Waite, 'The Dunedin Master Printers' Association 1889–1894', *Bibliographical Society of Australia and New Zealand (BSANZ) Bulletin*, 25.1&2 (2001): pp. 17–42 and most recently at the 2004 SHARP conference in Lyons in a paper entitled '"The Best Holidays on the Globe": Charles Francis in New Zealand'.

one of New Zealand's most significant industrial disputes, the Maritime Strike, is instructive. Both disputes, large and small, national and regional, emphasized the need for state intervention in order to ensure stability and equitable outcomes in the workplace. In terms of the New Zealand book trade, they also highlighted the twin poles of regional and national demarcation, private and public provision of educational resources that Whitcombe & Tombs was to prove so adept at navigating.

The dispute was set against the background of a Government Commission to enquire into the alleged existence of sweating in New Zealand. At the Christchurch hearing, witnesses gave evidence of George Whitcombe's strong anti-union views and it was suggested that the punitive system of fines operating in the company was simply a means of reducing the wage bill and no payments from a sick pay fund had ever been made. The result, according to the *Economic Journal* of 1891, was that evidence of the Company's treatment of its employees 'discredited the Company in the eyes of the public' at the commencement of the dispute.[25] George Whitcombe's own testimony before the hearing largely consisted of justifying his staffing policies in terms of practices adopted in England and America.

The dispute began in 1890 when the Canterbury Typographical Association issued a revised scale of wages with new minimum rates but also sought an end to the employment of women as compositors or to place them on the same footing as men as regards work and wages. After a meeting of Directors, George Whitcombe publicly 'stated his Company's intention of working the establishment on non-Union lines', and threatened to have work done in England.[26] The Typographical Association responded by going on strike and Whitcombe had the strikers replaced. The union encouraged a boycott of Whitcombe & Tombs products, going so far as request parents to vote only for Town School Committee candidates who pledged not to buy from the firm. The target here was Whitcombe's lucrative educational textbook market at a time when, as Anne Crighton points out, 'the Southern Cross Readers series was having marketing difficulties against stiff competition' and the call for standard national texts.[27] The union's call, however, had limited effect as many moderate unionists did not want to affect their children's education.[28] However, the Trades and Labour Council were instrumental in convincing the

25 W. T. Charlewood, 'Labour Troubles in New Zealand', *Economic Journal*, 1.4 (1891), pp. 710–20.
http://links.jstor.org/sici?+0013133%28189112%291%3A4%3C710%3ALTINZ%3E2.0.C O%3B2–F [accessed 9 July 2004].
26 Ibid., 711.
27 Anne Crighton, 'The Whitcombe & Tombs Dispute', p. 16.
28 Don McKay, 'The School Text-book Controversy', p. 146.

government of a need for a national school reader, or as the left-wing *Globe* newspaper put it, that if 'the children of New Zealand are ever to have a national spirit fostered in them, they must be taught the resources, beauties and romances of their own country'.[29]

At this point the regional Trades and Labour Council passed a number of remits aimed at Whitcombe & Tombs, including a recommendation 'that there should be uniformity of school books, which should be provided in the Colony, either at the Government Printing Office, or at an office employing union labour'.[30] Of perhaps more significance was the involvement of the Maritime Council, the national leader of the unions, in the dispute, which sought, but failed, to place a ban on handling consignments to or from the firm, either by rail or ship. Ironically, this action served to swing public opinion in favour of Whitcombe & Tombs. Whitcombe took advantage of this turn of events by claiming that boycotts of the company's manufactured goods in Dunedin compelled them, 'in self defence', to open an agency there.[31] George Whitcombe knew that the Railway Commissioners and the Union Steamship Company could not legally refuse his company's goods, which suggests that his intransigence had more to do with turning the dispute to his profitable advantage than a heavily principled stand.

The Maritime Council responded with its own form of brinksmanship by threatening a general strike, which would block the trade of Lyttelton and Christchurch. Other Christchurch companies tried to persuade Whitcombe & Tombs to relent, and George Tombs and a number of smaller shareholders supported arbitration. After a tense eleven-day standoff, the Maritime Council called off plans for a general blockade but not without claiming that Whitcombe & Tombs 'would be compelled to stand out in miserable relief as the only Firm in the colony who refused to recognize the rights of labour and true principles of Unionism'.[32] The boycott dwindled but in the meantime George Whitcombe had been to Dunedin and work had begun on fitting out the first of many branch shops.

Anne Crighton determined that the dispute 'revolved about the determination of George Whitcombe to obtain his labour at the cheapest possible rates without any interference from outside organizations'.[33] His success owed as much to the relatively uncoordinated activities of an embryonic union movement as to the solidarity of employers, but George Whitcombe's strength lay in his ability to court public opinion, or what today would be called public

---

29 Anon. 'A National School Reader', *Globe*, 24 March 1891.
30 Anon. *Press* (Christchurch), 16 June 1890.
31 Advertisement, *Press*, 1 August 1890.
32 Charlewood, 'Labour Troubles in New Zealand', p. 713.
33 Anne Crighton, 'The Whitcombe & Tombs Dispute', p. 11.

relations. He succeeded in maintaining a high public profile for his company throughout the dispute, even though it was initially a negative one. The result appears to have been an increase in jobbing work during a depression while minimizing labour costs. By 1893 he could 'congratulate shareholders upon the uniformly profitable nature and steady progress of the business' as he announced that dividends paid up during the previous ten years amounted to £2.10s.0d. thereby returning the full amount of shareholders' initial capital.[34]

It was also during this period that Whitcombe & Tombs painstakingly produced their first series of School Readers, handset and illustrated with woodcuts, which were then rejected by the Department of Education. Undaunted, the company set about producing a new series which was ultimately accepted and which Arnold Shrimpton claimed in 1933 'laid the foundation of the educational publishing business that now forms so important a branch of the firm's activities'. He also believed this example highlighted George Whitcombe's willingness to learn from his mistakes, although it must be noted that second chances are something of an exception in commercial publishing. Perhaps more significant was Shrimpton's observation that George Whitcombe 'realised now that every school book he published was expected to please the child, the teacher, the inspector, the parent and the Department of Education',[35] and this was clearly a factor in convincing the Education Boards to accept their Readers.[36]

George Tombs's son, Felix, who had been the first to manage the Dunedin branch opened in response to the strike, was appointed the company's first London representative in 1893.[37] He was there only a short time before he was joined by Whitcombe's sibling, Bertie, who had been sent to assist Felix and learn the London operation. Bertie, who was to succeed his father as Director and turn the firm into the pre-eminent national publisher, completed his managerial apprenticeship with twelve months at the Edinburgh warehouse of Alex Cowan and Sons Ltd, gaining a knowledge of the flat paper trade and paper making. He was recalled at the end of 1894 to manage the newly purchased Wellington branch.[38] According to Whitcombe & Tombs's Annual Report of 1895, the Wellington firm of Lyon and Blair was bought '[i]n order to preserve some of the most important contracts held by the company, and also to foster and extend trade connection in the North Island'.[39]

---

34 Circular, 18 September 1893, AWMM/WT.

35 Shrimpton, 'Whitcombe & Tombs Jubilee History'.

36 McKay, 'The School Text-book Controversy and the Development of the National School Reader: An Otago Perspective', 142.

37 G. M. Tombs, Letter to Arnold Shrimpton, 28 April 1933, AWMM/WT.

38 Shrimpton, 'Whitcombe & Tombs Jubilee History'.

39 Annual report, 1895, AWMM/WT.

Its extensive selling agency also covered Nelson and Westland in the South Island and its printery specialized in security printing.

The purchase of James Horsburgh & Co., a retail bookselling and stationery business, was to give Whitcombe & Tombs an especially strong position in the Otago province. James Horsburgh was an occasional publisher as well as a highly regarded bookseller and had worked hard to develop close connections with Otago University. He was engaged as London bookbuyer in 1898; his appointment reduced the firm's reliance on agents and put the buying in closer touch with the needs of New Zealanders.

Meanwhile Felix Tombs went north and opened an Auckland office in 1897. This completed the company's national expansion to all the major centres and resulted in the need for consolidation. The central quarter-acre Christchurch premises it had leased from its inception was purchased, serving the company to the present day as a hub for its rapidly expanding organization.

In 1901 Canterbury University College lecturer James Hight was appointed as the company's first editor. James Hight was a schoolteacher and examiner who had just had his *Introduction and Notes to Carlyle's 'Sartor Resartus'* published by Whitcombe & Tombs before joining Canterbury College in 1901 as lecturer in history and politics. Thus he was very familiar both with the business of teaching and the business of writing and was well placed, as Arnold Shrimpton described it, to 'distinguish the crank from the authentic educator of youth'.[40] As his later success as an administrator at Canterbury College attests, he was also meticulous and an able organizer – critical skills for an effective editor.[41] His experience and active engagement with contemporary educational issues gave Whitcombe & Tombs the opportunity to gain access to the Australian schoolbook trade. In 1902, a change took place in the Committee of Education in Victoria accompanied by changes to the syllabus. On Hight's recommendation, Whitcombe and Hight went to Australia, interviewing numerous heads of schools in Victoria and other states. As a result Whitcombe & Tombs opened a branch in Melbourne in October.

More books, especially general educational texts, began to be published and Whitcombe & Tombs's list reflected a more consistent and professional approach. Dennis McEldowney confirms in the *Oxford History of New Zealand Literature* that Whitcombe's authors were signing standard contracts, some with generous royalty provisions, at the turn of the century, well before this was standard practice. For example, James Drummond, whose *Animals of New*

---

40 Shrimpton, 'Whitcombe & Tombs Jubilee History'.

41 N. C. Phillips, 2003. 'Hight, James 1870–1958' *Dictionary of New Zealand Biography*, (updated 16 December 2003). <http://www.dnzb.govt.nz/> [accessed 9 July 2004].

Zealand (1904) is described in the *Dictionary of New Zealand Biography* as 'a standard reference work for generations of New Zealanders' would be one of the authors Dennis McEldowney estimated made the considerable sum of £300–400 per year in royalties.[42] This book, along with *Nature in New Zealand* (1902) was based on material Drummond had written for newspapers and originally intended for adults but, as Drummond recalled in the 1930s, 'Mr Whitcombe said that success would be more assured if the book was made suitable for schools ... [and] We were delighted to find it appealed to both young people and grown-ups.' Drummond found George Whitcombe to be 'shrewd, frank and straightforward', concluding 'In my association with him, he impressed me as a man of high courage, of determination, of sound judgement, and of enterprise restrained by caution. He did not tolerate carelessness or incompetency, but he was eager to reward merit if he could do so'.[43]

In order to meet the growing demands of the business, increases in both plant and machinery were required. The mechanization of printing equipment and motive power were undergoing rapid change. Linotype type-setting machines had been introduced for newspaper printing in the late 1890s, while steam- and gas-powered presses appeared in the larger New Zealand firms in the 1870s. George Whitcombe's approach had always been cautiously pragmatic but, recognizing the necessity for change, he embarked on a six-month fact-finding trip in 1904 to the United Kingdom, concluding with a month each in Canada and Australia.[44]

He spent much of April personally approaching as many of their suppliers as possible, doggedly seeking to enhance the terms on which they did business. Clearly, some of their existing arrangements bore the hallmarks of colonial deals dictated from the uncompromising stronghold of the colonial centre, but, given the opportunity to put his case face to face, George Whitcombe experienced little in the way of colonial cringe. He realized that discounts of an extra five per cent could account for significant savings, particularly if they were achieved across a range of products, and his ambitious plans for the company came to fruition.

He extracted better terms from all their suppliers and was not averse to sourcing one company's product from a competitor at a discounted rate. He even attended to such details as the choice of Christmas cards, taking time to

---

42   R. K. Dell, 'Drummond, James Mackay 1869–1940', *Dictionary of New Zealand Biography* (updated 16 December 2003) <http://www.dnzb.govt.nz/> [accessed 9 July 2004]; Dennis McEldowney, 'Publishing, Patronage and Literary Magazines' in *The Oxford Companion to New Zealand Literature*, ed. by Terry Sturm (Auckland, 1998) pp. 641–2.

43   J. Drummond, Letter to Bertie Whitcombe, 26 September 1933, AWMM/WT.

44   This information is drawn from George Whitcombe's voluminous Duplicate Letter Book, in which he meticulously recorded details of his travels. AWMM/WT.

explain New Zealand requirements. In a letter to Christchurch, he had little difficulty justifying his efforts: 'We have always been told by the London office that everything had to be paid for in London of this description, this is quite a fallacy, which, as you see, I am proving every day. All that people want is confidence, and when they know that our position is indisputable they are indifferent to the exact terms of settlement'.[45]

He arranged to visit eighteen factories in Bristol, Birmingham, Wolverhampton, Leicester, Sheffield, Manchester and Scotland, but after attending a printing exhibition obtained a number of other invitations. These ranged from publishers to equipment manufacturers and paper and ink suppliers. While a number of firms had strict policies on factory tours, initial reluctance was quickly overcome when the competition resided half a world away. These courtesies even extended to stints on the shop floor to operate machines and assess their complexity. He presciently observed that rotary lithography was the method of the future and made a detailed critical study of the relative merits of Linotype and Monotype composing machines, recognizing the quality advantages of the latter for book production. With a long list of equipment purchases for the London office to finalize at the end of his tour, he confidently concluded, 'I can see that with improved machinery we could do the whole work of New Zealand without any fear of possible competition if we only liked to lay it out for ourselves'.[46] In addition, there was also the opportunity to wrest lucrative specialist work back from the colonial centre.

He also visited the paper mills of John Dickinson & Co, and was particularly impressed with the Apsley factory which covered six acres – just as Whitcombe & Tombs's own factory in Christchurch would in a few short years. He paid special attention to motive power for the factory and machines, the machines themselves, as well as pay rates, the use of minors and hours of work. With regard to industrial relations, he clearly liked the more docile approach of the English:

I could not help but notice the very nice feelings which existed between the employees and the house. All whom I came into contact with in the shape of foreman and managers ... seem to think of their employer's welfare before their own, and of course to me it was particularly noticeable considering the very different relationship which exists between employer and employees in New Zealand, or indeed Australia.[47]

He also observed modern factory conditions, recording the latest developments in lighting and ventilation, but was most impressed by the prevalence of piecework, convinced that it was the key to efficient production. He stayed

---

45 Letter, 23 April 1904, AWMM/WT, pp. 15–16.
46 Letter, 4 June 1904, AWMM/WT, p. 122.
47 Letter, 23 April 1904, AWMM/WT, p. 14.

overnight with Sir Henry K. Stephenson, who was pleased with Whitcombe & Tombs's handling of their agency. He discussed in depth the Point Lining System with both partners over dinner and was deeply impressed with their comprehensive grasp of the management and production aspects of their business. A more immediate result of their conversation was a directive to New Zealand to replace type only in the Point system.

Finally, he met with a number of publishers, including Maurice Macmillan, whom he had met twice previously, in Christchurch in 1884 and again in London in 1888. He also visited George Newnes and Hodder & Stoughton to obtain illustrations for the *Southern Cross Readers*. He sought co-publishing arrangements with Simpkin Marshall, Hodder & Stoughton, Hutchinsons and Grant Richards, regarding joint imprints with Australian rights as important in raising their profile with the Australian book trade. Most were prepared to publish an edition of 2000 if half the sales were guaranteed by Whitcombe & Tombs. Having touted an advance copy of Drummond's *Animals of New Zealand*, he regarded it 'as good as anything that could be done on this side' and concluded hopefully 'I might say that I believe that the possibilities of publishing books of New Zealand interest on this side are very great if they were properly handled'.[48]

The result of George Whitcombe's ambitious plans is perhaps best captured by Denis Glover's soubriquet, 'The Octopus'.[49] W. E. Channing famously asserted that 'the diffusion of these silent teachers, books, through the whole community is to work greater effects than artillery, machinery or legislation. The culture which is spread, whilst an unspeakable good to the individual, is also to become the stability of nations.' The diffusion of silent teachers in the form of educational publishing and bookselling ensured a dominant role for Whitcombe & Tombs in the developing New Zealand book trade. The firm's rapid growth from regional to national to international publisher seems sufficient basis for a more modest claim to the stability and independence of a national book trade.

---

48 Letter, 25 June 1904, AWMM/WT, p. 192; Letter, 16 July 1904, AWMM/WT, p. 217.
49 Denis Glover was a well-known poet and founder of New Zealand's dominant literary publisher, the Caxton Press.

Cole's Book Arcade: Marvellous Melbourne's 'Palace of Intellect'[1]

WALLACE KIRSOP

ALTHOUGH IT IS OFTEN INADVISABLE to pay too much heed to items published on the Internet, a short article headed 'Before Barnes Met Noble' put out on 17 November 2001 by one David Minor makes a point that lies at the heart of the investigation on which the present paper offers a preliminary report. Mr Minor recalls the story of Cole's Book Arcade in four slightly jokey paragraphs and ventures the opinion that in Melbourne's Bourke Street Mall, in other words in the very centre of the modern city's commercial precinct, there 'once stood the first bookselling superstore'.[2] We came across this trans-Pacific contribution when at Monash University's Centre for the Book we were preparing a little celebration in November 2003 of the one hundred-and-twentieth birthday of Cole's arcade in its ultimate location. Apart from the nostalgia that seizes Melburnians old enough to have visited as children – *especially* as children – a business that closed its doors three-quarters of a century ago, there was and is a very serious reason for remembering Cole's long and flamboyant career as a bookseller. John Arnold notes in volume two of *A History of the Book in Australia* that he was 'a fore-runner of contemporary book superstores',[3] but it must be added that this fact seems to have escaped the trade in London and in New York in more recent decades. Vision is no doubt selective and at times appears to have some difficulty in crossing the Equator, to South America as well as to Australasia, let it be said. However, we all know that thoughts of distant external markets are not entirely absent from metropolitan boardrooms, especially those populated by expatriate Canadians and Australians, and it behoves us as historians to confront problems of distribution that are too often neglected in the search for producers on the one hand and readers and audiences on the other.

Before looking at the nature and the significance of Cole's innovations, it is necessary to give a brief account of his life. Inevitably this will emphasize the

---

1 Once again I am in debt to the State Library of Victoria and to its specialist collections. In particular my thanks go to Sandra Burt, Pam Pryde and Des Cowley.

2 <http://www.home.eznet.net/~dminor/TM011117.html [accessed 15 November 2004].

3 *A History of the Book in Australia 1891–1945: A National Culture in a Colonised Market*, ed. by Martyn Lyons and John Arnold (St Lucia, 2001), p. 132.

extent to which he started as an outsider in a trade that, even in the Australian colonies of the nineteenth century, was dominated by people trained in the British Isles. George Robertson and Samuel Mullen, who arrived in Melbourne on the same day – 12 November 1852 – as Cole, are notable examples of this transplanting of skills and of ready access to key networks in London, Dublin and Glasgow. It could be, of course, that Cole's very lack of experience, except as a customer and would-be author, was what made him able to think new thoughts about how books should be marketed and to dare to strike out in fresh directions and to revive old practices suited to the specific circumstances of Melbourne.

Predictably Cole has not been neglected by writers in Australia, although few of them have been practitioners of academic book history. Most recently *Australian Garden History* carried an article by Ken Duxbury, 'With Mirrors and Rainbows' (the latter being the bookseller's favourite symbol), documenting a life-long interest in flowers and gardens.[4] None the less the only substantial work is *Cole of the Book Arcade: A Pictorial Biography of E. W. Cole*, written and published thirty years ago by Cole Turnley, repository of the family's memories and heir to his grandfather's copyrights.[5] The author was obviously hampered by the lack of a solid corpus of business records, and the narrative is filled out with a certain amount of hypothesizing as well as many things derived from oral tradition. Despite this the book is no mere hagiography and provides a useful basis for further research on its subject. Its great strength, reflected in the title, is its use of pictures from various sources. In a sense the whole Cole enterprise has to be seen to be believed and to be grasped in all its complexity. Readers seeking more than a modest recourse to illustration must go to Cole Turnley's biography, which is notably and deplorably absent from most great British libraries.

One early document, a diary kept partly in shorthand in the first half of the 1860s, was available to Turnley. It was recently acquired by the State Library of Victoria at the John Chapman sale.[6] Its principal interest in the present context is that it records the beginning of Cole's career selling books from a stall in Melbourne's old Eastern Market in the last months of 1865. Until the 1990s it was believed that the Cole archives, like those of his leading

---

4   14.6 (May/June 2003), 20–24 and 15.1 (July/August 2003), 14–19.

5   (Hawthorn, Victoria: Cole Publications, 1974). See also his article on Cole in the *Australian Dictionary of Biography*, III: *1851–1890 A–C* (Melbourne, 1969), pp. 438–40, and Richard Aitken's brief notice in *The Oxford Companion to Australian Gardens*, ed. by Richard Aitken and Michael Looker (South Melbourne, 2002), p. 147.

6   *The Library of Dr John Chapman: Australiana, Printed & Manuscript, & Books on Various Subjects to be Sold by Auction Melbourne 24–25 February 2004* (Prahran, Victoria, 2004), lot 281 (with illustration).

contemporaries in the Melbourne book world of the 1860s and later – George Robertson, Samuel Mullen and Henry Tolman Dwight – had vanished. Then, one day and by chance, an astute collector came across the library and papers of Henry Williams, Cole's employee from 1891, later departmental manager and eventually trustee, in a skip at the docks. In time, therefore, it will be possible to reconstruct aspects of the history of the business through the 1890s and on to its demise in 1929, eleven years after Cole's own death.

Beyond fading memories and personal testimonies the way forward also lies through more systematic exploitation of the printed record: the magazine published over a period of thirty years between the 1880s and the First World War[7] along lines familiar in the Australian trade before D. W. Thorpe centralized such material in 1921 in his *Australian Stationery and Fancy Goods Journal,* which soon embraced bookselling and eventually became the *Australian Bookseller and Publisher;*[8] the advertisements that appeared for many years chiefly in the Melbourne *Herald,* an evening newspaper with a more popular audience than its august and politically committed morning rivals the *Argus* and the *Age.*[9] Then, too, there is the daunting task of compiling a descriptive bibliography of Cole publications from the religious, political and ideological – *The Real Place in History of Jesus and Paul, Religious Sects of all Nations* and *A Discourse in Defence of Mental Freedom* in the 1860s, *Spiritualism* in the 1870s, *Federation of the World* in the 1880s, *A White Australia Impossible* in the 1900s, and *Evils of the Drink Traffic* in the 1910s – to the entertaining scissors-and-paste classics like *Cole's Funny Picture Book* first released to an enduring juvenile market in 1879.[10] These and other compilations, often produced from Cole's own printing department, are not to be confused with the many titles from British firms that were distributed in substantial quantities from the Book Arcade's address and with its imprint on the title-page. They pose other problems, for which John Turner's Walter Scott Publishing Company bibliography and some other recent work provide merely the beginnings of answers.[11]

The man who arrived in late 1852 in what came to be known as 'Marvellous Melbourne', the 'Chicago of the South' – and this long before the deeds of Squizzy Taylor in the 1920s and a recent spate of spectacular gangland

---

7 The fragmentary holdings of *Cole's Book Buyers' Guide* in the State Library of Victoria run from volume IV of 1889 to numbers 77 and 79 of 1917.

8 See Joyce Thorpe Nicholson and Daniel Wrixon Thorpe, *A Life of Books: The Story of D. W. Thorpe Pty Ltd 1921–1987* (Middle Park, Victoria, 2000). Thorpe (1889–1976) sets down his own memories and impressions of Cole, pp. 45–8.

9 By the 1880s Cole was advertising every day on page one of the *Herald* and once a week, on Saturday, in the *Age.*

10 For a brief checklist see Turnley, *Cole of the Book Arcade,* p. 190.

11 John R. Turner, *The Walter Scott Publishing Company: A Bibliography* (Pittsburgh, 1997).

murders! – came from unlikely origins for an impresario of the book world. He was born in 1832 at Woodchurch, near Tenterden in the Kentish Weald.[12] His mother and his Methodist stepfather ensured that he had an elementary education, but he then began to earn his keep by farm-labouring. At the age of eighteen he went off to seek his fortune in London and quite soon decided to emigrate to the Cape Colony, an experience that was to influence his later advanced views on race relations. The attraction of the Victorian gold rush became irresistible and Cole embarked on a long apprenticeship in Australian life, almost thirteen years, before turning to bookselling at the age of thirty-three. They were adventurous times, during which he tried his hand at a number of occupations: digger on the goldfields, seller of cordials to thirsty miners, property speculator in a slight way, traveller down the Murray and early photographer of the customs of the Aborigines, proprietor of a pie-stall in Melbourne's Eastern Market after spending several years in and around Castlemaine with visits to Adelaide and Sydney. More important for his later development were his contacts with rationalist circles and his reading in 'public libraries', most likely mechanics' institutes rather than what we now understand by the term, even if it should be noted that the Melbourne Public Library opened its doors on 11 February 1856. In Castlemaine he had the opportunity to come into contact with enterprising booksellers, including the interesting Charles Glass,[13] but his own move into the trade in 1865 seems to have been almost fortuitous, the end-result of vain attempts to find a commercial publisher for his first pamphlet. From selling or giving it away from his pie-stall he progressed to building up a small stock of secondhand works and to dealing in them. As the laconic and partly misspelt entries in his early diary say:

	1865		
Saterday Sep 30 reguarly			
started Book shop in			
Eastern Market took	1	14	5½
Bought old books		6	
at starting			
Books in stock about			
600 volumes and 600			

---

12 The following account of Cole's career is unavoidably much indebted to Cole Turnley but, where possible, original documents have been consulted independently.

13 See the brief entry in *A Biographical Register 1788–1939. Notes from the Name Index of the Australian Dictionary of Biography*, ed. by H. J. Gibbney and Ann G. Smith (Canberra: *Australian Dictionary of Biography*, 1987), I, 264, and *Australian Almanacs 1806–1930: A Bibliography*, comp. by Ian Morrison, Maureen Perkins and Tracey Caulfield (Hawthorn East, Victoria, 2003), pp. 92–3.

periodicals both of avarage sample			
and cost about	17	0	0
Monday Oct 1th took		11	6 [14]

Note that he was already his own man, not an employee, and that things were to remain thus until his death more than half a century later. His rise was rapid: to a larger and more prominent stall in the Eastern Market – 'Cole's Cheap Book Store' – and then ten doors down Bourke Street in 1873 to the first 'Cole's Book Arcade', a space twenty feet by ninety feet reshaped as a place where everything was inviting and perfectly accessible to customers and visitors. As before, the public was invited to 'READ FOR AS LONG AS YOU LIKE. NOBODY ASKED TO BUY'; in other words Cole was maintaining the popular culture of the stall, as distinct from traditional, genteel bookshops where barriers and obstacles were *de rigueur* in this and later times. The Arcade's appeal was reinforced by the ingenious pictorial typography of its regular advertising on the front page of the *Herald*. In brash and boastful Melbourne of the 1870s and 1880s, contrasted by overseas visitors with a relatively discreet and refined Sydney, Cole's voice was one of the loudest and most extravagant. Hyperbole and publicity were key factors in his bids to attract and hold a mass audience. In 1875 he used his appointed spot to advertise, quite successfully, for a wife. The household settled in a flat above the shop. Cole's publishing ventures turned away from his private hobby-horses to books destined to appeal to his broad market, and in particular in 1879, to the *Funny Picture Book*. By late 1883 he was ready for the final move, to a new arcade a few doors east of the Royal Arcade, the city's oldest, built at the end of the 1860s. The grand opening on Melbourne Cup Day, the first Tuesday in November, came as the crescendo of an intensive advertising campaign:

COLE'S NEW BOOK ARCADE WILL OPEN ON CUP DAY. It is the FINEST SIGHT In MELBOURNE, And the GRANDEST BOOK SHOP IN THE WORLD. Intellectual non-racing People are invited there instead of going to the RACES. [15]

Through the boom decade that took Melbourne's population to over 400,000 (a phenomenon comparable to the growth from next to nothing in the nineteenth century of places in the Northern Hemisphere like Lodz, Odessa and Chicago) Cole's Book Arcade continued to prosper. Eventually, through freeholds and leaseholds, Cole was able to achieve an arcade that ran from Bourke

---

14   State Library of Victoria, MSS PA 04/55.
15   Reproduced in facsimile in *Cole of the Book Arcade*, p. 74. The advertisement appeared in both the *Herald* and the *Age* on Saturday 3 November 1883. The *Argus*, meanwhile, was announcing in Cup Week George Robertson's 'first and last CLEARANCE SALE' and a picnic to commemorate the fourth centenary of the birth of Martin Luther.

Street across Little Collins Street to Collins Street, thus extending over two city blocks. Claims were made that there were two million volumes on the shelves and half-a-mile of walkways. Certainly there was, in keeping with old traditions, a great diversity of stock: new and secondhand books, music, stationery, fancy goods, ornaments. At various times the arcade had other features as well: a lending library, a printing shop, a wholesale department, a tea salon, a fernery with a large aviary, funny mirrors, a cage of monkeys, a band. Over a hundred chairs were available for people who took literally the invitation to read without restriction. Engravings and photographs allow us to glimpse cluttered but planned interiors such as those of the Bourke Street arcade or of Mrs Cole holding court. The proprietor's taste for the sentimental and the whimsical was nowhere so obvious as in the doggerel and jingles he composed as part of publicity campaigns that also included medals and plates (all of them now collectors' items).

The relentlessness with which Cole sought the custom of children and of the great mass of the population is obvious. The Arcade was a place of popular entertainment and its owner was intent on overcoming the *Schwellenangst* that kept most people out of daunting cultural institutions. That he was largely successful is clear from the fond memories of older Melburnians and from the fact that he was able to weather the terrible crash of the early 1890s. Indeed he was able to take over the failed business of E. A. Petherick, who had been George Robertson's London manager from 1870 to 1887, and to run shops in both Adelaide and Sydney.

The inherent weakness in a business dependent on the energy and the inventiveness of one person became more obvious as Cole approached his eighties. His wife died in 1911, and Cole took the opportunity to move out of the shop apartment and to take up a suburban residence. He chose Earlsbrae Hall in Essendon, a 27-room mansion built by a brewer in the 1880s for £35,000. Being more remote from the office and the day-to-day running of the shop, Cole seems to have lost his grip. There was a great deal of over-ordering, and things began to slide, so that the debacle of the 1920s was hardly avoidable. For all its diversity – Cole had sold the Public Library of Victoria Sir Redmond Barry's annotated copies of his speeches and antiquarian law books from the library of John Macgregor in the 1880s – the enterprise was not able to withstand new pressures and ultimately collapsed.[16]

Let us turn to the rationale of this high-pressure showmanship. What were Cole's sources of inspiration? Where and how did he learn about the trade and

16 See the 1885 Stockbook of the State Library of Victoria. See also Wallace Kirsop, '"The Finest Private Library in Australia": John Macgregor's Collection', *The La Trobe Journal*, no. 69 (Autumn 2002), 30–38, and 'Redmond Barry and Libraries', *The La Trobe Journal*, no. 73 (Autumn 2004), 55–66.

its possibilities? The answers are far from obvious, and a number of contexts need to be considered.

To begin with, a word is required about my own reasons for being interested in the wider significance of the Cole phenomenon. As I indicated above, I have long thought that we give insufficient attention to questions of distribution in book-history studies in general, but that reproach hardly applies to the *Print Networks* series.[17] For a variety of partly accidental reasons, I have been involved in studying subscription publication in eighteenth-century France, hence networks of many kinds, and in supervising and doing research on discount and remainder bookselling in that country between 1750 and 1830. In addition anyone with experience editing journals and publishing academic monographs cannot fail to be acutely aware of the central role of the distributor.

The 'book superstore' is, therefore, fascinating, especially since many people in Australia seem to have forgotten that the Very Large Bookshop was part of their cultural heritage, not just through Cole, but also through Dymock's Book Arcade, founded in Sydney in the mid-1880s, and through the stores of Angus & Robertson and Robertson & Mullens (as the Melbourne firm became in the twentieth century). In London, of course, there was Foyles, founded in 1903. What do we read in the centenary celebratory volume of last year about 'the world's greatest bookshop'?

William's vision was a bookshop for the people – not just for academics, collectors, specialists or the gentry but for every man, woman and child, of any station in life: 'The People's Bookshop'. He was inspired by James Lackington's Temple of the Muses at Chiswell Street in London in the late eighteenth century, whose galleried bookshop was so large that, it was said, a coach and six could drive around inside it. William was an authority on the lives of booksellers of the past, and he modelled himself on Thomas Guy and James Lackington.[18]

Cole with his arcade 'three stories high, 600 feet deep, and an average width of 45 feet' is absent from this genealogy. Should we be surprised? There does not appear to be any notice of the November 1883 opening in *The Bookseller*, which, in publishing news and gossip about the trade, by no means ignored the Australian colonies. Thus, on 3 May 1884, a report was included on the 'sixth annual picnic of the booksellers and stationers of Sydney'. A month later it was the arrival of Ward Lock on the Australian scene that was recorded.[19]

When one remembers that the premises of Lackington, Allen, & Co. in Finsbury Square, conveniently just outside the City of London and the

---

17 See Wallace Kirsop, 'Booksellers and their Customers: Some Reflections on Recent Research', *Book History*, 1 (1998), 283–303.
18 Penny Mountain, with Christopher Foyle, *Foyles: A Celebration* (London, 2003), pp. 8–9.
19 *Bookseller* (1884), 459, 572.

jurisdiction of the Stationers' Company, had burnt down almost a decade before Cole tried his luck in the metropolis in 1850 and generations before the arrival on the scene of the Foyle brothers, one can wonder how much influence a distant memory of past hyperbole can have had. For the moment nobody, including James Raven,[20] has laid hands on the elusive plans of the undoubtedly impressive Finsbury Square structure.[21]

We know that Tenterden in Kent already had a bookseller in the eighteenth century.[22] We have to admit ignorance about most of what Cole did and saw in London before he shipped out to South Africa. How much did he discover about the Great Exhibition being prepared in the Crystal Palace? What contact did he have with London's arcades and covered markets? It is easy to agree with David McKitterick and Michael Winship, with whom I have discussed these matters, that such institutions have to be considered among the possible sources of inspiration, especially if one looks closely at certain decorative elements present in the interior of the Book Arcade. The Great Exhibition hypothesis has indeed been examined by David Farrar of Monash University Library in an unpublished paper. Cole's only renewed direct contact with Britain was during a buying trip in 1886, seventeen years before he and his wife went to Japan at the invitation of the Imperial Government. The author of attacks on the White Australia Policy deserved no less! By the middle of the 1880s, however, Cole could have claimed legitimately that he had a thing or two to teach about merchandizing techniques.

It is perhaps necessary to point out that Australia was much less isolated from and uninformed about the Northern Hemisphere in the 1870s and 1880s than earlier. A telegraphic link with the outside world had been completed in 1872, and sailing, or rather steaming, times between Melbourne and London had been reduced from three months in the early 1850s to under six weeks in the 1880s. As trade publications and catalogues prove abundantly, colonial readers had access to a vast range of books and periodicals. Think of the over 50,000 titles in stock at the warehouse of George Robertson, Cole's great wholesaler competitor, in the 1870s. Think, too, of a local press, the *Argus* and the *Age* with their weekly editions the *Australasian* and the *Leader*, that earned the unfeigned respect of Anthony Trollope and, three decades later, of Sidney Webb.[23] In these circumstances one could read about, and see pictures of, all

---

20 See his *London Booksellers and American Customers: Transatlantic Literary Community and the Charleston Library Society, 1748–1811* (Columbia, 2002), plates 9 and 10.

21 See *Lasting Impressions: The Grolier Club Library* (New York, 2004), pp. 44–5, where the frontage is noted as 140 feet.

22 See R. J. Goulden, 'Print Culture in the Kentish Weald', in *The Reach of Print: Making, Selling and Using Books*, ed. by Peter Isaac and Barry McKay (Winchester, 1998), p. 8.

23 *The Webbs' Australian Diary 1898*, ed. by A. G. Austin (Melbourne, 1965), pp. 113–14.

pertinent developments in the great European and North American centres. In addition one could profit from the fact, aptly recalled during our proceedings, that 'physical distance is also critical distance'. The immigrants of Cole's gener-ation were not afraid to innovate and to invent however attached they were to their British heritage. At the periphery one could pick and choose the elements one wanted from a centre that had lost its coercive and regulatory powers after Lord Campbell's determination on free trade in 1852. The native-born like David Scott Mitchell and Isaac Isaacs could be highly and delicately cultivated or internationally and pertinently informed without ever having left the Southern Hemisphere, as Beatrice Webb remarked with some surprise in 1898.[24] Even in Adelaide the Braggs could lay the basis of their joint Nobel Prize in Physics.

The gold rush decade of the 1850s attracted plenty of low-level adven-turers, but also people of enterprise and imagination. What contacts did Cole have with John Speechly Gotch, founder of the multinational firm Gordon & Gotch *from* and *in* Melbourne? Did he know Benjamin S. Nayler, who has recently been claimed as the inventor of the remainder trade in books in the Netherlands in the early nineteenth century?[25] Lisa Kuitert does not mention that Nayler had a second career in Melbourne in the 1860s and 1870s.

There is much that is uncertain in all this. The documents do not allow much more than guesses. We badly need an international and comparative study of the Very Large Bookshop, with its updating of the multiple attractions and distractions of the small provincial stores of the late eighteenth and early nineteenth centuries. Were there big shops in New York, say?[26] Were the cus-tomers able to read at their leisure without buying or were they kept at bay by counters? One has to be attentive to the iconography gathered by Sigfred Taubert in *Bibliopola* and to try to find more images. Pictures of the interior of H. T. Dwight's shop in the 1860s[27] and Sir Redmond Barry's robust defence at the International Conference of Librarians in London in 1877 of the freedom allowed to users of the Melbourne Public Library[28] suggest that in Victoria

---

24 *The Webbs' Australian Diary*, p. 68.

25 See Lisa Kuitert, 'B. S. Nayler and the Emergence of the Remainder Trade', in *The Bookshop of the World: The Role of the Low Countries in the Book-Trade 1473–1941*, ed. by Lotte Hellinga, Alastair Duke, Jacob Harskamp and Theo Hermans ('t Goy-Houten, 2001), pp. 277–84.

26 Roger Stoddard has reminded me of William Gowans, whose career in the previous gener-ation had curious parallels to Cole's. See *'Put a Resolute Hart to a Steep Hill': William Gowans, Antiquary and Bookseller* (New York, 1990).

27 See Ian F. McLaren, *Henry Tolman Dwight: Bookseller and Publisher* (Parkville, 1989), pp. xiv, 18.

28 See 'Redmond Barry and Libraries', passim.

people expected to have untrammelled access to the bookstock. In many places elsewhere things were different.

Some assertions are possible. Cole was familiar with the culture of stalls and of covered markets. Indeed, before he moved to his new Book Arcade in 1883, he had tried the experiment of leasing and running the whole of a refurbished Eastern Market. Conflicts with the owners, the Melbourne City Council, led him to retreat to a sphere he could control absolutely. However, his commitment to the freedom of access of these informal venues was obvious. Arcades had become part of the Melbourne scene, and Cole was able to adapt this modern form of shopping to his own purposes. Exhibitions were a regular feature in Australian cities in the second half of the nineteenth century, and the building put up in 1880 for Melbourne's own International Exhibition is the last surviving example of these palaces of industry from before 1900.[29] There were, then, multiple influences at work to reinforce Cole's combination of generosity and of skill in self-publicity. The undeniable individual flair took advantage of the moment and of the society's hunger for a shopping experience that was supremely entertaining.

If, in conclusion, we are to draw any general lessons from a case that remains *sui generis*, with Cole the precursor as its inimitable focus, they concern the relationship between the book and print worlds and modern consumer society. Before the twentieth century print was the dominant medium of advertising.[30] Booksellers freeing themselves from guild control gravitated to the new shopping centres, after 1780 in Paris to the Palais Royal, where the arcade was first developed. Even in the seventeenth century, the Galerie du Palais of a celebrated engraving by Abraham Bosse was a location where books took their place in a world of luxury consumption some distance away from the Latin Quarter and the University, the controlling authority. A recent Bosse exhibition in Paris described the Galerie du Palais as 'a sort of fashionable big store'.[31] In the long history of modernization, in which I see bookselling playing a pioneer part wherever it is freed from guild restraints, Cole's Book Arcade is an internationally significant episode.

---

29 See David Dunstan *et al*, *Victorian Icon: The Royal Exhibition Building Melbourne* (Melbourne, 1996).

30 Recent treatments of advertising in Australia, e.g. Robert Crawford, 'The Quest for Legitimacy: The Growth and Development of the Australian Advertising Industry, 1900–1969', *Australian Historical Studies*, 36 (2004), 355–74, can be said to pay insufficient attention to the nineteenth century.

31 *Abraham Bosse savant graveur, Tours, vers 1604–1676, Paris*, ed. by Sophie Join-Lambert and Maxime Préaud (Paris; Tours, 2004), p. 187.

Collins and the Commonwealth: Publishers' Publicity and the Twentieth-Century Circulation of Popular Fiction Titles

NICOLE MATTHEWS

THIS PAPER DISCUSSES the post-war publicity and promotion strategies of William Collins and Sons, an important and longstanding British publisher.[1] Despite the fact that Collins's turnover and output was one of the most significant in the twentieth century, little has been written about the company. One intriguing difference between Collins and more fully documented twentieth-century publishing houses is that a great deal of Collins's success, at least in the twentieth century, was derived from its middle-brow or mass market publications. By the late 1970s it was the largest general publisher in Britain, but one which was without a literary fiction or educational publishing list. In the post-war period its paperback imprint Fontana was particularly successful, running neck and neck for British third biggest paperback house along with Pan.[2] Yet many of these paperbacks were not the esteemed 'eggheads' of Penguin, but were often bestsellers of a less highbrow kind. According to Barron 'in traditional publishing circles, the firm is regarded as uncomfortably professional, very (some would say excessively) commercially-oriented in the way it goes about its business'.[3]

This commercial orientation of Collins provides a useful corrective to the sometimes articulated view that the British publishing industry was a gentleman's industry, coy about marketing, at least until the increasing influence of the USA in the 1960s. Taking a focus on a publisher like Collins requires scrutiny of publicity and marketing practices and a close examination of the role of bestselling middlebrow or popular fiction. Paying such close attention

1 This paper has been completed with the help of staff at the Glasgow University Archive Services and the Princeton University Special Collections and Rare Books. Research towards the paper was completed with the financial assistance of a Library Research Grant from the Friends of the Princeton University Library. Thanks to Eugenia Duarte Cunha de Freitas, Josh Matthews, Derrick Cameron, Joe Moran and Nickianne Moody for help with researching and revising this paper.
2 Ken Gofton, 'Canny Collins' controlled change', *Financial Times*, 25 August 1971, p. 15.
3 C. Barron, 'How Collins was magnified', *Management Today* 34 (1978), p. 107.

to the publishing history of bestsellers, it has been argued, might transform accounts of national publishing industries.[4] The significance of popular fiction titles for Collins were such that when they hit financial difficulties in the late 1970s, the broadsheet press suggested that the absence of bestsellers by writers like Hammond Innes and Alistair MacLean from that year's list could be held partly responsible, while the first threats of Collins's take-over by Rupert Murdoch in the early 1980s were countered with threats by popular writers like Innes to take their publications elsewhere.[5] Thinking about Collins as a company really requires us to engage with their bestselling fiction.

A focus on Collins enables us to identify some important trends in twentieth-century British publishing through a firm that both exemplifies and, perhaps, exaggerates these trends, anticipating developments that would occur later in other parts of British publishing. In particular, taking Collins as the subject of this paper forces us to consider very carefully publicity and marketing as key elements of publishing, and, intertwined with this, both the role of popular fiction within twentieth-century British publishing and the relationship between export and domestic markets. Taking this focus on publishers' publicity, as I will suggest later, presents some difficulties in tracing sources which will lead me to propose a particular focus on the materiality of books, and especially book dust jackets, as a useful source of information.

W. A. R. Collins, the Chairman of Collins for much of the postwar period, was seen within and without the company as particularly interested in marketing and publicity for books. His obituary in the in-house paper *Collins News* in November 1976 gives a vivid description of his passion for sales and publicity:

Sales representatives are not traditionally the most impressionable of men, yet under his chairmanship, a sales-meeting took on some of the quality of a revivalist meeting with targets zooming through the roof as the latest, greatest Collins bestseller was expounded in a whirlwind of excitement... It was this enthusiasm which would send him, late on a cold January night after a dinner party, pacing the pavements of London with his plaid cape flying behind him as he inspected the bookshop windows and denounced the iniquities of booksellers who devoted less than half their space to Collins' books: which would lead him, as he walked from the Central Hotel to Cathedral Street to pounce on some luckless assistant at John Smiths', still only half-awake and cross-examine her on how many copies she had sold of book X and why there was such an inadequate display of books Y and Z.

---

4   Richard Nile and David Walker, 'The Mystery of the Missing Bestseller' in *A History of the Book in Australia, 1891–1945: a National Culture in a Colonised Market*, ed. by Martyn Lyons and John Arnold (St. Lucia, 2001), p. 253.

5   'Collins booked for recovery', *Daily Telegraph*, 25 March 1980.

There is a danger here, perhaps of subscribing to hagiography, a danger to which, according to disgruntled employees writing to *Private Eye* in the mid 1970s, the House of Collins was particularly susceptible. However, other sources support this view of 'The Chairman' as particularly concerned with publicity and marketing. The *Daily Telegraph* obituary of Collins in 1976 described him as a brilliant promoter of books, citing his establishment of the Collins Crime Club series in the 1930s. Rogers and Rogers, in their account of bookselling in New Zealand comment that Collins' enthusiasm was infectious and many booksellers, anxious to please the distinguished publisher, ordered excessively as a result, often having to cancel their orders later![6] The very status of Collins as a paternalistic family firm throughout this period suggests that this enthusiasm by its chairman reflects on the practices of the company more broadly. For example, as early as the 1930s, Collins was viewed as exceptional in moving beyond notices in the trade papers and Sunday newspapers in its advertising of new books. In the 1950s its publicity campaigns were seen as leading the industry by commentators outside of the company as well as within it. Collins went on to embrace formal market research earlier than many other British publishing houses. Hardback sales director Iain Ogston commented in 1978: 'Unlike some other publishing houses, the sales people in Collins are not hidden away in some woodshed at the back, but are made to feel an important and integral part of the business'.[7]

In yet another way Collins represented a trend in the British book industry, but to an exaggerated extent through its reliance on exports. The British publishing industry has for a long time been particularly reliant on exports, compared, for example, to the US industry but Collins, particularly since the World War Two, has had a more globalized market than most. While around 25 per cent of the British publishing industry's book stock was exported during this period, 40 per cent and upward of Collins books were for export while by the late 1970s well over half of Collins's sales were made overseas.[8]

Australia was Collins's largest export market, as it indeed has been the largest market for British books more generally since at least the late nineteenth

6   Anna Rogers and Max Rogers, *Turning the Pages: the Story of Bookselling in New Zealand* (Auckland, 1993), p. 266.

7   Barron, 'How Collins was Magnified', 209. See also Linda Lloyd Grant, 'Fifty Years of Penguin Books' in *50 Penguin Years* (London, 1985), p. 23; Sydney Goldsack, 'Taking the Wooden Horse to Market' from *Fontana*, 4 (1950), 18; Sydney Hyde, 'Looking back on Publishers' Publicity – II", *The Bookseller*, 13 January 1973, 98; Sue Williams, "Agatha Christie and the mystery of the declining sales", *The Bookseller*, 24 March 1989, 1070–74.

8   Alison Baverstock, *Are Books Different?: Marketing in the Book Trade* (London, 1993); 'Publishers have good prospects' *The Scotsman*, 21 May 1969; Jan Collins 'The Future Looks Bright', *Collins News Annual Report*, 1 April 1977, p. 1.

century. One commentator described this relationship in the late 1960s: 'British publishers hold dominion over the book publishing business in Australia, a territory in which they have planted their colophons like flags'.[9] The importance of the antipodes for Collins's sales is reflected in the fact that the firm from the 1870s had permanent staff in Sydney and from late 1880s in New Zealand. In a 'fifties issue of *Fontana* this 'Australia-conscious' perspective was such that export staff were urged not to 'neglect our many other markets'.[10] By the late 1970s, no less than 25 per cent of Collins's turnover occurred within the Australian market. Sales figures for some of Collins's most important writers highlight the importance of exports generally and the Australian market more specifically, particularly for popular fiction. Alistair MacLean's *The Way to Dusty Death*, for example, released in September 1973, had sold after eight weeks over 26,000 copies in the home market, but over 34,000 overseas, including 11,000 in Australia, a pattern which very closely copied sales of his *Bear Island*, published in 1971.[11]

Given the great significance placed on publicity and marketing by Collins, one would expect such a large number of exports to impact on the way in which the firm marketed its books. Certainly publicizing and selling books in export markets played an important role in the culture of the firm. The importance of exports was hammered home in the news from the Chairman in virtually every issue of *Fontana*, Collins's in-house magazine of the 1940s and 1950s, while from this period onward Collins himself made many overseas trips, highlighted in the firm's internal publications. British publishers like Collins were described by industry commentators as arriving on antipodean shoes in the northern winter 'as regularly as the mutton birds from Siberia'.[12] Collins also laid great importance on authors' overseas visits, urging reluctant writers like MacLean to undertake them and celebrating them on the pages of in-house journals. Comments on publicity within the Commonwealth features heavily in the post-war archived correspondence of the firm. Hammond Innes

---

9   Helen Frizzell, 'The British stake in Australian publishing', *The Bookseller*, 21 June 1969, 2884. Also Graeme Johanson, *Colonial Editions in Australia, 1843–1972* (Wellington, New Zealand, 2000), p. 5.

10 'News from Afar', *Fontana* 6 (1952), 5–6 (p. 5). Also *Books and Print in New Zealand: A Guide to Print Culture in Aotearoa*, ed. by Penny Griffith, Ross Harvey and Keith Maslon (Wellington, New Zealand, 1997) and David Keir, *The House of Collins: the Story of a Scottish Family of Publishers from 1789 to the Present Day* (London, 1952).

11 Glasgow University Archive Service – Collins Archive – GB248 UGD243 William Collins, Son and Co. Ltd. Also Henry Eagles, 'Good reading from Collins', *The Scotsman*, March 1979 [note: no exact date or page, from clippings collection in the Collins archive]; *Annual Report* 1977, p. 2 (see Collins above).

12 O'Neill cited in Frizzell, 'The British stake in Australian publishing', p. 2884.

and W. A. R. Collins in the late 1940s and 1950s, for example, corresponded at length about the appearance of Fontana books in Canadian bookshops, about Sydney and Durban bookshops' window displays for Innes's book *Mary Deare*, and the importance of ensuring a supply of Innes's books to the South African market.[13] However, outside such commentary in authors' correspondence and in-house journals, there are significant difficulties in documenting the kind of publicity used to promote Collins books, even publicity for the bestselling, season-heading books like the popular fiction discussed here. As John Tebbel in his overview of publishing history notes, the archives of particular publishing houses, even for the twentieth century, are often fragmentary.[14] This seems to be especially true of records of publicity meetings. The history of publishers' publicity falls uncomfortably between the concerns of literary history with its focus on authorial intent and the more overtly commercial concerns of the advertising industry. This disciplinary awkwardness is reflected in archives and collections.

The Collins archive, part of the Glasgow University Scottish Business Archive, for example, preserves correspondence between authors, editors and publisher. Unfortunately, little record of the processes of devising publicity can be found within the catalogue of the papers. But a careful look at the 'scrap' paper bundling together the correspondence reveals some copies of minutes of publicity meetings and the bi-annual notes on books for export from the company's Chairman, notes found nowhere else in the archive. Other elements of publicity are still more elusive or ephemeral even than these formal minutes: showcards and streamers for booksellers' windows, bus advertisements, and the mostly unindexed advertisements and book reviews in mass-circulation magazines and newspapers. A few of the most prominent of these publicity campaigns are documented in editorial and advertising material in trade journals like *The Bookseller* and the *Australian Bookseller and Publisher*, and some are recorded in the papers of particular writers. However, one traceable and very useful source for supplementing such archival material and making sense of later twentieth-century publishers' publicity, I shall argue, are the jackets of the books themselves.

Recent writers on the history of the book have drawn attention to the value of the materiality of the book, and particularly its visual dimensions, as a key to understanding the book and of the experience of reading. Dorothy Collin cites Robert Darnton's comments that 'one could learn a great deal

---

13 Glasgow University Archive Service – Collins Archive – Hammond Innes correspondence 1/11/10.
14 John Tebbel, *A History of Book Publishing in the United States*, vol. IV (New York, 1981), xi.

about attitudes towards books by studying the way they are presented'.[15] Curiously, while this interest in the materiality of the book is evident in a number of explorations of print culture and practices of reading, it is rarely to be found in approaches to twentieth-century books. This absence is curious not just because the material of twentieth-century books is undoubtedly more readily available to the researcher than rarer earlier books, but also because of the way the visual becomes important in a new and obvious way to twentieth century books, with the emergence of the dust jacket and illustrated paperback covers.

The increasing importance in the period after World War Two of the jacket in the selling of books is testified to in a heated exchange of letters in the *Bookseller* of 1958. A bookseller from Durban forwarded to the British trade magazine a complaint from an active young sales assistant about the lack of detail about plot and colour in the cover image in some recent popular fiction. The questionable status of eye-catching jackets in the British publishing industry even at this stage was highlighted by the defensive retort of one of the publishers so critiqued, Michael Howard of Jonathan Cape: 'Perhaps nothing but a bare-bosomed blonde depicted in four-colour half tone will enable Mr Mace to sell a novel to his customers'.[16] Around the same time, L. S. Truepenny in his regular column in *The Bookseller*, 'On the Mailing List', both highlighted the growing importance of book covers as an element of advance publicity to booksellers and admitted some shame about that importance:

The world is impelled by pretty faces more than it cares to admit, I suspect and certainly book buyers (and of course, booksellers) are perilously sensitive to book jackets... a few words on what it was intended that the jacket should look like [would be useful]. In the absence of a picture, even a description would be better than nothing.[17]

The uncatalogued export notes and minutes of publicity meetings from the Collins archive highlight the centrality of book jackets for Collins in particular. Sales successes and failures were regularly predicted by and ascribed to the quality of book jackets. As early as 1958, the first response of an editorial committee to declining sales of the mystery and adventure series was to change the wrapper. Along similar lines, the November 1969 export notes on Collins's

---

15 Cited in Dorothy Collin, 'Bookmaking: publishers' readers and the physical book', *Publishing History* 44 (1988), 61. See also Michelle Moylan and Lane Stiles, 'Introduction' in *Reading Books: Essays on the Material Text and Literature in America*, ed. by Michelle Moylan and Lane Stiles (Amherst, 1996), p. 2; Gerard Curtis, *Visual Words: Art and the Material Book in Victorian England* (Aldershot, 2002); John Mansfield, *Book/Cover* (unpublished Masters thesis, Monash University, 2004).

16 'Letters: Jackets and Blurbs', *The Bookseller*, 3 Sept 1955, 899.

17 L. S. Truepenny, 'On the Mailing List', *The Bookseller*, 18 Oct 1958, 1583.

Spring 1970 list describes the publicity campaign around Catherine Gaskin's latest book, highlighted as particularly important for the Australian market: 'Everything has been centred around a very attractive jacket featuring the heroine and a portrait of the author. On this joint campaign we are spending the best part of 3,000 pounds to put over this author and all her books...'.

As this export note suggests, book jackets are a significant source of evidence not just of the way the book itself was packaged, but also about wider approaches to publicity. By the 1950s, they had become a central part of broader publicity campaigns. We can borrow a summary of important forms of publicity for this period from an article in *The Bookseller* from the mid 1960s. These forms of publicity included book reviews, printed publicity (such as catalogues), space advertising, point of sale promotion and editorial publicity such as 'news releases, gossip paragraphs ... interviews on television and so on'.[18] Many of these forms of publicity drew in important ways on book covers as source material.

While images inspired by, or photographs of, book jackets themselves are more prominent in US newspaper reviews and advertising, book jackets are occasionally used in advertising and reviews in UK and Australian newspapers, even as early as the mid-1950s. Perhaps more significantly, jackets play a notable role in publishers' advertising in the trade press, in both UK and Australia. Export issues of *The Bookseller* from the 1950s and 1960s, for example, incorporate cover images on a great many pages of its listings of books to be released in the upcoming season, interspersed with photographs of authors. Similarly, advertisements and information about upcoming publications and promotions in *Ideas* (later *The Australian Publisher and Bookseller*) feature, from the 1960s onwards, photographs of book covers. The use of book jackets in the trade press was all the more important because of the role of publications like *Ideas* as a way of contacting often far-flung booksellers who may not receive frequent visitors from publishers' representatives.[19]

Book jackets were also seen by Collins as a central element of in-store promotion. Much of the meditation on book jackets in the Collins archive of correspondence and minutes from the 1950s onwards consists of discussions of how particular jackets will work in a massed context at the point of sale or in window displays. The decision was made, for instance, in an editorial meeting concerning publicity in 1961 to trim the advertising budget in order to afford the purchase of more racks and stands for bookshops. Hammond Innes, in response to a query from Billy Collins, provides in a letter from 1956 a very

---

18 John White, 'Publishers' Publicity and the Library Market', *The Bookseller*, 27 November 1965, 2280.
19 Joyce Nicholson, 'Promoting a book', *Australian Bookseller and Publisher*, March 1979, 48.

detailed account of the impact of the way Fontana paperbacks are displayed *en masse* on shelves in Canadian bookstores. Again, the middle 1950s, around the time Fontana paperbacks begin to be produced, seems to be a turning point in the kinds of display techniques used in bookshops. Front facing displays in bookshops were starting to be used in New Zealand, for instance, by 1956.[20]

So what can we see from paying close attention to the covers of Collins's most popular fiction? One of the most striking features is that the covers and associated publicity for many of these books and authors were identical in Britain and markets within the Commonwealth, such as Australia. Collins was not one of the publishers who produced physically different 'colonial editions' for export; such practices were on the wane by the post-war period in any case.[21] Drawing on advertising and articles in the *Australian Bookseller and Publisher*, contemporary advertisements in *The Bookseller* and the covers of UK paperbacks themselves, it is clear that from at least the late 1960s, identical editions of books by writers like MacLean, MacInnes, Bagley and Innes were being used in the two markets.

While explicitly put together to alert overseas booksellers to the forthcoming publications of the next six months, the Spring and Autumn export editions of *The Bookseller*, were also used by UK retailers. Anthony Wilson, a UK-based bookseller, for instance, in a talk to the Publishers' Publicity Circle in 1965 commented on the great usefulness for bookshops of the comprehensive indexing of new titles and the publishers' advertising in the export editions of *The Bookseller*. *The Bookseller* itself acknowledged this dual purpose for the export issues, with its move 'to meet the wishes of booksellers' of the index to books announced, 'which has developed as a kind of reference catalogue of forthcoming books' to the front of the magazines.[22] These advertisements and editorial notes were heavily illustrated with photographs of book jackets. Thus the publicity used to alert retailers internationally of forthcoming books was the same as that sent to British booksellers.

The centrality of book jackets to publishers' publicity makes it unsurprising that there are convergences between the wider publicity campaigns around popular books in Britain and Australia. For example, we find not just that the editions of Ngaio Marsh's book *Photo Finish* and Helen MacInnes' *The Hidden Target* were released in Australia featuring the same jackets as in the UK, but that a similar press campaign, pairing the books and using their

---

20 Rogers and Rogers, *Turning the Pages*, p. 32. See also Glasgow UBA, Collins papers, Innes GB248 UGD253 1/11/10.

21 Johanson, *Colonial Editions in Australia*, p. 51.

22 'Notes and News', *The Bookseller*, 24 July 1965, 237–9 (p. 237). See also 'Publishers' Publicity – its Use and Uselessness to Booksellers', *The Bookseller*, 27 March 1965, 1586.

cover images, was used in both countries.[23] The similarities of book jackets in Britain and Australia tell us, then, not only something about the way the books themselves might have been received by booksellers and consumers, but frequently gives us a guide to the other kinds of publicity that were produced to support the marketing of these books.

One way of seeing this convergence would be as an indication of the lack of respect by British publishers for the independent concerns of overseas sales markets, an extension of the view that Frizzel articulates of the colonial attitude of British publishers towards Commonwealth markets. There is perhaps some truth to this view. A reading of the 'Letter from Australia' in *Fontana*, for instance, points to the heavy steering hand of the Chairman in the selection of books to publicize internationally. The books that regular correspondent Doris Bush and her boss Freddie Howe mention in their letters are invariably those emphasized in the articles by the Chairman at the beginning of each issue of *Fontana*: *King Cotton* in 1948; *The Sea Chase* and *The Wooden Horse* in 1949 and 1951, *The Struggle for Europe* in 1952. At times there is a plaintive tone to these 'Letters' suggesting an attempt to please against the odds. *Rommel* was the new book that Collins was particularly keen to mention in the July 1950 edition of *Fontana*, and Bush comments apologetically '*Rommel* got away to a slow start, the pace is now accelerating, enthusiasm is mounting, and we are very optimistic that we shall hold our own with the other markets'.[24] Given the many comments about the paternalism of Collins as a firm, we might see such comments as reinforcing the view that Australia was seen as a dumping ground for books produced with the British market in mind.

However, I would like point to some countervailing evidence which suggests an alternative interpretation of this convergence of UK and Australian publicity for Collins books. Rather than simply seeing the use of similar covers and publicity in the Commonwealth as indicative of a continuing dominating influence of the UK publishers' domestic agendas on the book scene of Australia, we could follow Johanson's argument that the Australian market had a shaping influence on the British one such that 'the colonial tail wagged the imperial lion'.[25] The ways in which commissioning, marketing and packaging choices were made for UK editions of particular books were, I shall argue, shaped by the awareness of Collins's staff that their products would have to sell in overseas markets.

One nice example can be found in the choice of name and packaging for a thriller called *The Contaminant*. There was some debate over the choice of

---

23 'Current Promotions', *Australian Bookseller and Publisher*, March 1982, 52; Princeton University Special Collections and Rare Books, Helen MacInnes Papers, Box 2, Folder 3.

24 Doris Bush 'Letter from Australia' *Fontana*, 4 (1950), 9.

25 Johanson, *Colonial Editions*, p. 7.

name for the book, with the initial name referring more closely to the institutions of the international intelligence community. Ultimately, however, it was decided to give the book the same title in the UK as in the USA. Ronald Clarke, design manager, explained the importance of consistency in titles and packaging: 'Australia and New Zealand are influenced by advertising and news coverage in American papers and magazines. Imagine the confusion if a much publicized book called *The Contaminant* was being produced under another title. All publicity has to be the same'.[26] This instance illustrates the way in which decisions about the packaging and publicity for books for sale in the home market were shaped by the needs of export markets, particularly the Commonwealth.

Collins made quite a point of encouraging US publishers of their titles to adopt similar jacket designs and associated publicity posters, and in many cases were successful, as the identical jacket designs of MacInnes's *The Salzburg Connection* (1969) and *Prelude to Terror* (1978), published by Collins in the UK and Harcourt Brace and World in the USA, illustrates. This emphasis on making sure the names, images and packaging for mass market fiction was consistent internationally was also present in the earlier sixties and the fifties. Very strong similarities of iconography and design are to be found as early as 1960, for example, in the sketch line drawings of columns adopted as the key note for both Collins and Harcourt Brace and World's covers for *Decision in Delphi*. In 1958, Hammond Innes, who was acknowledged by Collins to sell very well internationally, felt strongly enough about the consistency of publicity to fight with film producers over the title of the film made of one of his books.[27]

Marketing director Michael Hyde explained the philosophy that underpinned such consistency in marketing very clearly in an interview cited in Collins's in-house paper:

we are an international company and we feel the need to capitalize on this at the planning stage of new books... I am thinking particularly of the Australian and New Zealand market...Wherever possible we are taking a much broader look a new titles to ensure that the strategy behind them will maximize world wide sales.[28]

The emphasis here is on consideration of exports not simply at the stage at which packaging and publicity takes place, but much earlier in the planning of books. To give just one example, at the editorial board meeting of 28 March 1971, with Billy Collins in the chair, the potential export sales for publications were minuted in no less than nine of the twenty books discussed. This concern at the commissioning and editorial stage with the international market for books

---

26   'Collins News presents: The Life Story of a Bestseller', *Collins News*, May 1978, p. 2.
27   Glasgow UBA, Collins Papers, Innes corresp. GB248 UGD243 1/11/11.
28   'Aiming to turn over and international leaf', *Collins News*, 1977, 1.

Fig. 1. Tourist and cold war iconography side by side on the covers of Collins's UK and Australian editions of popular fiction. (HarperCollins Publishers Ltd)

was not a new concern for Collins in the 1970s. For instance Ronald Politzer, acclaimed publicity manager of the 1940s and 1950s, stressed that his role began even before books had been written.[29]

One intriguing example which illustrates Collins's concern, at the earliest stages of shaping a book, with selling books to an export market comes from this same period. As part of a short but warm correspondence between W. A. R. Collins and Helen MacInnes, the Scottish-born writer of popular fiction who had begun to publish her work in the UK with Collins in 1951, Collins makes some suggestions about MacInnes's future work. Her very successful first novel, *Above Suspicion*, was set in the Alps, Mont St Michel formed the backdrop to her second, and the Dolomites to her third. Each of the first two was made into a Hollywood film. However, by the time of this correspondence, MacInnes had set three of her novels in the USA, where she had been living since the late 1930s. Collins commented:

I wonder what chance there is of your writing a novel with a European setting for your next book. Quite a number of people have raised this point, remembering your earlier books. From the American point of view this may not be so good, but from the point of view of this country particularly, and I think the Dominions, it would be a real help to sales.[30]

Why did Billy Collins encourage MacInnes to set her work in Europe? One argument might be that Collins sought to tap into the increasing interest in travel after the war, with greater discretionary income, and flights by jet aeroplane. Selling popular adventure and spy fiction through the burgeoning tourist industry certainly became a standard strategy for a range of publishers later in the 1960s. Hodder and Stoughton in 1969, for instance, promised winners of a window display competition for Mary Stewart's *The Gabriel Hounds* a trip to Lebanon, while in the same year Gollancz offered a trip for two to Cornwall for winners of a Daphne du Maurier crossword in the *Sunday Times*.[31]

MacInnes took Billy Collins's advice and went on to set her novels in popular tourist destinations of Europe for more than twenty years. Having advised such settings, William Collins and Sons went on to promote MacInnes's novels centrally through the iconography of tourism, as amply visible in MacInnes's book jackets. From the early 1960s, the jackets of MacInnes's novels feature a series of travel and tourist themes. They often feature the signature architecture or scenery of a particularly popular tourist

---

29 'Collins personality: Ronald J. Politzer', *Fontana*, 6 (1952), 25.

30 Glasgow UBA, Collins Papers, MacInnes correspondence, 16 July 1953 GB248 UGD243 1/11/9.

31 'Points from Publishers', *The Bookseller*, 15 March 1969, 1750; Advertisement for Mary Stewart's *The Gabriel Hounds*, *The Bookseller*, 25 January 1969.

Fig. 2. Tourist iconography – in particular women in national costume – promoting international sales. (HarperCollins Publishers Ltd)

destination: classical columns signifying Greece or canals and gondolas in
Venice, for instance. Other jackets highlight the iconography, like the paperback cover *Pray for a Brave Heart* with its edelweiss or the red rag and bull of
Message from Malaga (see Fig. 1); or scenery, for instance, the use of the Alps
on the cover of *The Salzburg Connection* (see Fig. 2). Women in the national
costume of Brittany or flamenco outfits feature in many of the Fontana paperbacks of MacInnes's in the 1960s and 1970s (see Fig. 2). These elements of
jacket iconography are often placed side by side with tourist iconography:
foreign currency, postcards, maps, cameras and film.

Collins's publicity strategy for MacInnes reflected the tourist iconography
of the covers. An article in *The Bookseller* on Helen MacInnes in February 1969
announced the British publication of MacInnes's *The Salzburg Connection*,
which topped the bestseller lists in the USA and Australia, and was later made
into a film. The article cites the opinion of a US review: 'A bonus that always
comes with each Helen MacInnes mystery is the new knowledge about
customs, people and beauties of a different area'.[32] This emphasis on setting
also appeared in advertisements for MacInnes's books. Advertisements in both
Hatchard's News and *The Bookseller* publicized *The Venetian Affair* with a quote
from *The New York Times*, which described it as a 'Baedeker thriller', while
MacInnes' novels were regularly advertised in *The Times* as ideal holiday
reading. Reviews also picked up on the connection between MacInnes's novels
and the tourist industry. *Punch*, for instance, describes *The Salzburg Connection*
as 'A powerful story with super backgrounds: Buchan plus Baedeker'.[33]

Such references to MacInnes's novels as appropriate substitutes for a travel
guidebook suggest that they might be consumed by those who might realistically visit their tourist settings. However, another interpretation of Billy
Collins's advice to MacInnes to set her work in Europe could be that her work
might be enjoyed not just by actual travellers but also by armchair tourists.
Another of Collins's most successful writers saw remote and inaccessible
settings, those visited only by the armchair traveller, as a selling point in his
novels. Hammond Innes's work, like that of MacInnes, sold well on export
markets and was promoted very heavily in terms of the writer's own travelling
adventures. Both Innes and his editor at Collins agreed that 'as escape reading
is concerned, [people] would much prefer a good adventure story in more
remote places'.[34]

---

32 'Points from Publishers', *The Bookseller*, 1 Feb 1969, 373.
33 Princeton RBSC, MacInnes Papers, Box 25, Folder 3: *Hatchard's News*, 1964, 2; advertisement from *The Bookseller*, 18 Jan 1964, 125; advertisement from *Punch*, 5 March 1969.
34 Glasgow UBA, Collins Papers, Innes GB248 UGD243 1/11/7, letter of 14 December
1950.

Collins anticipated that readers in the Dominions would enjoy work set in European locations, and this expectation may have been fed by a vision of readers with dreams of travel to Europe. Certainly staff at Collins perceived antipodeans, even those born and bred in New Zealand and Australia, as viewing Europe as 'home'.[35] Whatever the reason, MacInnes' work, publicized using the same tourist iconography as in the UK, fared very well in Australia. Successful novels like *The Salzburg Connection* spent longer at the top of the bestseller list there than in the UK.

Billy Collins's advice to MacInnes on the settings of her books certainly demonstrates that, far from Commonwealth markets being a dumping ground for books published with a domestic audience in mind, questions of export sales were central to Collins's key figures when commissioning and editing popular fiction. If we see the armchair traveller as the central focus of Collins's publicity for MacInnes's books, we might even argue that the reader in 'the Dominions' was at the centre of Collins's strategy for publicizing books by authors like Innes and MacInnes, as well as other popular authors such as Alistair MacLean, whose jackets were also rich in tourist iconography during this period. The heavy reliance of Collins on exports to the Commonwealth, as well as archival evidence, certainly supports this interpretation.

This example also demonstrates that book jackets can provide a helpful supplement to scarce archival resources on the publicity and marketing of popular books. In the case of some of Collins's most popular writers, evidence of publishers' intentions and marketing strategies can be seen through the Collins Papers in Glasgow and the Helen MacInnes Papers in Princeton. These archival sources tell a very similar story to that of the book jackets themselves. Our broader exploration of publicity strategies in the period after the Second World War has suggested that during this time book jackets played a pivotal role in marketing and selling popular novels. Altogether, then, the arguments of this essay have suggested that the materiality of books, and book covers in particular, are a resource well worth closer attention from scholars of twentieth-century literary and media history.

---

35 'Australasian Journey', *Fontana*, 3 (1949), 17.

Chepman and Myllar:
The First Printers in Scotland

LUCY LEWIS

O N 15 SEPTEMBER 1507, James IV granted a patent to Chepman and Myllar to import a press and produce mass books for domestic consumption, granting them, moreover, exclusive rights to sell such books in the city of Edinburgh. However, religious books were not the first to issue from the Chepman and Myllar press newly set up in Edinburgh. Instead, the first year of business saw a flurry of short pamphlet-style publications of vernacular poetry, and it is these that will form the subject of this paper. These pamphlets have already attracted a fair amount of attention from literary scholars because they preserve good, early witnesses for key texts from the Middle Scots canon (notably works by Dunbar and Henryson). However, the reasons for the pamphlets appearing in the physical form that they do, and at the moment that they do, have not been as widely discussed as their literary content. In the following discussion I shall argue that they were produced with a view to binding up in the same volume, and that they can therefore be compared with the examples of English *sammelbände* that were produced by Caxton and Wynkyn de Worde. This investigation resumes the discussion I presented at the British Book Trade History Conference in Worcester in 2001.[1] My argument here has two parts: I shall argue firstly that the production of separate pamphlets with the potential to be bound together was sound strategy from a marketing point of view but also, secondly, that the form of the Chep-man and Myllar pamphlets reflects a dialectic between individuality and com-munity. This dialectic helped to express a changing sense of Scottish identity within the international community.

The composite volume now held in the National Library of Scotland consists of eleven copies of black-letter editions, nine of which were printed in Edinburgh by Chepman and Myllar, another by an unknown printer, and the eleventh on the continent. The whole volume has been produced in facsimile by W. Beattie and selected pages of it are now available to view online at the

---

1 Lucy Lewis, "'For No Text Is an Island, Divided from the Main": Incunable Sammel-bände', in *Light on the Book Trade: Essays in Honour of Peter Isaac*, ed. by Barry McKay, John Hinks and Maureen Bell (London; New Castle, DE, 2004), pp. 13–26.

National Library of Scotland's website.[2] It should be remembered that the order in which the texts are currently bound is not necessarily the order in which they were printed. Beattie revised his view of the order of printing after he wrote the introduction to his facsimile, and this revised order has recently been corroborated by Catherine van Buuren in her essay about the typographic features of the texts.[3] The texts, according to this revised order, are: Dunbar's *Tua Mariit Wemen and the Wedo* (STC 7350: this the work of an unknown printer), Dunbar's *Flyting of Dunbar and Kennedy* (STC 7348), Henryson's *Orpheus and Eurydice* (STC 13166), Lydgate's *The Maying and Disport of Chaucer* (also known as the *Complaynt of the Black Knyght*: STC 17014.3), *Golagrus and Gawayne* (STC 11984), *The Porteous of Noblesse* (5060.5), Dunbar's *The Goldyn Targe* (7349), Dunbar's *Ane Ballat of Lord Barnard Stewart* (STC 7347), a romance called *Sir Eglamour* (STC 7542) and a poem called the *De Regimine Principum* (STC 3307). The eleventh text is a *Gest of Robin Hood* printed by Jan van Doesborch of Antwerp. Two other editions of Chepman and Myllar survive but are preserved elsewhere: the *Acts and Deeds of Wallace* composed by Blind Harry the Minstrel (preserved in Cambridge University Library: STC 13148), and the *Book of the Howlat* by Richard Holland (preserved also at Cambridge University Library as well as in Dundee City Archives: STC 13594).

It would be a difficult task to attempt to estimate the original print-runs of these editions, though they cannot have been large. Copies of these editions which were bound together (as these apparently were from an early date, judging by the manuscript annotations and signatures) would stand a better chance of survival than those kept separately in loose, unbound form.[4] Early owners' reasons for collecting the pamphlets together in this form may have been pragmatic – to ensure longevity in a strong binding – or more intellectual: an

---

2   William Beattie (introd.), *The Chepman and Myllar Prints: Nine Tracts from the First Scottish Press, Edinburgh 1508 Followed by Two Other Tracts in the Same Volume in the National Library of Scotland: A Facsimile. With a Bibliographical Note by William Beattie* (Edinburgh, 1950). A plain edition (with some facsimile plates) is also worth consulting. This is by George Stevenson, *Pieces from the MakCulloch and the Gray MSS together with the Chepman and Myllar Prints*, Scottish Text Society, 65 (Edinburgh, 1918). Online at <http://www.nls.uk>.

3   Catherine van Buuren, 'The Chepman and Myllar Texts of Dunbar', in *William Dunbar, "The Nobill Poyet": Essays in Honour of Priscilla Bawcutt*, ed. by Sally Mapstone (East Linton, East Lothian, 2001), pp. 24–39.

4   Most of the manuscript annotations are transcribed by J. Durkan and A. Ross in *Early Scottish Libraries* (Glasgow, 1961). I was very grateful to be helped, in my own study of the volume and its annotations, by Brian Hillyard of the National Library of Scotland, who made available scans from the negatives for the facsimile edition.

attempt to enhance the perceived unity of a particular body of work. The question of whether or not there really is unity in this series of publications is one which I shall pursue throughout this paper. The argument for unity needs to come to terms with the fact that these publications did not appear simultaneously (though they were produced within a short space of time) and that they are discrete bibliographical entities. Myllar's printer's device (a windmill) appears seven times among the items now found in the National Library of Scotland volume, each time marking a break, the end of a text. Printers' devices were traditionally used in the early print era as a way of signing off. Title pages (as Margaret Smith has recently demonstrated) were less common in this period, and ways of beginning a text were not standardized.[5] The items in the National Library of Scotland volume mostly lack prefatory matter, and it is not clear whether this is because they are defective or because they were never present. Catherine van Buuren assumes that they are defective. She writes:

> To be complete, each tract in the Chepman and Myllar prints would have had an introduction (e.g. 'Her begynnys the Maying and Disport of Chaucer'), then Chepman's device, the poem, Myllar's printer's device, and a colophon, neatly giving the two men's names and the place and date of printing. The Maying is the only piece in the collection that has them all.[6]

It is possible that prefatory matter (everything before the poems themselves) was removed when the editions were bound together. Certainly the first pages of books are the most subject to wear and tear so they may have degraded more quickly, before the pamphlets were bound up together. The volume as we see it today was rebound in 1951, with the original printed leaves all separated and set in surrounds of modern paper. The previous binding, made by Charles Hering of London, was made no earlier than 1798 (some of the paper used is watermarked with this year) and no later than 1808, the date of the ex-libris.

Myllar's device is an obvious visual allusion to his name. The image of the mill also evoked (for the present reader at least) another structure described in medieval poetry, Chaucer's rumour mill from the dream-vision poem, The Hous of Fame. The structure described in Chaucer's poem receives and recycles all manner of pieces of speech, however trivial, and is an object of fascination to the aspiring poet who is the narrator of the poem. The poet perceives that the mill can provide him with subjects to write about and may help him on the way to joining the elite company of canonical authors listed earlier in the poem. The rumour mill is described in terms of a wondrous marvel:

---

5   Margaret M. Smith, The Title-Page: its Early Development 1460–1510 (London; New Castle, DE, 2000).
6   See van Buuren, 'The Chepman and Myllar Texts of Dunbar', p. 27.

Tho saugh y stonde, in a valeye
Under the castel, faste by,
An hous, that Domus Dedaly,
That Laboryntus cleped ys,
Nas mad so wonderlyche, ywis,
Ne half so queyntelych ywrought,
And ever mo, as swyft as thought,
Thi queynte hous aboute wente,
That never mo hyt stille stente.
And therout com so so gret a noyse
That, had hyt stonden upon Oyse,
Men myghte hyt han herd esely
To Rome, y trowe sikerly.[7]

The noisiness of the house of rumour immediately evokes a mill (and indeed a printing press, another mechanical device, although the printing press was obviously unknown to Chaucer).[8] Like a mill, the house of rumour produces chaff as well as grain: ephemeral nonsense as well as more edifying information. Made of twigs and branches, it also resembles a nest, as if the sounds that enter and leave it are the chirpings and twitterings of the birds Chaucer loved to write about in his dream vision poems, especially *The Parlement of Foules*. Chaucer's dream visions were certainly known in Scotland and it is quite likely that Chepman and Myllar, in printing Scottish descendants of the dream vision genre like *The Goldyn Targe* and *The Tua Mariit Wemen and the Wedo*, were consciously extending the campaign of vernacularization inaugurated by *The Hous of Fame*. The mill device could be read as a half-conscious allusion to the Chaucerian tradition of vernacular 'makyng' (that is poetic composition), since Chepman and Myllar's texts do indeed open the doors of the rumour mill wider, democratizing the world of letters further by publishing examples of Scottish eloquence to rival those of England.

Chepman had a device too, and examples of this can be seen in the National Library of Scotland volume. His device depicts a man and a woman clad in leaves standing on either side of a heraldic tree. They are semi-wild beings (the man perhaps reminiscent of the 'wodwo' who is a figure from folk mythology in northern England and Scotland) who seem at the same time to

---

7   See *The Hous of Fame* as printed in *The Riverside Chaucer*, ed. by Larry D. Benson (Oxford, 1987), pp. 347–73 (p. 370).

8   The similarities between water mills and printing presses were borne out when the delegates of the 2004 British Book Trade History Conference visited the works of Robert Smail (now owned by the National Trust for Scotland) in Innerleithen on 28 July 2004. Two water-wheels, running off a mill-lade diverted from Leithen Water, originally powered the press.

evoke Adam and Eve and pagan spirits. An interesting interpretation of this device is given by David Parkinson in his essay about court culture in the reign of James IV.[9] He notes that, although Chepman's device is modelled on that of the French printer Philippe Pigouchet, the way it is used in the context of the Chepman and Myllar texts makes a particular statement about Scottish national identity. He demonstrates that the wild man costume alludes to the tournament known as the 'Emprise du Chevalier Sauvage à la Dame Noire', which took place in 1508 and in which James IV took the part of the 'wild knight'. Presiding over this tournament as adjudicator was Lord Bernard Stewart, who is celebrated in a poem of Dunbar's printed by Chepman and Myllar in that same year. Dunbar also wrote a rather bawdy ballad dedicated to a negro serving girl (a parodic version of the 'Dame Noire' of the tournament) which was not printed, possibly (Parkinson speculates) because it was too scurrilous. Parkinson argues that the semi-wild state evoked in the Chepman device reflects the desire of the printers' royal patron to embody the native side of Scottish national identity as well as its more sophisticated side:

Counterfeiting savagery enabled James IV to lay claim to Arthurian tradition on Scottish terms, as had been done in the Middle Scots romance printed by Chepman and Myllar, *Golagros and Gawane*; it also expressed his claim to be direct ruler over those 'wild Scots' of the Highlands and Islands, not securely contained within the realm as late as 1508.[10]

Parkinson concludes: 'Chepman and Myllar's little prints of 1508 reaffirm the bond of what is courtly and international, to what is regarded as local and popular, a bond which is as characteristic of Middle Scots literature as it is of the court of James IV.'[11] It also seems that this dialectic between the local and the universal, between microcosm and macrocosm, is reflected in the physical structure of the book now preserved in the National Library of Scotland.

A strong argument in favour of regarding the publications of 1508 as a deliberate sequence, planned and conceived almost as a whole, is that several of them are found together elsewhere, in analogous manuscript anthologies. We can infer from this that Chepman and Myllar were working in a tradition of conjoining texts in certain ways: they may even have used such a manuscript as printer's copy, though no particular manuscript stands out as a probable candidate. The Maitland Folio (now in the Pepys Library of Magdalene College, Cambridge) contains many of the same texts printed by Chepman and Myllar, though in slightly variant versions, and dating from the second half of the

---

9   See David Parkinson, 'Scottish Prints and Entertainments, 1508', *Neophilologus* (75) 1991, 304–10.
10   Ibid., p. 307.
11   Ibid., pp. 308–9.

sixteenth century rather than the first.[12] The Maitland Folio contains a version
of the *Tua Mariit Wemen and the Wedo* which is very close to that printed by
Chepman and Myllar, and also a version of the *De Regimine Principium Bonum
Consilium*, and of *The Goldyn Targe* by Dunbar, both also in the Edinburgh
volume. Another manuscript anthology which is significant for this discussion
is Bodleian Library MS Arch.Selden B.24 which contains, among various Scottish items, *The Maying and Disport of Chaucer* by Lydgate in a version remark-
ably close to that printed by Chepman and Myllar. In a discussion exploring
the textual tradition, A. S. G. Edwards writes:

The relationship between the two texts, one manuscript, the other print, extends
considerably beyond identity of title. It seems clear that if Selden was not the direct
source for Chepman and Myllar, the print derived from a copy not very far removed
from it. The manuscript and the print share over a hundred common variants against all
these witnesses, in addition to their close dialectal connections.[13]

As Edwards acknowledges, *The Maying and Disport of Chaucer* (also known as
The Complaynt of the Black Knyght) was a key text linking the English and
Scottish traditions. The Asloan manuscript, compiled early in the sixteenth
century, contains *The Maying and Disport of Chaucer* in a version 'that seems'
(Edwards writes) 'textually related to both the Selden and the Chepman and
Myllar print, the only other copies of Lydgate's poem with which it shares this
title'.[14] A full description of the Asloan manuscript, which notes the texts it
shares with the Chepman and Myllar group, has been given by I. C. Cunningham.[15] It is almost as if Lydgate's pseudo-Chaucerian poem, *The Maying and*

---

12 For a good description of the Maitland Folio, see Julia Boffey, 'The Maitland Folio
Manuscript as a Verse Anthology', in *William Dunbar, 'The Nobill Poyet'*, ed. by Sally
Mapstone, pp. 40–50.
13 See A. S. G. Edwards, 'Bodleian Library MS Arch. Selden B.24: a "Transitional"
Collection', in *The Whole Book: Cultural Perspectives on the Medieval Miscellany*, ed. by
Stephen G. Nichols and Siegfried Wenzel (Ann Arbor, 1996), pp. 53–67 (p. 60).
14 Ibid., p. 61.
15 See his essay, 'The Asloan Manuscript', pp. 107–35 in *The Renaissance in Scotland:
Studies in Literature, Religion, History and Culture Offered to John Durkan*, ed. by A. A.
MacDonald, Michael Lynch and Ian B. Cowan (Leiden, 1994). After careful examination,
Cunningham concludes that it is unsafe to assume that either the Asloan text or the Chepman and Myllar version are copies of one another. Cunningham also notes that the
anonymous poem before the colophon of *The Maying* in the Chepman and Myllar print is
not present in Asloan whereas it is in the later Bannatyne manuscript. For further discussion
of the Bannatyne manuscript, see Theo van Heijnsbergen's essay in the same volume, 'The
Interaction between Literature and History in Queen Mary's Edinburgh: the Bannatyne
Manuscript and its Prosopographical Context', pp. 183–225. Heijnsbergen notes the many
social and professional links that connected the Bannatyne family and its circle with Chep-

Disport of Chaucer, acted as a threshold between one culture and another. A text which uses eavesdropping as a dramatic device, it is also about the ways in which different authors and different literary communities eavesdrop on each other.

Lydgate's *Maying and Disport of Chaucer* imitates *Chaucer's Book of the Duchess*, in which a wandering poet overhears the lament of a love-sick knight dying of melancholy. In Chaucer's poem the melancholy is caused by the death of the lady, whereas in Lydgate's the grief is caused by the indifference of the love-object. There are shades too, in Lydgate's poem of Chaucer's *Troilus and Criseyde*, especially in the way that the narrator-poet invokes names from classical literature to inspire him to write about love:

> O Nyobe! Let now this teres reyn
> Into my penne, and eke helpe in this nede
> Thou woful Mirre, that felist my herte blede
> Of pitouse wo, and my honde eke quake,
> When that I write for this mannys sake.[16]

Like the narrator of *Troilus and Criseyde*, Lydgate's poet-narrator claims to have no first-hand experience of love:

> But I, alas, that am of wytte but dulle
> And haue no knowyng of such mater,
> For to discryve and wryten at the fulle
> The woful compleynt, which that ye shul here;
> But euen-like as doth a skryuener,
> That can no more what that he shal write,
> But as his maister beside dothe endyte.[17]

Within the context of the Chepman and Myllar texts, the Lydgate poem acts as a touchstone, linking texts otherwise disparate in tone and style. The theme of melancholy in love is picked up in Henryson's *Orpheus and Eurydice*, and the theme of cruelty and heartlessness (of which the Black Knight complains) is picked up in *The Goldyn Targe* and in a more extreme form (bordering on sadism) in the grotesque *Tua Mariit Wemen and the Wedo* (which also adopts eavesdropping as the basis for its dramatic structure). Of course, we need to remember that *The Tua Mariit Wemen* may not be a Chepman and Myllar production, so should only provisionally be regarded as part of a planned sequence.

---

man, the printer and notary. For example, Chepman's wife, Agnes Cockburn, is named as a Bannatyne godmother for 1540 in the 'memoriall buik' appended to the manuscript.

16 See H. N. MacCracken (ed.), *The Minor Poems of John Lydgate*, Early English Text Society, original series, 192 (London, 1934), 2 vols, II: *Secular Poems*, 390.

17 Ibid., p. 390.

In the Edinburgh volume the exchange is not only between England and Scotland but between Scotland and France, a long-established and complex relationship. The French influence is exemplified by Chepman and Myllar's edition of *The Porteous of Noblesse*, which was based on a poem by Alain Chartier. Positive relations with France are attested in Dunbar's *Ballad of Lord Bernard Stewart*, which mentions Bernard's service to the French king, giving thanks for his temporary return to his native land at the same time as it compliments his continental masters. The volume now preserved in the National Library of Scotland is a truly international volume. Henryson's *Orpheus and Eurydice* shows the influence of Italian Neoplatonism as well as of traditional, Aristotelian scholasticism.[18] We should not be surprised by this internationalism, since Myllar seems to have learnt his trade at Rouen before he set up the press at Edinburgh, and he probably brought over French compositors to work with him on these early editions. Catherine van Buuren is convinced that the compositors were French, and adduces as confirmation of this the fact that ampersands are expanded to 'et', not 'and'.[19] The fact that one of the texts in the tract volume, the *Gest of Robin Hood*, was printed on the continent (in Antwerp) is further evidence of cosmopolitanism. A version of this was available in a 1506 publication of Wynkyn de Worde's, so it is somewhat surprising that the continental edition, rather than the English one, found its way into the Scottish collection, but further confirms that the Scottish literary community at the time was as European in outlook as British. The *Gest* seems on the face of it to be a rather anomalous inclusion in the collection – it is not a dream vision nor is it moralistic like many of the other items. The piece with which it seems to have most in common is *Golagrus*, since, like *Golagrus*, it is a tale of adventure in a somewhat lighthearted vein. Although elements of Arthurian pastiche in the *Gest* afford parallels with *Golagrus*, there is little point labouring the connection: its presence in the volume may be due to random chance rather than to careful selection.[20] Interestingly, the manuscript annotation 'Robyn Hude', which is on the facing page to the start of the *Gest* and on the last leaf of *The Testament of Mr Andro Kennedy*, seems to be in a hand at least

---

18   On the possible connections between Henryson and Italian culture and writers, see John MacQueen, 'Neoplatonism and Orphism in Fifteenth-Century Scotland: the Evidence of Henryson's "New Orpheus"', *Scottish Studies*, 20 (1976), 69–89.

19   See 'The Chepman and Myllar Texts of Dunbar', p. 31.

20   The interweaving stories that make up the *Gest* involve adventures coming to and spreading out from Robin's forest base, much as knightly adventures do in Arthur's court. The parallels with Arthur's court seem deliberate. For example, the poet presents Robin's desire to have an adventure before he can feast as an imitation of Arthurian tradition. Arthurian stories climax with royal praise for the hero, and this is also the case here.

contemporary, if not identical, with the handwriting found at the end of the *Golagrus*.[21]

Given that certain common strands and concerns can be seen to run through the collection of Chepman and Myllar publications, and that they were all made within a short space of time, one may ask why the Scottish printers chose to preserve separate signature sequences for the different texts rather than simply printing them as a single edition. One answer is that they may have wanted to give themselves the opportunity of perfecting their craft through a series of experiments. It has been observed that the standard of type-setting and general appearance improves with subsequent editions. It should not be forgotten that the printers had been commissioned by James IV to print Mass books (a commission they did subsequently fulfil) and may have regarded the early poetic texts as a way of practising for more serious work. Printing a series of short pamphlets in rapid succession would have given them a chance to get feedback and learn by experience as well as the marketing advantage of being able to offer their customers options for semi-customized anthologies. Purchasers of early copies might well have been flattered by the invitation to chose for themselves which texts to combine in a personal selection, almost as if they were noble patrons commissioning a manuscript collection. The stigma of print would still not quite have worn off at this stage. Some of the pieces in the volume, especially the ballad for Lord Bernard Stewart, were particularly topical, suiting a particular occasion, and would have been suitable for sale as individual items, though still retaining an interest after the occasion had passed.

Precedents for this type of *sammelband* configuration from the English tradition are numerous and instructive. In my previous British Book Trade History Conference paper, I discussed some examples from the printing presses of Caxton and Wynkyn de Worde. Among these were devotional texts (the pairing of John Mirk's *Festial* with the *Quattuor Sermones*, and the *Treatise of Love* with the *Chastysing of Goddes Children*) and secular ones (the *Polychronicon* with the *Description of Britain*, and the grammatical texts *Synonyma* and *Equivoca*).[22] I concluded that paper with the suggestion that distinctions should

---

21 The annotation relating to the *Gest* is on page 196 of Beattie's facsimile of the National Library of Scotland volume, and the colophon of *Golagrus* on page 51 (see figure 1). *The Testament of Mr Andro Kennedy* is one of three short Dunbar poems following the *Tua Mariit Wemen and the Wedo* in the edition by the unknown printer. The other short poems are: *Lament for the Makars* and *Kynd Kittok*.

22 For a good recent discussion of devotional *sammelbände* printed by Wynkyn de Worde and the connections with the manuscript tradition of the texts concerned, see Julia Boffey's discussion of the *Abbey of the Holy Ghost* and John Alcock's *Mons Perfectionis* in her essay 'The Charter of the Abbey of the Holy Ghost and Its Role in Manuscript Anthologies', *Yearbook of English Studies* (33) 2003, 120–30 (p. 126).

be made between texts which appear together regularly and those which may be conjoined more casually with a range of other texts. The regular, almost systematic, pairing of certain editions can be regarded as an early form of marketing strategy on the part of printers and booksellers, whereas the same cannot be said of all the textual combinations that we find within early bindings.[23] Since there are no other surviving copies of the Chepman and Myllar publications found in the Edinburgh volume, we cannot assert with any confidence that they were always intended to be sold together as a sequence. Indeed, the ballad for Lord Bernard Stewart might well have circulated independently as an occasion piece, sold at the arrival of the renowned countryman back in Edinburgh specially to mark the event. However, there is reason to believe that the Chepman and Myllar publications were conceived loosely as a sequence, and recognized as such by early readers who had them bound up together, for they form a vernacular anthology of a type that had already been seen in England. Of particular relevance here are the quarto editions printed by Caxton in 1476, which have been discussed by Alexandra Gillespie in an article for the Cambridge Bibliographical Society.[24] Among these are texts by Chaucer such as the dream vision known as *The Parliament of Fowls* (there entitled *The Temple of Bras*), *Anelida and Arcite* (a lament) and various moral lyrics, as well as pieces by Lydgate such as *The Temple of Glas* and the *Churl and the Bird*. Gillespie concludes:

Caxton's quartos were deliberately designed with a dual function: they supplied a market with English poetry 'good chepe' in pamphlet form, and they were also the component parts of the first, overlooked, printed miscellanies in England, bridging the gap between manuscript anthologies and famous Renaissance books such as Tottel's *Songs and Sonnets*. Although Caxton's printing of these quartos was itself innovative, it is clear that his textual choice was informed by the example provided by the English manuscript trade.[25]

The same is patently true of the Chepman and Myllar texts.

As has already been mentioned, a strong manuscript antecedent for the Chepman and Myllar publications is the Bodleian Library MS Arch. Selden B.24, produced at the end of the fifteenth century, which has a distinctively

---

23 On this topic, see A. S. G. Edwards and C. M. Meale, 'The Marketing of Early Printed Books', *The Library*, sixth series, 15 (1993), 175–86.
24 Alexandra Gillespie, 'Caxton's Chaucer and Lydgate Quartos: Miscellanies from Manuscript to Print', *Transactions of the Cambridge Bibliographical Society* (12:1) 2000, 1–25.
25 Ibid., p. 24.

Scottish character, without being parochial.[26] It contains the sole text for *The Kingis Quair of James Stewart*, as well as *Troilus and Criseyde* and the *Parlement of Foules* along with other courtly texts by different authors. It is likely that Chepman and Myllar had such manuscripts in mind when they conceived their sequence of vernacular Scottish texts. The texts present examples of Scottish eloquence ranging from the fanciful and colourful to the stately and dignified, and also show that Scottish culture was not inward-looking but open to influence from, and dialogue with, its European neighbours, including England. Dunbar, who is well-represented in this volume, is in some ways typical of this protean Scottishness: the sheer diversity of styles and manners he adopts across his oeuvre has attracted much comment. His development of a strong, lyric voice that speaks out of, but not always in harmony with, court culture is a notable achievement, and in many ways the Chepman and Myllar sequence showcases that achievement, giving it a context and a setting. Individuality and community, parochialism and cosmopolitanism, are integrated and reconciled in the Edinburgh volume almost as if setting out the terms of a constitution.

This project – of defining and mapping Scottish national identity – would have been appreciated by the volume's early readers who seem to have been members of the legal profession. The early readers who sign their names in the volume – Florentine Martin of Gibbieston, Thomas Pratt and Alexander Borthwick of Gordonshill – are mentioned in early sixteenth-century Fife legal records. Such men would perhaps have seen the unity in these otherwise diverse texts, seeing that in books, as in states or commonwealths, there must be room for different voices all to be heard. Interestingly, a fragment of another Chepman and Myllar publication now surviving in Cambridge University Library, formed part of a collection that contained several legal texts.[27] This is the fragment of the *Book of the Howlat* by Richard Holland. The Cambridge fragment was described by William Beattie in a paper for the Edinburgh Bibliographical Society in 1946, and an interesting addendum was made to this by Robert Donaldson in 1983.[28] The collection of miscellaneous pieces now in Cambridge University Library was in the possession of William Spooner

---

26 See the facsimile edition introduced by Julia Boffey and A. S. G. Edwards, *The Works of Geoffrey Chaucer and the Kingis Quair. A Facsimile of Bodleian Library, Oxford, MS Arch. Selden. B. 24* (Cambridge: Brewer, 1996).

27 The shelf-mark is CUL Sel.1.19.

28 Beattie's original article is in vol. 2 of the *Transactions* (1938–45), published 1946, 393-7, and Robert Donaldson's piece is entitled 'An Early Printed Fragment of the *Buke of the Howlatt* – Addendum', *Edinburgh Bibliographical Society Transactions*, V.3 (1980–3, published 1983), 25–8. Donaldson shows that fragments in the binding of a protocol book in the Dundee City Archives are from the same leaf as the fragment in Cambridge University Library.

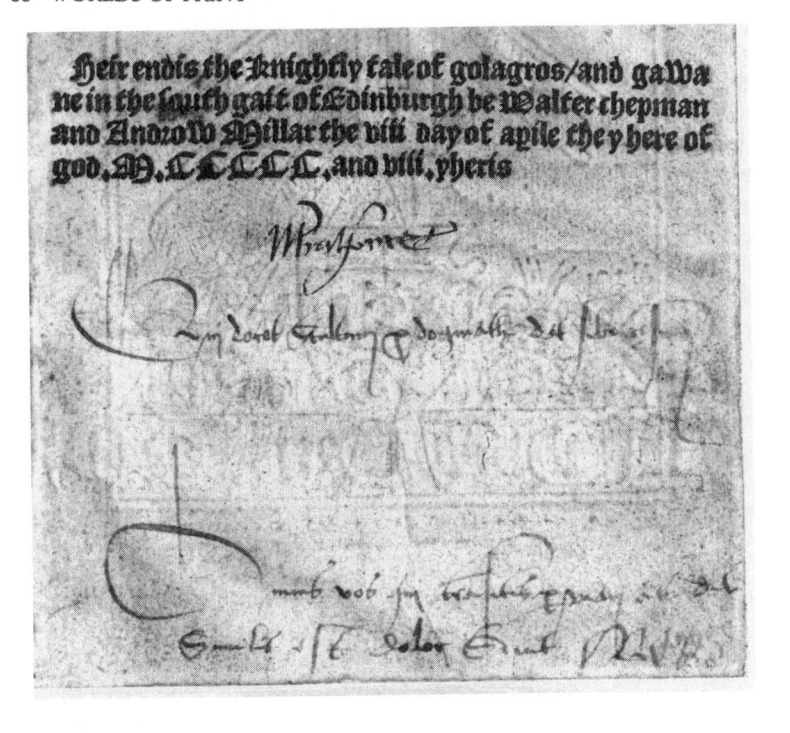

Fig. 1. Some examples of annotations in the Chepman and Myllar volume

Brough of Leek and was then bought from his nephew, H. H. Brindley of St
John's College, Cambridge, in 1920, since when it has been in the University
Library. In addition to the *Book of the Howlat*, there is a fragment of a copy of
Barbour's *Robert the Bruce*, printed in 1616.[29] Also found in the volume are
several Scottish legal texts: STC 21878 and 21900/21901. The first of these is
a book of Acts of Parliament printed in 1611 by Thomas Finlason, and the
other, printed by Finlason in 1621, prints further Acts of Parliament. There are
also title pages from two works of John Skene, the first an exposition of
difficult terms contained in the *Regiam Maiestatem* printed by Robert Walde-
grave in 1597 at Edinburgh, the other a Scottish legal text book. Also in the

---

29   This seems to be from the edition published by Andro Hart, STC 1378. However, the
Cambridge fragment appears to have been unrecorded hitherto and is not listed along with
the other extant copies in the National Library of Scotland, the British Library, the Bodleian
Library and the Folger Shakespeare Library.

collection is an interesting item, STC 140, which is entitled: *The Muses Welcome to the High and Mightie Prince James ... at His Most Happy Returne To His Old and Native Kingdome of Scotland*. Another text to be found amongst these miscellaneous papers is Chaucer's *Troilus and Criseyde*, in the 1532 edition of William Thynne. The combination of texts in this Cambridge volume suggests that, for a certain kind of seventeenth-century reader, an interest in legal forms sat easily side-by-side with an interest in British courtly, vernacular literature. Of course, members of the legal profession often harbour literary tastes, and it is worth noting that Chepman himself was a lawyer (a notary public) as well as a printer. The annotations (other than the signatures) in the Edinburgh, Chepman and Myllar volume are mostly in Latin, a language in which legal men had need to be fluent, and are serious in tone. For example, a saying from the Ash Wednesday liturgy appears next to the text of Henryson's *Orpheus and Eurydice*: 'Memento homo quia cinis es et in cinerem Reuerteris'.[30] Elsewhere, the annotator copies another phrase with Lenten associations, a fragment from Lamentations: 'Omnes vos qui transitis per viam attendite ... Similis est dolor sicut ...'[31] Here the writing becomes almost illegible (see Fig. 1: the annotation follows the tale of *Golagrus and Gawayne*). The serious nature of the annotations suggests that the volume was not simply taken up as light entertainment, that perhaps it stimulated its early readers to sober reflection on the temporality of human existence. Whether or not these early readers considered nationhood, in particular the Scottish nationality reflected in this Edinburgh volume, to be more stable and lasting than selfhood, would be interesting to know.

The Chepman and Myllar copies provide a good example of a pheno-menon characteristic of early print culture: the production of texts to be bought, and bound, together. Although I might stop short of calling the Edinburgh volume a *sammelband*, since there is no concrete evidence that the combination of texts it contains existed elsewhere, it seems almost certain that these texts were printed as potential companion pieces for each other. As Seth Lerer has recently noted, medieval literature was essentially anthologistic in nature, and so these combined forms would have seemed perfectly natural to early readers.[32] The kind of anthology offered in the Edinburgh volume is one that showcases the richness of Scottish literary tradition while at the same time putting it in its European context.

---

30 'Remember, oh man, that you are dust and that to dust you will return'.
31 'All you who travel by the way, take heed ... this pain is similar to ...'
32 See Seth Lerer, 'Medieval English Literature and the Idea of the Anthology', in *PMLA: Publications of the Modern Language Association of America* (118:5) 2003, 1251–67.

Scottish Freemasonry and Learned Printing in the Later Eighteenth Century

STEPHEN BROWN

THE PRINTING OF MASONIC TEXTS in Scotland during the eighteenth century lagged far behind that in England, a seemingly minor point and, not surprisingly, unnoted in any of the major academic studies of Enlightenment masonry. However, when one considers that masonry's authentic written records in Scotland predate those in England by well over one hundred years, that the only reliable historical accounts of pre-eighteenth-century masonic rituals reside in Scottish archives, and that Scotland is the acknowledged birthplace of freemasonry, this lack of printed texts at the very point in time when freemasons were establishing lodges all across Europe, in Canada and America, and from the West to the East Indies, should strike the book historian as odd.[1] During the first half of the eighteenth century, only one masonic text of genuine note was published in Scotland, as opposed to scores of works printed in London and a number in Dublin during the same period. Even the colonies were far ahead of Scotland in this respect, Benjamin Franklin having published at Philadelphia in 1734 the first masonic book to be printed in America. The vast majority of these publications were editions, versions, and piracies of James Anderson's seminal *Constitutions of the Free-Masons* (London, 1723),[2] usually taking the form of pocket companions or

---

1 The best academic studies of early freemasonry are: Douglas Knoop and G. P. Jones, *A Short History of Freemasonry to 1730* (Manchester, 1940); Margaret C. Jacob, *The Radical Enlightenment: Pantheists, Freemasons, and Republicans* (London, 1981); *Living the Enlightenment: Freemasonry and Politics in Eighteenth-Century Europe* (New York, 1991); David Stevenson, *The Origins of Freemasonry: Scotland's Century, 1590–1710* (Cambridge, 1988); *The First Freemasons: Scotland's Early Lodges and Their Members* (Aberdeen, 1988; rev. 2nd edn, Edinburgh, 2001); J. Smyth, 'Freemasonry and the United Irishmen'; *The United Irishmen: Republicanism, Radicalism, and Rebellion*, eds. D. Dickson, et al (Dublin, 1993); Steven C. Bullock, *Revolutionary Brotherhood: Freemasonry and the Transformation of the American Social Order, 1730–1840* (Chapel Hill, 1996); Peter Clark, *British Clubs and Societies, 1580–1800* (Oxford, 2000).
2 On Anderson as the source for the English and Scottish pocket companions, see Robert Cooper, 'The Knights Templar in Scotland: The Creation of a Myth' (Grand Lodge of Scotland, Edinburgh, 2002), pp. 7–16. See also, C. Adams, 'The Freemasons' Pocket Com-

handbooks and setting out the history, customs and ideals of masonry, together with continually updated and expanded collections of masonic songs and lists of the lodges and their officers around the world.

For some reason, the Scots appear not to have felt a need for such instructional texts, at least before 1752; the only significant masonic publication in Scotland before that date was a fine octavo edition in 1739 of Charles Leslie's *Masonry: A Poem. To which are added several Songs.* Published by the firm responsible in that same year for launching Scotland's first true magazine,[3] the *Scots Magazine*, the poem is dedicated to the just elected third Scottish Grand Master, John Earl of Kintore, and coincided with the opening of the Royal Infirmary, largely funded through masonic donations.[4] As a material artefact, the edition itself is extravagant for that time in Scotland, its layout, font, and paper quality consistent with the best work done by the Foulis Press, and the surviving copy in the library of the Grand Lodge of Scotland is a fine example of the best Scottish bookbinding during the period. The text of the poem in turn makes no mention of the fabulous history of masonry that was current in England and extensively disseminated through several printings of Anderson's two editions of his *Constitutions* (1723, 1738),[5] and at least two editions of William Smith's adaptation of Anderson (1735, 1736) and, in particular, Anderson's own widely circulated poem on the history of masonry. Instead, it takes for its theme the parallel between the applications of geometry in Europe's classical architecture and the masonic ideal of using the example of such beauty as a metaphor for human moral potential. Charles Leslie uses rhyming couplets as effectively as Alexander Pope at his best, and moves his theme ultimately towards a call for masons to acknowledge 'fair Liberty ... Virtue and Science' as their primary pursuits and obligations. In this respect, by eschewing the myth making that was predominant in English masonic writing, and especially Anderson's fabricated histories of masonry which locate the organization's origins in Adam and the Creation, while establishing its rituals at the site of King Solomon's Temple, this Scottish poet assumes that his native

---

panions of the Eighteenth Century', *Ars Quatuor Coronati*, 45 (1932), pp. 165–203. Adams, however, is far more focused upon English than Scottish examples.

3   The publishers of all the masonic pocket books printed in Edinburgh in the eighteenth-century were also all publishers of successful newspapers and magazines.

4   The Grand Lodge of Scotland was established in 1736. According to David Brewster in *The History of Freemasonry* (Edinburgh, 1804) not only were freemasons the chief benefactors of the new infirmary, but 'out of gratitude to the society of Free Masons ... the Royal Infirmary had unanimously agreed, that preference should always be given to distressed and infirm Free Masons' (pp. 155–9).

5   Anderson is generally accepted to have originated freemasonry's legendary history for his 1723 text. See Cooper, pp. 7–8.

audience will recognize freemasonry as a recent and modern institution, rooted in the old stonemasons' guilds but reflecting the contemporary values of the nascent Enlightenment in Scotland. Thus Leslie finds in the most monumental achievements of actual stonemasons, a metaphor for the modern moral life.

One other interesting aspect of this work is the two songs included with the poem. The publishers – William Sands, Andrew Brymer, Andrew Murray, and James Cochran – all masons, have chosen not to append the four songs written by James Anderson and reprinted in every English pocket companion, after their first appearance in the 1723 *Constitutions*. Anderson's songs respectively named for the freemasonic Master, Warden, Fellow Craft, and Entered Apprentice had immediately become the musical standards of masonry everywhere – with the apparent exception of Scotland, if this unique text is accepted as typical of Scottish sentiment. In place of Anderson, it prints two humorous songs, specific to masonry but celebrating the joys of social fraternity, as opposed to the symbolic and ceremonial obligations of the various masonic offices that one finds in Anderson. And, as we shall see, this divergence in attitude with its emphasis on the ethics of democratic fellowship will continue to be a feature that distinguishes Scottish masonic literature from English until the appearance of David Brewster's *History of Free Masonry* in 1804, the first book actually published in Scotland on the authority of the Grand Lodge and by its first truly official printer, Alexander Laurie.[6]

When the first version of Anderson's *Constitutions* made its appearance in Scotland in 1752, it did so in the form of a reprint of William Smith's adaptation entitled, *A Pocket Companion for Free-Masons* (London, 1735), which was published at Edinburgh by William Cheyne, the proprietor of two of the city's earliest periodicals, *The Thistle* (1734–36), a weekly newspaper, and *Letters of the Critical Club* (1738), a magazine of monthly political commentary.[7] There are at least two sound reasons for the delay in issuing a masonic pocket companion in Scotland, one cultural, the other judicial. In the first instance, as the 1739 edition of *Masonry: A Poem* seems to suggest, Scottish masons were in no hurry to acquire such texts. Unlike their counterparts in England who originated histories and pocket companions, Scottish masons had no need to invent a history for their institution. While there is no reputable evidence to indicate any direct and immediate connection between English eighteenth-century masonic lodges and the guild societies of earlier

---

6   David Brewster, *The History of Free Masonry, Drawn from Authentic Sources of Information; and with An Account of the Grand Lodge of Scotland ... and an Appendix of Original Papers. For Alex. Lawrie, Bookseller and Stationer to the Grand Lodge of Scotland* (Edinburgh; London, 1804).

7   James Callendar, *The Free Mason's Pocket Companion* (W. Cheyne, Edinburgh, 1752). See Appendix I.

English stonemasons, the written records in Scotland demonstrate a clear line of evolution from the associations of Scottish stonemasons in the 1590s into the freemason lodges of the early eighteenth century. Minute books and other archival sources tell the story of how Scottish stonemasons came to allow other tradesmen, professionals, and aristocrats to join their lodges, beginning some time in the seventeenth century.[8] The 1720s appear to have been the period of greatest disruption and ultimate change in Scotland from 'operative' (or guild-based) to so-called 'speculative' masonry, a process that Lisa Kahler has demonstrated was effectively completed by the late 1740s, even in those cases like that of the Edinburgh Lodge where there had been futile but nonetheless fierce resistance to change in the early decades of the century. Thus, because masons in Scotland were immersed in their history and had for an extended period been struggling both constitutionally and ideologically to give form to modern Scottish masonry, they had no cause to acquire a pseudo-history of the sort that the London-based James Anderson – ironically, perhaps, a Scot himself and originally from Aberdeen – offered English freemasons in his *Constitutions*. One might therefore suggest that by 1752 Scottish masonry was sufficiently altered from its original state and so far evolved into a speculative institution that both the use of pocket companions and the opportunity they provided to fashion a Scottish origins myth that reflected its English precedent were timely. This would fit with Lisa Kahler's argument that a new social order was apparent in Scottish masonry by 1750.[9] By 1761, however, Scotland had produced a largely native pocket companion that included the first narration of a distinctly Scottish legend of national masonic origins and Scottish companions began in turn to influence their English counterparts.

But there is a second and far more fundamental reason for the delay in printing a pocket companion for masons in Scotland, and one which may also explain the absence of Anderson's original songs from the appendix of the 1739 Edinburgh edition of *Masonry: A Poem*. Throughout most of the eighteenth century, the book trades in Scotland and England disagreed about the matter of copyright, with Scottish printers holding to a strict interpretation of the law that protected published materials in Britain for a period of only twenty-eight years.[10] In the 1740s, arguments about copyright and Scottish reprints went to

---

8 See David Stevenson, *The First Freemasons* (Aberdeen, 1988), and Lisa Kahler, 'Free-masonry in Edinburgh, 1721–1746' (unpublished dissertation, St. Andrews, 1996), especially her discussion of the Lodge of Edinburgh, 1598–1746, pp. 58–110.

9 See Kahler's concluding chapter, in particular, pp. 295–308.

10 For the definitive study of Scottish interpretations of copyright during this period, see Warren McDougall, 'Smugglers, reprinters, and hot pursuers: the Irish-Scottish book trade, and copyright prosecutions in the late eighteenth century', in Robin Myers and Michael

court in Edinburgh, because Andrew Millar, again ironically a Scot, whose publishing ventures were based in London, sued his colleagues in Scotland for infringing on his copyrights. The case was not settled until 1749, and not finally processed by the Lords until 1751, when the Scottish booksellers' interpretation of the statutory period of twenty-eight years for copyright was allowed to stand.[11] This situation may explain why 1752, and not 1750 or 1754, was the date for the first Scottish publication of a pocket companion for masons.[12] Since the original for all of the English companions was Anderson's *Constitutions* of 1723, the year 1751 would have been the first time when Scottish publishers felt free to reprint the work, since the twenty-eight-year statutory period for the copyright on Anderson's text had then expired. But since the court's response to Millar's legal action was still awaiting acknowledgement by the Lords in 1751, William Cheyne's determination to publish in 1752 makes some sense. Cheyne is also the first to print James Anderson's ceremonial masonic songs, suggesting again that copyright perhaps more than taste was the reason for their absence from the 1739 edition of *Masonry: A Poem. To which are added several songs.* Certainly, after this date, as we shall shortly see, Scottish pocket companions were printed at regular intervals for two decades.[13]

No doubt a combination of social and cultural circumstances arising from the unique historical nature of Scottish masonry, together with the statutory restraints of copyright, go a fair distance in explaining the apparently belated appearance of pocket companions in Scotland. But with William Cheyne's publication in 1752 of *The Free-Mason's Pocket Companion*, edited by his St David's Lodge brother, James Callendar, Scottish masonic printing quickly came of age. Furthermore, it is not surprising that publishers in Scotland eschewed commissioning a history or companion of their own during the early to mid-eighteenth century; the Scottish book trade at the time relied almost exclusively on reprints to generate its profits and the cost of an original text would likely have been viewed as prohibitive. Even the editorial work Callendar did for Cheyne is limited, and he is not credited for it on the work's title page; Callendar simply used William Smith's text, which had in turn been

Harris, eds, *The Stationers' Company and the Book Trade, 1550–1990* (Winchester and New Castle, DL, 1997), pp. 151–83.

11   McDougall, 'Smugglers', p. 155.

12   William Smith's 1735 edition was clearly viewed as a piracy of Anderson, and its printing in 1735 resulted both in court action by Anderson and intercession on the part of the Grand Lodge of England. See Adams, pp. 169–72.

13   See Appendix I for a full list of Scottish pocket companions. Note that the Smith and Entick versions in Scotland can initially be identified by the mottoes on their title pages: *'Deus Nobis Sol & Scutum'* for Smith, and *'Per bonam famam & infamam'* for Entick.

derived from Anderson's. Callendar's name, however, does appear on the separate title page for the collection of songs which was appended to the volume, and it was here that he did his most original and lasting work. As masonic texts began to be printed in Scotland over the next few decades, collections of songs, both included with companions and published separately, would be crucial to the success and expansion of the masonic literary marketplace. Only in the nineteenth century would that market command an original history of Scottish masonry, when, as previously mentioned, David Brewster's *History of Free Masonry* (1804) would appear.

Between 1752 and 1754, three pocket companions were published in Scotland by three different firms, all essentially reprints of William Smith's 1735 London version of Anderson. After Cheyne in 1752, there was an edition printed by James Reid at Leith in 1754 and another printed at Edinburgh in 1758 by Alexander Donaldson, probably the king of the eighteenth-century Scottish reprint trade, a very active mason, and the publisher of the lucrative newspaper *The Edinburgh Advertiser*. Donaldson's efforts are the most interesting, because he is quick to recognize the potential market for Callendar's *Collection of Free Masons Songs* in its own right.[14] The collection had been published in part and without acknowledging Callendar in Glasgow in 1755, but Donaldson restores Callendar's name and identifies him as a Master Mason (an infrequent designation in Scottish masonry at the time) for his own 1758 edition, while taking the further step of including London on the imprint for the songs, which he makes available through 'Mess. Wilson and Durham at Plato's head, in the Strand'.[15] He is also alone in declaring his own masonic status on the title page ('Printed by Br. A. Donaldson and Company'), something one sees rarely in Scottish masonic imprints in the eighteenth century.

Other than their use of Callendar's songs, these first Scottish pocket companions had little in the way of native content, and reflected no original masonic scholarship. That would change with the publication of the next Scottish handbook, William Auld's *The Free Masons Pocket Companion* (Ruddiman, Auld and Company, Edinburgh, 1761). If there was any question of Donaldson having flooded the market with his reprint of Smith, Auld and his printing partner, Walter Ruddiman, addressed this by using a more recent and more scholarly version of the *Constitutions*, John Entick's *The Pocket Companion and History of Free-Masons*, edited for and published by Jonathan Scott (London,

---

14 See Appendix II for a bibliography of Scottish editions of masons' songs in the eighteenth century.

15 The third degree or Master Mason's degree was not often conferred in Scotland before this point in the eighteenth century, having been originated by English lodges. See Lisa Kahler's discussion of the unusual circumstances surrounding Provost George Drummond's receipt of this degree, and the account in *The History of Free Masonry*.

1754).[16] As with Smith's earlier work, Entick's new text proved popular and was pirated, leading to a revision and enlargement by Entick for an edition in 1759.[17] However, Scott and Entick also demonstrated a Scottish predisposition in their companion, however modestly, by including on the final page and set apart from their own collection of masonic songs, a specifically Scottish mason's anthem, 'sung at the laying of the Foundation of the New-Exchange, at Edinburgh', thus beginning a dialogue between English and Scottish pocket companions that would continue through two additions of Auld's work into Wellins Calcott's quite unique 1769 London publication. Along with this new source text, taken from Entick, Auld provided his readers with three original, native features: the first history of Scottish masonry to go beyond Anderson's superficial efforts into a detailed account that came down to the establishment of the present Grand Lodge of Scotland and printed the names of all the office bearers and Scottish lodges up to the publication date of the handbook; an appendix that reprinted the act of the Associate Synod of Scotland against freemasons, together with a response examining the flaws in the act (reprinted from the *Scots Magazine* and other Scottish periodical sources from 1756 through 1758); and an expansion of Callendar's forty-three songs by the addition of a number of new Scottish songs. Auld further declares his serious intent as a publisher of Scottish masonic history through an advertisement facing the title page of his pocket companion:

earnestly requesting that all persons possessed of any ancient records, or other writings relative to the Society of Free Masons in *Scotland* would please to communicate them to William Auld Printer in *Edinburgh*, who will readily acknowledge the obligation, and give assurance that this request is intended for a public concern, and that no improper use shall be made of them.[18]

Auld goes on to indicate that receipts shall be issued for all submitted materials from himself in his capacity as the Master of the Lodge of Grand Stewards, and from the Masters of the Ancient Lodge of Mary's Chapel and the Thistle Lodge. Here we see some of the first evidence of a concerted effort on the part

---

16 After editing the pocket companion for Jonathan Scott, Entick went on to produce the weekly anti-government newspaper *The Monitor* for him from 9 August 1755 to 30 March 1765. A relationship with the radical press was not unusual among masons in the eighteenth-century book trade.

17 John Entick, *The Pocket Companion and History of Free-Masons* (R. Baldwin, London, 1759), 2nd edn, revised and enlarged.

18 Probably the first indication in print of a Scottish antiquarian interest in native freemasonic history. Significantly, this initiative comes from two Edinburgh lodges, and not the Grand Lodge of Scotland itself, demonstrating once again that in Scotland individual lodges still tended to make the sort of decisions that were centralized through the Grand Lodge in England (emphasis is Auld's).

of some Edinburgh lodges to pursue a scholarly history of Scottish masonry from original sources, as well as a suggestion that William Auld and his pocket companion had something of an official status that had not been granted to previous Scottish printers and their histories. Indeed, some of the materials acquired by Auld through his advertisement in the 1761 edition were later used by him in his new editions in 1765 and 1772. Auld's scholarly methodology and his perspective on history and the value of retrieved documentation and artefacts are very close to the positions taken by contemporary antiquarians and indicate the beginning of a learned approach toward masonry in Scotland, an approach that would have been quite congenial to both Auld's printing partners, William Ruddiman and William Smellie.

The popularity of Auld's new pocket companion was immediately apparent. Donaldson printed it for sale at his London as well as his Edinburgh premises, first in 1761 and again in 1763, when Ruddiman and Auld printed their second edition, to be followed by a Glasgow printing in 1765 by Joseph Galbraith. All three Scottish publishers associated with Auld's first attempt at a pocket companion – Walter Ruddiman, Alexander Donaldson, and Joseph Galbraith – were canny businessmen who would have long, successful careers in the Scottish book trade, and their strong interest in the Auld edition easily suggests that the work's popularity was matched by its profitability. In his new partnership with William Smellie in 1765, Auld published a generally revised edition of the *Free Masons Pocket Companion*, with some rewriting of the Scottish history, particularly in the final paragraph, the increase of the songs to fifty-five, besides the anthem, and significantly, the deletion of the material on oath-swearing and the act of the Associate Synod. He also inserted new materials about the Charter. This edition is, perhaps, the first Scottish companion to have an impact upon its English counterparts in London. The chapter on the institution of the Grand Lodge of Scotland appears with only minor alterations in Wellins Calcott's *A Candid Disquisition* (1769), the first English companion to go beyond its source in Anderson in narrating a masonic history for Scotland. But the inclusion of Auld's chapter is only part of a larger strategy behind Calcott's volume, one which needed to establish the historic legitimacy of Scottish masonry in order to achieve its grander purpose in England.

Immediately after the 'Account of the Establishment of the Present Grand Lodge of Scotland' (pp. 104–16), which is derived wholly from Auld with only modest editorial changes, Calcott inserts a letter from James Galway, an English Past Master (pp. 116–22), applauding Calcott's inclusion of the Scottish material and reminding the readers that masonic proceedings in Scotland are

assembled in buildings, which [are] their own property, set apart for that purpose alone, whereby [unlike the English] they not only [are] secured from every danger of molestation, or the insults and disrespectful treatment of publicans, but accumulate *considerable* funds.

This he contrasts with English lodges, most of which were then established in taverns and inns where 'our meeting at the houses of publicans, gives us the air of a *Bacchanalian society*, instead of that appearance of *gravity* and *wisdom*, which our order *justly* requires', and which Galway associates with the Scots.[19] Galway's letter and Calcott's companion have a not very well concealed ulterior motive behind their apparent Scottish interests which is to encourage masons in England to support and subscribe to their Grand Lodge's recent initiative to establish a purpose-built national lodge, which would be the first such masonic building in England. Calcott's volume is also unusual for its long list of subscribers, thirty-two pages in all and accounting for several hundred fellow masons, including James Boswell, newly arrived in London and described in the list as the 'author of the history of Corsica' (p. 4). It is one of the few masonic histories since Anderson's in 1723 to be published in octavo as well as duodecimo, with large octavo editions on fine paper supplied to subscribers.

Along with its remarkable influence on English masonic publications, Auld's history and pocket companion had a long tenure as the preferred text in Scotland. It was reprinted at Glasgow twice in 1771, first by Peter and John Tait in partnership with James Brown, and immediately afterwards by Robert and Thomas Duncan. Perhaps in response to these publications, Auld revised his text and printed a third edition in 1772, entitled *The History of Masonry*, which remains the authoritative edition in Scotland until 1804, when it was supplanted by David Brewster's *History of Free-Masonry* by authority of the Grand Lodge. When he became Scottish Grand Master in 1788, Lord Napier was presented with a copy of Auld's 1772 third edition, which now rests, with its inscription to Napier in the rare book collection at the National Library of Scotland. Its presentation to Napier is at least circumstantial evidence asserting the claim of Auld's work to still be the 'authorized version' in Scotland at that date. In the years intervening between Auld and Brewster, at least three other Scottish pocket companions were printed, which owe their historical accounts to Auld: one by John Donaldson in London in 1775, and offered for sale in both London and Edinburgh, another by John and Peter Wilson at Ayr in 1792, and a final one by William Bell at Glasgow in 1798.[20] The Wilsons and Bell both justified their publication by including new Scottish songs, but neither attempted to enhance or abridge Auld's scholarship.

---

19 Calcott, *A Candid Disquisition*, p. 118 (emphasis Calcott's).
20 As in 1763, Auld's work is again pirated by a Donaldson, this time Alexander's brother John, at London in 1775, another indication of the volume's continued popularity and profitability.

Apart from their inclusion after 1761 of a narrative history of Scottish masonry, pocket companions printed in Scotland differed from their English sources in their greater emphasis on popular songs. Where compilations of masonic songs in England tended to be more conservative in what they judged to be appropriate material[21] and adhered more closely to the standards first set out by James Anderson in 1723 and then by the next most important scholar of English masonic history, William Preston beginning in 1772,[22] their counterparts in Scotland celebrated the native tradition of popular song through an ever-expanding repertoire of materials.[23] William Smith's *A Collection of Songs of the Masons* (London, 1734), perhaps the first English publication devoted entirely to masonic music, includes only fifteen songs in addition to the full versions of Anderson's four official pieces from 1723.[24] On the other hand, in *A Collection of Free Masons Songs* (Edinburgh, 1754), James Callendar reprints all of the lyrics from Smith, while adding twenty further songs. The intro-

---

21 One scholar has remarked that 'curiously, the Exeter Collection is the only Masonic one of its kind to include a song which falls short of the high moral tone so conspicuous in all Masonic verse of the eighteenth century' (A. Sharp, 'Masonic Songs and Song Books of the Late Eighteenth Century,' *Ars Quatuor Coronati*, 65 (1953), p. 88). This is certainly true of English publications which regularly advertised the decorum of their collections, but it cannot be applied to Scottish masonic song books which included popular and vernacular material from the beginning and featured a good many bawdy songs. See especially the Scottish songs appended to Joseph Galbraith's 1765 Glasgow *Pocket Companion*.

22 Preston was born in Edinburgh (28 July 1742) where he was a clerk to the scholar and librarian Thomas Ruddiman (1757) before becoming a printing apprentice with Walter Ruddiman (1758–9), who in partnership with William Auld published the first authentically Scottish pocket companion in 1761. Both Ruddimans were masons, and Walter wrote the letter of recommendation in 1760 that secured Preston his lifelong position in London with the printing firm of the highly successful publisher and mason, William Strahan. Preston produced nine separate editions of the *Illustrations* during his lifetime. All nine can be accessed through Andrew Prescott's CD-Rom edition, *Preston's Illustrations of Masonry* (Academy Electronic Publications Ltd, 2001). Preston did not include any songs in the first edition of his *Illustrations* (1772), with songs only appearing in modest numbers with the second edition (1775).

23 Burns's songs are fixtures in late eighteenth-century masonic collections, his 'Farewell to the Brethren of St. James's Lodge, Tarbolton' becoming a standard even in English anthologies by the time of Stephen Jones's seminal *Masonic Miscellanies* (Vernor and Hood, London, 1797). However, from the 1760s, Scottish collections had always favoured popular music in a way that nicely prefigured the appearance of James Johnson's *Scots Musical Museum* (1787–1803).

24 The only detailed history of masonic songs in the eighteenth-century is Sharp's 'Masonic Songs and Song Books of the Late Eighteenth Century,' which has little to say about the distinctiveness of Scottish song books. Also Clark, *British Clubs and Societies*, pp. 227, 326–7, 333, 344, 348.

ductions and advertisements to the various Scottish collections of masons' songs often address the crucial place of songs in Scottish pocket companions, and not just for their marketing value. In his 1758 preface, Callendar writes about the gift of 'entertainment' that singing brings to masonic gatherings, a point repeated by the editors of other Scottish collections of masons' songs. Singing was a defining feature of Scottish masonic lodges, just as it was a fundamental aspect of Scottish popular culture. James Boswell wrote about one poorly attended lodge meeting during his term as Master in 1774, which was only redeemed because everyone present had an opportunity to sing a song. On the occasion of another lodge meeting in 1775, he wrote in his journal: 'my spirits were vigorous and I sang my non-sensical Scotch song, *Twa Wheels*.'[25] The agenda of Scottish masonic meetings always put business ahead of pleasure, making the latter all the more delightful when it arrived. But the English were often hard-pressed to establish any decorum for their proceedings, *dulce* or otherwise. Indeed, their practice of meeting in taverns meant that drinking and feasting often came before the business in English masonic lodges, usually leading to no business at all, something complained about by continental visitors.[26]

There was also an assumption among Scots printers that the market for masonic materials went far beyond the masons themselves to include women prominently among the non-masonic readership. In fact, several surviving copies of eighteenth-century Scottish pocket companions and song collections are inscribed by women. Thus the Advertisement to *The Young Free-Mason's Assistant. Being a Choice Collection of Masons Songs ... Scotch and English* (Dumfries, 1784) reports that:

as this Collection may fall into the hands of some who are not initiated into the mysteries of Free-Masonry, of course, to them, many of the Songs will be unintelligible: It was therefore thought advisable, to subjoin a few of the most Celebrated Scotch and English Songs for their amusement (pp. 5–6).[27]

Such is clearly the strategy shared by most Scottish publishers of collections of masonic songs, including *The Entertaining Songster* (Aberdeen, 1791) and evident in the circulation of masonic songs in chapbooks in Scotland throughout the eighteenth century. Of particular interest, however, is the pocket companion printed at Ayr in 1792 by John Wilson who published the Kilmarnock Edition of Robert Burns's poems. Wilson advertises his text as including

25 *Canongate-Kilwinning Lodge Minute Book*, 7 July 1774; and Boswell, *Edinburgh Journals*, 13 February 1775.
26 Clark, *British Clubs and Societies*, pp. 325–7.
27 The National Library of Scotland's copy has a disputed Robert Burns signature on its title page.

Irish songs, along with English and Scottish, a politically interesting inclusion at a time of increasing national confrontation over the Irish question and, doubly so, since his publication coincides with the surge of radicalism in Scotland in 1792 that led to the first arrests under the new act to suppress seditious libel. Freemasons, in fact, dominated the list of those indicted and tried in Scotland for seditious libel in the 1790s.

If the editors of masonic song collections in Scotland were active participants in the increasingly institutional effort to bring together in print a representative body of the nation's traditional songs, some of the more learned activities among masons in Britain were decidedly radical in purpose. These included everything from the more modest social radicalism of Lord Buchan's formation of the Society of Antiquaries of Scotland in 1780, with its initial intent to establish a socially inclusive space for legitimate academic pursuits in science and history outside the preserves of Edinburgh University, particularly emphasizing free public lectures in direct competition with those given by professors occupying the university's most prestigious Chairs, to the far more dangerous intent stated by the mason and MP Thomas Erskine in his speech on the liberty of the press at the Free-Mason's Tavern in London in December 1792.[28]

Scottish masonry in particular had always presented a set of social values that coincided perfectly with the ideals of the Enlightenment: a belief in the human capacity for improvement, the promotion of the liberal arts and sciences, social liberty, charity and fraternity, and the commitment to a moral imperative for the universal dissemination of all useful learning. In key published documents, Scottish freemasons carefully distinguished between their attitude toward human nature and that of the Church of Scotland. This distinction is nowhere more eloquently set out than in the learned *Principles of Free Masonry Explained in a Discourse Delivered before the very Antient Lodge of Kilwinning in the Church of that Place and in the Year MDCCLXVI* (probably printed by Joseph Galbraith, Glasgow, 1768):

> From the short account given, my Brethren, which you have heard
> of Christianity; and from that now given you of the principles
> of Free Masonry, you may see how differently these two institutions
> aim at removing the cause of these evils which spring from society....
> Christianity, in short, would render mankind pious and virtuous, by
> reforming human nature; and Free Masonry would lay a check upon

---

28 Lord Buchan would become the Scottish Grand Master in 1782; his chief supporters among the active founders of the Society of Antiquaries of Scotland were mostly masons. See also, *The Speech of the Hon. Thomas Erskine ... at Free-Mason's Tavern, Dec. 22, 1792* (London, 1792); and Thomas Erskine, *The Declaration of the Friends of the Liberty of the Press* (London, 1793).

the malicious and unsocial passions of mankind, and encourage their kind affections without changing their nature.

This appears to me, as far as I am able to judge, to be the vast difference between Christianity and Free Masonry. The first of these institutions is, beyond all dispute, worthy of the wisdom and goodness of God ... the second does honour to the wisdom and goodness of man....

(pp. 27–8)

This Hutchesonian emphasis on the benevolent doctrine of improvement aligned Scottish masonry at the mid-eighteenth century with the reform agenda of moderate churchmen like Dr William Robertson, who were effectively modernizing Scottish universities and scholarship by moving theology from the centre of the curriculum – and thus social life – while simultaneously freeing universities from the controlling hand of the church's most conservative members. At the high point of the Scottish Enlightenment, freemasons and masonic principles stood behind projects like the *Encyclopaedia Britannica* and nurtured the speculations of Adam Ferguson, Lord Monboddo, and Joseph Black within their lodges. Many of the early learned efforts in antiquarianism were also closely allied to the interests of Scottish masonry, while the practice of Scottish masonic history by William Auld was decidedly antiquarian in its scholarly bent. And Scotland's learned printers, as we have seen, from Ruddiman to Smellie, along with an easy majority of the country's book trade were active masons. The Scottish masonic promotion of native poetry and popular songs did much to establish the career of Thomas Blacklock, arguably the first poet laureate of Scottish masons before Robert Burns, and contributed significantly to the acceptance and success of the vernacular writings of Ramsay, Fergusson and Burns in the eighteenth century, and of Hogg early in the next century.[29] But by the 1780s freemasonry increasingly found itself opposed by the establishment in the universities and the government. That opposition did much to arrest the development of Lord Buchan's masonically oriented Society of Antiquaries, and came together with melodramatic insistence in the curious but popular attack on freemasonry by the Edinburgh University Professor, John Robison, in his somewhat hysterical bestseller *Roots of a Conspiracy*

---

29 Freemasons did a great deal to support and promote music in Scotland, and native musicians in particular, during the eighteenth century. Evidence for this can be found throughout the surviving minute books for the period, where the various lodges record the names of musicians employed at lodge functions and money paid out on such occasions. Masonic lodges also sponsored many public concerts, advertisements for which appear regularly in Edinburgh's newspapers throughout the period.

(Edinburgh, 1797) – printed by two masons, Thomas Cadell (London) and William Creech (Edinburgh).[30]

Whereas Scottish masonic publishing, as we have seen, had demonstrated an increasingly learned and socially-engaged inclination from its beginnings in 1739 with *Masonry: A Poem*, by the close of the eighteenth century, it began with deliberate intent to turn inward and look away from issues of social improvement. Throughout the Enlightenment, Scottish masons printed the country's most important newspapers and magazines – without outcries about conspiracies – as well as writing some of Scotland's most enduring scholarly works. Even the discipline of Scottish masonic history, begun by William Auld, shared the contemporary, learned antiquarian mandate – in common with its English counterpart – first through a late-Augustan style of nationalistic legend-building derived in part from Virgil's *Aeneid* by way of Dryden, and later through the specifically Scottish phenomenon of Ossian. But these masonic forays into social improvement and scholarship of all sorts were disrupted by 1800 because, as David Brewster writes:

after the publications of Barruel and Robison, the progress of Free Masonry in Britain was retarded by an act of Parliament in 1799, for the suppression of seditious societies, in which the fraternity were virtually prohibited from erecting new lodges in the kingdom (p. 145).

Brewster then goes on to argue passionately that British freemasons are patriots, thus laying the foundation for what would become Victorian domestic masonry (pp. 145–6). Freemasonry nationalized and allied to empire would differ vastly from the individualism of Scottish masonry in the eighteenth century.

When the brief Whig government of 1806 rewarded the celebrated Scottish mason and philosopher Professor Dugald Stewart with a preferment in the form of the newly created office of 'Writer, Printer, and publisher of the *Edinburgh Gazette*', Scottish masonry began a long association with this rather dull government organ through its official Stationer to the Grand Lodge, Alexander Lawrie. Since Stewart had neither the experience nor the interest to edit and publish a newspaper, however official and predictable its content, the Whigs gave that task to Lawrie, a fellow mason who had not only printed Brewster's

---

30 Although freemasons dominated the Scottish book trade in the eighteenth century, there is no real evidence for collusion among the brotherhood. Indeed, Creech, a lodge Master, would otherwise surely have suppressed Robison's book rather than making a significant profit from its many editions. Further, the publisher and adventurer Peter Williamson complains that despite being an active mason, his lodge brothers will not give him any sort of assistance in establishing his printing concern, a circumstance that also applied to James Tytler in his attempts to set himself up as a publisher in Edinburgh.

History of Free Masonry in 1804, but was for a very long while credited with having written it. Still, the *Edinburgh Gazette*, established by the government in 1793 to speak on its official behalf, at the height of Edinburgh's radical unrest, was a far cry from the sorts of socially aware and controversial periodicals that masons like William Smellie, Peter Williamson, James Tytler, Dr James Anderson and William Johnston had launched in Edinburgh during the later eighteenth century.[31] But masonry was growing evermore self-absorbed and inward-looking in its intellectual interests after the crises of the late 1790s, and most of the promise held out by the social agenda and learnedness of Enlightenment Scottish masonry was displaced by an intellectually arcane and socially conservative form of the Craft. David Brewster's 1804 *History* announces this changing of the guard succinctly when he substitutes proto-Victorian 'heroes at the head of our fleets and armies' (p. 146) for the likes of Hutcheson, Stewart, and Burns.[32] When masons become generals and admirals, there is far too little space left for thinkers and writers.

---

31 Their periodicals included, respectively: *The Edinburgh Magazine and Review* (1773–6), *The Scots Spy* (1776), *The Bee* (1790–4), *The Historical Register* (1792–3) and *The Edinburgh Gazetteer* (1792–4). Both Tytler and Johnston were indicted for sedition in 1792. Dr Anderson was summoned before the Sheriff for publishing dangerous materials, but was not formally charged, in part because of his learned reputation.

32 Brewster himself became the editor of an important periodical with his appointment to *The Edinburgh Magazine* in 1802, becoming for some time the editor of the *Scots Magazine* when it was combined with *The Edinburgh Magazine* in 1804.

Appendix I

Sources and Examples of Eighteenth-Century Scottish Masonic Pocket Companions

(All texts duodecimo unless otherwise indicated)

Primary English Sources for all Scottish Companions

James Anderson, *The Book of Constitutions* (London, 1723); *The New Book of Constitutions* (London, 1738). Sources for two subsequent versions by William Smith and John Entick. Quarto and octavo.

William Smith, *A Pocket Companion for Free-Masons* (E. Rider, London, 1735). A piracy, contested by Anderson. Also printed by Smith in Dublin, where it had Grand Lodge of Ireland approval.

W. Smith, *The Free Mason's Pocket Companion* (John Torbuck, London, 1736). Reprint of William Smith's *A Pocket Companion for Free-Masons*.

John Entick, *The Pocket Companion and History of Free-Masons* (Jonathan Scott, London, 1754). Sanctioned by Grand Lodge of England.

The Pocket Companion and History of Free-Masons (R. Baldwin, London, 1759). Revised and enlarged 2nd edn of Entick.

Scottish Companions Derived from Smith

(Usually found with Smith's motto–*Deus Nobis Sol & Scutum*)

James Callendar, *The Free-Mason's Pocket Companion* (W. Cheyne, Edinburgh, 1752). Taken from Torbuck's printing.

The Free-Mason's Pocket Companion (James Reid, Leith, 1754). Taken from Cheyne.

A Pocket Companion for Free-Masons (Archibald McLean, Glasgow, 1754). Title page describes this as the '4th edition', probably because McLean has gone back to Rider's disputed 1735 printing and then counts Torbuck's reprint (1736) and that by Cheyne (1752) as the '2nd and 3rd editions'.

James Callendar, *The Free-Mason's Pocket Companion, A Collection of Free Masons Songs* (Br. Alexander Donaldson, Edinburgh 1758).

Scottish Companions Derived from Entick

(Usually found with Entick's motto – *Per bonam famam & infamam*)

William Auld, *The Free Masons Pocket Companion* (Ruddiman, Auld, and Company, Edinburgh, 1761; 2nd edn, 1763). The Appendix which contains materials on the Associate Synod and a collection of songs has its own title page and imprint.

The Free-Masons Pocket-Companion (Alexander Donaldson, Edinburgh and London, 2nd edn, 1763; 3rd edn, 1771). Assumes Ruddiman and Auld as its 'first edition'.

William Auld and William Smellie, *The Free Masons Pocket Companion* (Auld and Smellie, Edinburgh, 1765; 2nd edn, 1768).

The Free Masons Pocket Companion (Joseph Galbraith, Glasgow, 1765).

[NOTE: Wellins Callcot, *A Candid Disquisition of the Principles and Practices of ... Free and Accepted Masons* (Br. James Dixwell, London, 1769) derives its section on Scottish masonry verbatim from William Auld, and is influenced in many other ways by Scottish masonry.]

The Free Masons Pocket Companion (Peter Tait, James Brown, & John Tait, Glasgow, 1771).

The Free Masons Pocket Companion (Robert & Thomas Duncan, Glasgow, 1771). Exact reprint of Tait.

William Auld, *The History of Masonry* (William Auld, Edinburgh, 1772). Listed as the 3rd edn of Auld and Smellie, but actually Auld's original work for Walter Ruddiman, incorporating the edition published with William Smellie, retitled, and including revisions, additions, and updating through 1771. This remains the standard edition until 1792. See the copy in the National Library of Scotland which was given to Lord Napier during his tenure as Grand Master of Scotland in 1788–9.

The History of Masonry (John Donaldson, London, 1775). Sold in London and Edinburgh. Reprint of Auld's 1772 edition with the imprint of Alexander Donaldson's brother, John.

The Free Mason's Pocket Companion (John & Peter Wilson, Air [*sic*], 1792; sold in Edinburgh, Stirling, and Glasgow).

The Free Masons Pocket Companion (William Bell, Glasgow, 1798).

Appendix II

Editions of Masonic Songs in Eighteenth-Century Scotland
(All texts duodecimo unless otherwise indicated)

The following texts have their own title pages and imprints. Although some (identified by asterisks) were initially bound together with *Pocket Companions,* all were available for sale separately as distinct publications.

NOTE: James Anderson's *Constitutions* (London, 1723) appends the four essential ceremonial songs of eighteenth-century masonry. These are first expanded upon in print by *A Collection of the Songs of Masons* (London, 1734), which added fourteen other songs, 'in praise of Masonry'. This collection forms the basis for the songs appended to the histories and companions that follow, including the songs in the various editions of Preston's *Illustrations of Masonry;* however, Scottish texts, beginning with Cheyne in 1752, expanded this canon significantly with the addition of popular Scotch songs, usually outside masonic themes.

Masonry: A Poem. To which are added several Songs (Sands, Brymer, Murray, and Cochran, Edinburgh, 1739).

**A Collection of the Songs of Masons* (W. Cheyne, Edinburgh, 1752).

**A Collection of the Songs of Masons* (James Reid, Leith, 1754). Reprint of Cheyne, 1752.

A Choice Collection of Songs to be Sung by Free-Masons: Some of which were never before published (Glasgow, 1755).

*James Callendar, *A Collection of Free Masons Songs* (Br. Alexander Donaldson, Edinburgh, 1758). Sold by George Paton in Edinburgh and by Mess. Wilson and Durham in London

A Collection of Free Masons Songs (Robert Bremner, Edinburgh, 1760). Reprint of Callendar.

William Auld, *Appendix to the Masons Pocket Companion: containing ... a complete collection of all the Free Masons songs, with several new ones never before published* (William Auld, and Company, Edinburgh, 1761). The *Appendix* has its own pagination, separate from that of the Companion and the imprint bears only Auld's name, excluding that of Ruddiman.

*William Auld and William Smellie, *A Collection of Free Mason Songs, many of which were never before published* (Auld and Smellie, Edinburgh, 1765). The 'Contents' (pp. v, vi) listing the songs appears ahead of the 'Contents' (pp. vii, viii) for the Companion itself, suggesting that the songs were a primary selling feature of the volume, despite the extraordinary, new

Scottish material in the Companion. Adds fifteen songs to those in Ruddiman and Auld.

A Collection of Scots and English Songs (Joseph Galbraith, Glasgow, 1765).

A Collection of Scots and English Songs (Peter Tait, James Brown & John Tait, Glasgow, 1771).

The Young Free-Mason's Assistant. Being a choice collection of Mason Songs ... to which are added celebrated songs, Scotch and English. (Robert McLachlan, Dumfries, 1784).

A Collection of Masonic Songs (Gavin Wilson, Edinburgh, 1788). Includes 18 songs by Wilson himself.

The Entertaining Songster; consisting of the best Masonic Songs (A. Shirrefs, Aberdeen, 1791).

*A Collection of the Most Approved English, Scottish, and Irish Songs (John & Peter Wilson, Air [sic], 1792).

*The Free Masons Pocket Companion ... to which is added a variety of humorous songs (William Bell, Glasgow, 1798).

The Kail-Brose of aula Scotland. To which are added ... The Free-Mason's Song (C. Randall, Stirling, n.d./late-18th century). Chapbook. Masonic songs will have appeared in this format regularly throughout the period.

'Forming the Literary Tastes of the Middle and Higher Classes': Elgin's Circulating Libraries and their Proprietors, 1789–1870

JANE THOMAS

ELGIN IS THE COUNTY TOWN of Moray in the predominantly rural North-East of Scotland. The economy of this area was based almost entirely around agriculture and fishing in the nineteenth century and, although there was some rural, domestic manufacturing in the shape of flax dressing, spinning, knitting and weaving, these industries were on a small scale and declining by 1790.[1] Any manufacturing of scale was located in Moray's two royal burghs, Elgin and Forres, and this was limited to industries supplying local needs such as food and cloth milling, iron founding, sawmilling and tanning.[2] While these industries expanded during the nineteenth century, none of them was ever a major employer and neither Elgin nor Forres could have been considered industrial.[3] On the contrary, Elgin has been labelled a 'douce' burgh (i.e. genteel and respectable), and had a high proportion of professional males amongst its inhabitants.[4]

---

1 The proportion of males occupied in these industries in the Grampian region (Aberdeenshire, including Aberdeen, Banffshire, Buchan and Moray) is estimated to have been 52.04 per cent in 1851, whilst the Scottish average was only 29.86 per cent. Only the Highland region had a higher figure at 64.59 per cent. J. H. Treble, 'The Occupied Male Labour Force', *People and Society in Scotland, Vol II, 1830–1914*, ed. by W. Hamish Fraser and R. J. Morris (Edinburgh: John Donald, 1990), pp. 167–205 (p. 200); *Statistical Account of Scotland 1791–99*, Vol XVI, ed. by D. J. Withrington and I. R. Grant (Wakefield, 1982). Also online: <http://edina.ac.uk/stat-acc-scot/>

2 Leather working had a long tradition in the area, but never on a large scale. See Jane E. Thomas, 'The Burgh of Elgin in Early Modern Times', Unpublished MLitt thesis (University of Aberdeen, 1990).

3 J. and W. Watson, *Morayshire Described: being a Guide to Visitors* (Elgin: Russell and Watson, 1868). Facsimile edition published by Moray District Libraries, 1983, pp. 131–243; *Statistical Account*, vol. XVI, p. 694.

4 In 1901, 6% of adult males were engaged in professional employment in the burgh. R. J. Morris, 'Urbanisation and Scotland', in *People and Society in Scotland*, vol. II, 1830–1914, ed. by W. Hamish Fraser and R. J. Morris (Edinburgh, 1990), pp. 73–102 (p. 81). This trend was noticeable even in the sixteenth century, see Thomas, 'Burgh of Elgin'; Jane E.

Although by no means an industrial centre, Elgin was a burgh with some influence and served not only as the economic, social and administrative capital of Moray but, from the time of its foundation in the twelfth century had also operated as a local and regional centre for much of the North-East of Scotland. The nineteenth century saw Elgin's position strengthen still further as its population grew and it became the centre for new road and rail networks.[5] The burgh's traditional service economy also expanded with the foundation of bookshops, newspapers, libraries and educational establishments. Elgin's merchants, craftsmen and professionals had always served an area which extended well beyond the bounds of Moray, but changes in society and developments in communications meant that they became busier than ever. In 1863 it was commented that:

Strangers are often surprised how Elgin can support so many fine shops (and craftsmen) ... but the secret lies in the fact that all these are required for a wide district of the country, embracing not only Morayshire but, to a great extent, the adjacent counties of Banff, Nairn, and Inverness; while many of them have extensive business connections with Ross, Sutherland, and Caithness. Elgin also has a large number of professional men ... who are employed extensively in all the counties north of the river Dee.[6]

Isaac Forsyth, 1789–1846
It was perhaps to be expected that, as the hub of both the social and economic activity of the area, and with a willing audience of well-educated professionals, Elgin should be the location of Moray's first circulating library. This library's founder, Isaac Forsyth, was born in Elgin in 1768, the son of Alexander, a well-respected merchant and bailie in the town. In 1783 Isaac became apprenticed to Messrs John and Alexander Angus, booksellers, binders, stationers and circulating library proprietors in Aberdeen, where he learnt the binding trade. After four years in Aberdeen, and a few months perfecting his craft in London, Isaac Forsyth returned to Elgin in 1788 and established himself as a stationer, binder, and bookseller in The Tower, an imposing seventeenth-century building which adjoined the family's home on Elgin's High Street, and which still overlooks the burgh's church and market place.[7]

Thomas 'Elgin Notaries in Burgh Society and Government, 1540–1660', *Northern Scotland*, 13 (1993), 21–30.

5   By 1861 Elgin's population of 7543 accounted for more that 17% of Moray's total.

6   *Black's Morayshire Directory including the Upper District of Banffshire, 1863* (Elgin: James Black, Courant Office, 1863), p. 90.

7   Isaac Forsyth MacAndrew, *Memoir of Isaac Forsyth: Bookseller in Elgin 1768–1859* (London: Kegan Paul, Trench and Co., 1889).

Fig. 1. Portrait of Isaac Forsyth commissioned by the burgh in 1851 which had pride of place in the burgh's Assembly Rooms. Reproduced from Isaac Forsyth MacAndrew, *Memoir of Isaac Forsyth, Bookseller in Elgin, 1768–1859* (London: Kegan Paul, Trench and Co., 1889)

Forsyth quickly tired of practical bookbinding and took on an apprentice binder, John Dunbar, to enable him to concentrate on other aspects of the business.[8] He decided to take his business in a new direction and, by the end of 1789, he had established Elgin's first circulating library with an impressive collection of over 1000 volumes.[9] Forsyth's move to establish a circulating library at this time, in a relatively remote Scottish burgh, was a brave one. These libraries were much less common in Scotland than they were south of the border and the thirty one establishments in existence by 1801 were largely concentrated in the major towns.[10] Forsyth's move was undoubtedly influenced by his experience of the circulating libraries of Aberdeen and London, such as that run by his former employer, Mr Angus, but his friendship with Alexander Brown may also have played a part. Brown and Forsyth became friends while they were apprentices in Aberdeen, and Brown, who was to become a bookseller and library proprietor on a large scale, also founded his first library in 1789.[11]

Forsyth has been credited with being the first bookseller, 'properly so called', north of Aberdeen, and also with establishing the first circulating library in the 'North of Scotland'; unfortunately neither statement is strictly accurate as James Imlach of Banff and Alexander Davidson of Inverness both had well-established bookshops and libraries by 1788.[12] However, Forsyth may be counted amongst the first booksellers and library proprietors in the area and, in view of the town's extensive sphere of influence, his was certainly an important new establishment. Forsyth deserves credit for his willingness to try such a venture when only twenty-one years of age and his biographer was fully

---

8   MacAndrew, *Memoir of Isaac Forsyth*, p. 14.

9   *Catalogue of Books of the Elgin Circulating Library, Containing a Select and Valuable Collection of Books by the Latest and Best Authors* (Elgin: Isaac Forsyth, 1789), including later appendix believed to be 1795. Available at the National Library of Scotland, and at Moray Local Heritage Centre, Elgin.

10   John Crawford, 'The Community Library in Scottish History'. Paper delivered at the 68th IFLA Conference, Glasgow 18–24 August 2002. Online: <http://www.ifla.org/iv/ifla68/papers/063-111e.pdf >.

11   MacAndrew, *Memoir of Isaac Forsyth*, p. 13; *Elgin Courier*, 20 May 1859, p. 2; Iain Beavan, '"All New Works of Interest Received on Publication": Aberdeen and its Access to the Printed Word 1800–1850', in *The City and its Worlds: Aspects of Aberdeen's History since 1794*, ed. by Terry Brotherstone and Donald J. Withrington (Glasgow, 1996), pp. 94–114; McDonald, pp. 120–3, 124–9.

12   *Forres Gazette*, 25 May 1859, p. 3; MacAndrew, *Memoir of Isaac Forsyth*, p. 14; National Library of Scotland, Scottish Book Trade Index (hereafter NLS, SBTI). Online. Available: <http://www.nls.uk/catalogue/resources/sbti>; W. R. McDonald, 'Circulating Libraries in the North-East of Scotland in the Eighteenth Century', *Bibliotheck* 5 (1968), 119–37 (pp. 131–2).

Fig. 2. Elgin High Street *c.*1800 with The Tower to the left-hand side of the picture. Original in Billings' *Antiquities* (1845–52). Reproduced in *The Records of Elgin 1234–1800* compiled by William Cramond, 2 vols (Aberdeen: New Spalding Club, 1903), I, p. 504

justified when he commented that 'his ideas always expanded to the level of the day, and frequently carried him far in advance of it'.[13]

By the time his library opened in 1789 Isaac Forsyth had managed to amass quite a considerable collection of books and it is apparent that he must have gone to great pains to do so. There is believed to have been no production of printed material in Moray before 1821 when the printer, Robert Johnston, settled in Elgin from Greenock, and prior to this all Moray's printing had been

---

13 MacAndrew, *Memoir of Isaac Forsyth*, p. 14.

carried out in Aberdeen, Inverness or Banff.[14] When Isaac Forsyth published *A Survey of the Province of Moray* in 1798 it was printed for him in Aberdeen, and he is known to have formed a partnership with an Inverness printer, Lewis Grant, for the production of some of his other publications. However, it is clear from library catalogues and booksellers' lists of this period that the bulk of the material stocked by Moray booksellers and library proprietors was not, in any event, produced locally even after 1821.[15] Forsyth began his bookselling business with materials 'brought from London and Edinburgh, where he had the superior advantages of purchasing his goods on the spot with ready money, and from the best houses in Britain'.[16] It appears that Forsyth's father had stocked his own merchant's shop with goods brought mainly from London, and Isaac and his fellow booksellers continued this tradition.[17]

Forsyth continued his buying trips to the south but his stock was not always acquired without difficulty. He usually travelled by sea but when bad weather prevented this in 1791 he was forced to return from London over land – a journey which took him twenty-two days.[18] Elgin's other booksellers also obtained books from the south, with George Maitland receiving 'a Monthly Parcel regularly from London, and one once a fortnight from Edinburgh, per coach', and, in May 1830, Peter MacDonald had 'lately returned from the South where he ... purchased a large stock of BOOKS'.[19] It may be, however, that Isaac Forsyth possessed some advantages over his competitors when dealing with London's publishing houses. In the early years of the nineteenth century Forsyth took as an apprentice one George Smith, later co-founder of the publishing house Smith, Elder and Co of London.[20] Their friendship was life-long, with George accompanying Isaac on a trip to Paris in 1825, and it seems likely that this relationship had some advantages for Forsyth.[21] It must be noted, however, that Smith's partner, Alexander Elder, had learnt his trade

---

14 There is known to have been a printer in Aberdeen from 1622, and in Inverness from the 1770s. James Davidson, printer and bookseller in Banff was active by 1820. Robert Young, *Annals of the Parish and Burgh of Elgin from the Twelfth Century to the year 1876* (Elgin: Moray Weekly News, 1879), p. 515; *Forres Gazette*, 27 January 1864, p. 3. William Watt, *A History of Aberdeen and Banff* (London: Blackwood, 1900), pp. 226–7; Eveline Barron 'The Printed Word', in *The Hub of the Highlands*, ed. by Inverness Field Club (Edinburgh, 1975), pp. 291–305 (291).

15 *Survey of the Province of Moray: Historical, Geographical and Political* (Aberdeen: Isaac Forsyth, 1798). Facsimile edition: Moray District Libraries, 1984; NLS SBTI.

16 *Aberdeen Journal*, 8 July 1788, p. 1.

17 *Elgin Courier*, 20 May 1859, p. 2.

18 MacAndrew, *Memoir of Isaac Forsyth*, pp. 26–39.

19 *Elgin Courier*, 19 December 1828, p. 1; *Elgin and Forres Journal*, 6 May 1830, p. 1.

20 *Dictionary of National Biography*, vol. I (London: 1917), p. xxxi.

21 MacAndrew, *Memoir of Isaac Forsyth*, p. 78.

from Forsyth's near neighbour, Mr Imlach of Banff, who might also have benefited from a special relationship with this particular publishing house.[22]

Whilst Elgin's booksellers purchased a surprising amount of materials direct from publishers in London and Edinburgh, it seems likely that at least some books were supplied via wholesalers based in Aberdeen. Although I have come across no evidence of business dealings between them, Forsyth appears to have had links, either personal or professional, with at least one major Aberdeen book wholesaler, Lewis Smith, from the 1830s. When Smith's youngest son was born in 1850, he was named Isaac Forsyth Smith, which must indicate a close relationship of some kind.[23]

What was the nature of the books which Isaac Forsyth went to such pains to procure? It is fortunate that the library's first catalogue, dated 1789, survives in full, together with a supplement which probably dates from 1795.[24] Around 630 titles and 1406 volumes are listed in the 1789 catalogue and, although the nature of some of the works cannot be determined from a superficial examination of the titles alone, it is clear that light fiction, such as tales and romances, accounted for a large percentage of the library's original stock. Around 38 per cent of the titles listed in this catalogue can be described with some certainty as fiction, and several of the more ambiguous titles, such as *Dodd's Thoughts on Prison* and *Perry's Man of Business*, may also have fallen into this category. Fiction certainly made up by far the largest category of books and, as a large proportion of these works ran into many volumes, fiction must have dominated the shelves of Forsyth's library.

While the listing of books in catalogues does not necessarily imply their readership, the evidence would suggest that fiction was, indeed, very popular with Forsyth's customers. Novels and other light fiction made up almost 65 per cent of the titles listed in the 1795 catalogue supplement suggesting that these works had proved to be by far the most popular items out of the original stock. Neither did the appeal of fiction decline for the people of Elgin as 48 per cent of the titles listed in an 1830 appendix to the catalogue (printed in full in the local paper) also fell into this category. The titles which seemed to be most popular were novels and tales rather than literature, largely by unnamed or little known authors, and Scott and Galt are almost the only authors listed who have enjoyed enduring reputations.[25] Although it is not possible to be certain in the absence of borrowing records, it does seem likely that the people of Elgin

22 *Banffshire Journal*, 22 February 1876; *Annals of Banff*, pp. 299–300.
23 Iain Beavan, 'The Nineteenth Century Book Trade in Aberdeen, with Primary Reference to Lewis Smith', 2 vols (unpublished PhD thesis, Robert Gordon's University, 1992), pp. 401, 443.
24 *Catalogue of Books of the Elgin Circulating Library*.
25 *Elgin and Forres Journal and Northern Advertiser*, 4 November 1830, p. 1.

were partial to a good tale. Forsyth had to make a living and it is unlikely that the dominance of fiction titles would have continued, as it appeared to do, if the readers had not borrowed them.

It perhaps comes as no surprise to find that fiction dominated the shelves of the Elgin Circulating Library. The book-buying public in England at this time was, in general, less inclined to purchase fiction, which might only warrant one reading, than non-fiction.[26] However, fiction is believed to have been less popular in Scotland and the composition of Forsyth's library appears to have been somewhat unusual in a country where John Crawford believes non-fiction 'usually accounted for about 80 per cent of (the) stocks' of circulating libraries.[27] Only around 62 per cent of the stock in Forsyth's library in 1789 was non-fiction, and this was dominated by the five main categories of religion and moral philosophy, which accounted for 10.5 per cent of the stock, history and politics (9.7 per cent), poetry and drama (8.7 per cent), travel and adventure (7.5 per cent), and biography (6.2 per cent).

The non-fiction titles in Forsyth's library very much reflect the tastes of the day, and similar volumes are likely to have been found in most contemporary libraries, but it is perhaps noteworthy that titles of a religious nature should have been so numerous in a library from which books were leased at some expense and it would be interesting to compare these figures with those of similar libraries. Forsyth may well have been indulging a personal preference when he purchased these books, and possibly misjudged the appeal of this type of work to the readers of Elgin. Only four of the 284 titles added to stock in 1795 were of a religious nature, while history and politics, travel and adventure and biography all retained their importance in the collection, having apparently found a ready audience.[28] Forsyth's personal interest in farming may also have been responsible for the small, but significant, collection of works on practical husbandry which appeared as part of his opening stock. Forsyth was passionate about farming, was an active contributor to the *Farmer's Magazine*, and also served as secretary of the Morayshire Farmers' Club for twenty-seven years.[29] Some of Forsyth's neighbours undoubtedly shared his interest in agriculture

---

26 Christopher Skelton-Foord, 'To Buy or to Borrow? Circulating Libraries and Novel Reading in Britain, 1778–1828', *Library Review*, vol. 47, 7 (1998), 348–54; Guinevere L. Griest, *Mudie's Circulating Library and the Victorian Novel* (Newton Abbot, 1970), pp. 29, 79.

27 Crawford, 'Community Library'; D. Craig, *Scottish Literature and the Scottish People* (London: Chatto and Windus, 1961), pp. 149, 167, 200, 206, 209; A. R. Thompson, 'An Enquiry into the Reading Habits of the Working Classes in Scotland 1830–1840' (unpublished BLitt thesis, University of Glasgow, 1962), p. 132.

28 History and politics accounted for 9.2 per cent of the new titles added, travel and adventure 9.9 per cent and biography 3.9 per cent.

29 MacAndrew, *Memoir of Isaac Forsyth*, pp. 67, 72.

but, as there is no evidence of further additions to stock of works of this nature, perhaps few of them wished to read about it. It would be very interesting to know how many of Forsyth's subscribers chose to borrow titles such as *The Modern Farmer's Guide, or a new system of husbandry, from long experience in several kingdoms, by a real farmer.*

Forsyth added to his library's stock continuously. He frequently advertised new additions to stock in the press and is known to have published at least twelve supplements to his catalogue by 1841.[30] The library closed for a period in 1809 whilst Isaac Forsyth went on a buying spree in London, returning with 'nearly ONE THOUSAND VOLUMES of the newest and most valuable publications' to add to the collection, in order to 'keep pace with the increasing spirit of investigation with (*sic*) the improved state of society creates and demands'.[31] The library's stock is said to have stood at 3000 volumes by this time and Forsyth undertook to 'add every new publication of merit' to this core collection to ensure continued patronage.

Forsyth's regular additions meant that the stock of the Elgin Circulating Library continued to grow, apparently reaching over 4000 volumes by 1813, and possibly peaking at around 6000 volumes in 1830.[32] This appears to have been an impressively large collection for a remote town of such a modest size but holdings of 5000 or more were not uncommon in other Scottish circulating libraries of this period and perhaps a collection of this size was no more than the people of Elgin expected.[33] In addition, these figures must be treated with some caution as, although the 1830 appendix to the catalogue was said to contain 'about 1000 volumes', this appendix, which apparently appears in full in the local press, actually contains only 221 titles and 525 volumes.[34] There is nothing in the advertisement to suggest that this is other than a full listing of the appendix and so Forsyth must have slightly overestimated!

Who were the subscribers whom Isaac Forsyth tried so hard to please? In the introduction to his first catalogue Forsyth makes a clear statement about the types of people who may wish to subscribe to his library. He hoped that, in his carefully selected collection, 'the Man of Letters will see something not unworthy of his Attention, while those who are pleased with the lighter Species of Reading may find, in a beautiful Variety, Instruction judiciously blended

---

30 Supplements to the catalogue were advertised in 1791, 1798, 1809, 1811, 1813, 1821, 1827, 1829, 1830, 1837, 1838 and 1841.
31 *Aberdeen Journal,* 25 October 1809, p. 1; 28 November 1810, p. 1.
32 *Aberdeen Journal,* 25 October 1809, p. 1; 10 Nov 1813, p. 1; *Elgin Courier,* 19 November 1830, p. 1; *Elgin and Forres Journal,* 4 November 1830, p. 1.
33 Crawford, 'Community Library'.
34 *Elgin and Forres Journal,* 4 November 1830, p. 1.

with Amusement'.[35] Ladies were specifically noted as being among his customers in 1813 and they were clearly welcome from the outset as titles such as the
Young Misses Magazine and *Sir Isaac Newton's Philosophy Explained for the Use
of Ladies* formed part of his opening stock.[36] While none of the stock appears to
have been specifically aimed at children, some of the simple tales would certainly have appealed to them and in 1828 the library was stated to be source of
'rational instruction and entertainment' for families and individuals alike. It
seems very likely that, although not members themselves, children were able to
take advantage of their parents' memberships.[37]

It is apparent that, although Forsyth's library stocked a good deal of
popular reading material which would have appealed to the ordinary people of
the area, this was not his target audience. In 1809 he suggested his library was
of special value to those wishing 'to maintain a respectable appearance in
society, from the extent and accuracy of their information', and the library's
customers were also variously described as members of the 'liberal and discern-
ing public', and belonging to 'the middle and higher classes of the population'.[38] Forsyth's clientele almost certainly belonged to the educated elite of
society, and his opening charges of between 10s.6d. per year for one volume at
a time and 20s. for four volumes reflect this.[39] These charges rose gradually over
time and by 1830 a year's subscription cost 30s. for two volumes, a charge
which few ordinary folk could have afforded.[40]

Membership of the Elgin Circulating Library was not confined to resi-
dents of the burgh itself and, in common with many of the burgh's other
service industries, Isaac Forsyth actively sought to serve the community out-
with Elgin. From the outset country subscribers were welcomed and were per-
mitted to borrow twice the number of books as burgh subscribers were allowed
for the same charge.[41] In 1809 Forsyth advertised for subscribers from 'Inverness, Fort George, Nairn, Forres, Fochabers, Keith, Huntly and Cullen (and)
their respective neighbourhoods', and he also promised to serve customers in
Sutherland via, 'the Morayshire and Sutherland Weekly Packet'.[42] Forsyth's
network of contacts must have been extensive as agents were said to be located
in each of these places, allowing subscribers to avoid 'having anything

35 *Catalogue of Books of the Elgin Circulating Library.*
36 Ibid.
37 *Aberdeen Journal,* 10 November 1813, p. 1; *Elgin Courier,* 10 October 1828, p. 1.
38 *Aberdeen Journal,* 25 October 1809, p. 1; *Elgin Courier,* 10 October 1828, p. 1; *Forres
Gazette,* 25 May 1859, p. 3.
39 *Catalogue of Books of the Elgin Circulating Library.*
40 *Elgin Courier,* 19 November 1830, p. 1.
41 *Catalogue of Books of the Elgin Circulating Library* .
42 *Aberdeen Journal,* 25 October 1809, p. 1.

whatsoever to do with the carriers'.[43] In 1813 Forsyth promised to deliver 'to any place on or near the public roads, within 40 miles of the library, either to the east or west, or by packet to Sutherland and Ross-shire', and by 1829 he was promising to deliver as far afield as Aberdeen.[44] It is unknown how many rural subscribers Forsyth was able to attract but he was clearly not just making empty promises. Prior to her death in 1815, Mrs Elizabeth Rose of Kilravock, which is situated between Nairn and Inverness, was one of his subscribers, and the boxes of books which she received from him periodically were said to have given her 'infinite pleasure'.[45]

Isaac Forsyth continued to operate the Elgin Circulating Library along much the same lines, and with apparent success until the 1820s. During the 1820s, however, several factors combined to distract Forsyth from his bookselling and library business. He began to suffer from a serious hearing problem in the early 1820s, which was to render him deaf within a very short space of time; his wife died in 1826, and his multiple interests made increasing demands on his time. Apart from his bookselling and library business, Forsyth had moved into publishing, and was also heavily involved in farming, banking, insurance and burgh life in general. He periodically tried his hand at other business ventures with limited success.[46] He is known to have lost a good deal of money through his connection with the Aberdeen Bank, and also through diverse, ill-fated ventures such as his thread and straw hat manufactories.[47] Forsyth is known to have lamented the fact that his apprenticeship was in bookbinding, and believed he could have been much more successful in business had he received training in practical bookselling instead, but his biographer seriously doubts this would have made any difference.[48]

By the late 1820s Forsyth was clearly unable to devote sufficient attention to his library and I have found no evidence of any additions to stock for the six years following the publication of the fourth appendix to the catalogue in

---

43 Ibid.

44 *Aberdeen Journal*, 10 November 1813, p. 1; *Elgin Courier*, 16 January 1829, p. 1.

45 George Bain, *The History of Nairnshire*, quoted in 'The Northern Highlands in the Nineteenth Century, No IX'. Online: <http://www.electricscotland.com/history/highlands/no9.htm> (6 Jul 2004).

46 MacAndrew, *Memoir of Isaac Forsyth*.

47 Forsyth's link with the Aberdeen Bank proved particularly disastrous. He was to some known more as banker than bookseller and was, in fact, given the designation 'Banker' as opposed to 'Bookseller' by his acquaintance, Hugh Miller of Cromarty. Hugh Miller, *Memoir of William Forsyth, Esq: a Scotch Merchant of the Eighteenth Century* (London: Stewart and Murray, 1839), p. 123; MacAndrew.

48 MacAndrew, *Memoir of Isaac Forsyth*, p. 15.

December 1821.[49] Forsyth may well have been distracted and suffering financially but this situation unfortunately coincided with a noticeable increase in the number of booksellers, libraries and reading rooms in the area.[50] These factors combined to leave the library in a less than healthy state by the late 1820s. An injection of capital was urgently required, and Forsyth also needed someone to breathe new life into his library and to share the burdens of his businesses. In October 1827, Isaac Forsyth took Alexander Young, a banker and later Provost of Elgin, into partnership with him.[51]

The new partnership began well. In 1828 'very extensive additions' were made to the library's stock, which by then is stated to have reached over 5000 volumes. Further stock was added in 1829 and, in 1830, the latest appendix to the catalogue appeared in full in the local press, covering three full columns on the front page of the *Elgin and Forres Journal*.[52] The library's subscription rates were raised at some point, probably in an attempt to cover the cost of the new stock, and charges stood at 27*s.* per annum for two books by 1828, which was considerably higher than the 21*s.* that had applied in 1821.[53] In 1829 it was stated that this new rate was, 'the cheapest in Scotland', but this seems unlikely and Forsyth and Young may have risked pricing themselves out of the market.[54]

By 1830 the choice the library offered to its customers was very extensive but it is clear that it was the new books which were most in demand as, in that year, the partners pleaded with their subscribers to 'return the new books speedily to the library as that alone enables the proprietors to give general satisfaction'.[55] The failure to return books promptly was perhaps a new problem as, initially at least, it was anticipated that subscribers would wish to exchange their books as often as possible. The 1789 catalogue stated that books could be changed once a day 'but not oftener' and no maximum loan period was ever

49 *Aberdeen Journal*, 5 December 1821, p. 3.
50 e.g. Local newspaper proprietor, John Grant, opened a Reading Room in 1828, *Elgin Courier*, 18 January 1828, p. 1; the Literary Association had established a library in 1818, and a Reading Room by at least 1833, *New Statistical Account of Scotland, Vol XIII, Banff, Elgin and Nairn* (Edinburgh: Wm. Blackwood and Sons, 1845), pp. 22–3. Also online: <http://edina.ac.uk/cgi/StatAcc.cgi.> The number of active booksellers in Elgin increased from 2 during the 1810s to 6 during the 1820s, Jane E. Thomas, 'The Printed Word in Moray, 1790–1870'. (Unpublished MSc Econ dissertation, University of Wales, Aberystwyth, 2004).
51 *Elgin Courier*, 8 October 1827, p. 1.
52 *Elgin Courier*, 10 October 1828, p. 1; 11 December 1829, p. 3; 19 November 1830, p. 1; *Elgin and Forres Journal*, 4 November 1830, p. 1.
53 *Aberdeen Journal*, 5 December 1821, p. 3; *Elgin Courier*, 10 October 1828, p. 1.
54 *Elgin Courier*, 11 December 1829, p. 3.
55 *Elgin Courier*, 19 November 1830, p. 1; *Elgin and Forres Journal*, 4 November 1830, p. 1.

mentioned in the library's publicity.[56] In 1813 country subscribers were informed that they may exchange their books once a week for as little as 3s. to 5s. a year for carriage, the implication being that this was the normal loan period.[57] It was perhaps the case that subscribers chose to hold onto their books for longer only as new books became less frequently available.

In spite of the best efforts of Forsyth and his new partner Alexander Young, their problems seemed to continue. In 1829 subscription rates were temporarily reduced and the public was warned that the library could not continue to supply 'new and expensive books on the same liberal scale' without more subscribers.[58] The library began to face direct competition in 1831 when the Elgin Subscription Library was founded, and in 1832 two itinerating libraries were established in the town, supported financially by Samuel Brown and following the model of similar libraries in the Borders.[59] The introduction of these itinerating libraries was greeted with great enthusiasm and they were contrasted favourably with 'stationary libraries' which,

however actively (they) may be conducted (are) by universal experience found in the course of a few years to decline in interest and thenceforward (have) to maintain a hard and of course an ultimately unsuccessful struggle against the natural decline of novelty.[60]

It seems that there would never be enough new stock to please the readers of Elgin but it is doubtful whether the limited stock of fifty volumes apiece which the itinerating libraries offered would have seriously addressed this problem. The new subscription library seems to have been short-lived and so this was not the answer either, but it is clear that the people of Elgin were now looking for something different.

Despite Forsyth's obvious early commitment to the project and the library's considerable success in the early years, Forsyth and Young had to work hard to keep the library going in later years. Although it remained in their hands until 1844, by which time Forsyth was seventy-six years old, the library was rarely advertised after 1830 and adverts were noticeably smaller. Although a few new additions to stock were made as late as 1841, when Forsyth and Young moved their bookselling and stationery business into smaller premises in 1842, the library was not mentioned as moving with them, and perhaps it was

---

56 *Catalogue of Books of the Elgin Circulating Library.*

57 *Aberdeen Journal,* 10 November 1813, p. 1.

58 *Elgin Courier,* 13 November 1829, p. 3.

59 *Elgin Courier,* 11 February 1831, p. 1, 13 January 1832, p. 3, 30 March 1832, p. 3, 6 April 1832, p. 3, 16 November 1832, p. 3.

60 *Elgin Courier,* 13 January 1832, p. 3, 30 March 1832, p. 3, 6 April 1832, p. 3, 16 November 1832, p. 3.

no longer operational.[61] Forsyth and Young finally sold their bookselling and stationery business, together with the circulating library, to A. and R. Ferguson in 1844.[62]

A. and R. Ferguson 1844–1846

The Ferguson brothers came to Elgin from Edinburgh, having been employed in Oliver and Boyd's bookshop there for ten years. In February 1844 they moved the bookshop and circulating library to Roy Place, High Street. When they took on the library it had possibly not been operational for some time and it was noted that a considerable number of single volumes and sets were missing.[63] The brothers Ferguson would undoubtedly need their 'extensive connections all over England and Scotland' and 'full command of capital', if they were to revive its fortunes.[64]

The brothers made a considerable initial effort, and indeed outlay, to attract new subscribers to the library and by April 1844 over 200 volumes had been added to stock. A new catalogue was also being produced and it was promised that more volumes would be added 'from time to time, should the library receive that degree of encouragement which, from the reasonableness of the terms the Proprietors confidently anticipate'.[65] The subscription rates were substantially reduced to 2s.6d. per quarter, 'to afford the Public of Elgin and its neighbourhood improved facilities for the acquisition of useful knowledge, and to furnish them with a source of rational amusement'.[66] These charges were low but this was apparently insufficient to attract subscribers in large numbers as, by August 1844, it was noted that 'the subscriptions of those who have joined will barely cover the outlay for periodicals alone'.[67] Nevertheless, the Fergusons added forty-five titles to the library at this time, 'in order to give the project of an efficiently conducted library for Elgin a fair trial'. They did, however, warn that in future, 'the number and value of the works purchased for the library' would be 'in direct proportion to the number of subscribers'.[68]

The Fergusons possibly never stood much chance of success. They were incomers to the town with no local standing and are likely to have found it difficult to establish themselves in the community of a small burgh. In addition, although Forsyth and Young had struggled to maintain the success of their

61 *Elgin Courant*, 24 September 1841, p. 1, 20 May 1842, p. 1.
62 *Elgin Courant*, 9 February 1844, p. 1; *Forres Gazette*, 7 February 1844, p. 1.
63 *Elgin Courant*, 2 February 1844, p. 1.
64 *Elgin Courant*, 9 February 1844, p. 1; *Forres Gazette*, 7 February 1844, p. 1.
65 *Elgin Courant*, 19 April 1844, p. 1.
66 Ibid.
67 *Elgin Courant*, 30 August 1844, p. 1.
68 Ibid.

library, and faced some competition, the Fergusons were directly challenged by the establishment of the Elgin Literary Union Cheap Circulating Library. This library, of which mention is first made in late 1844, operated out of the newly opened High Street bookshop of James Allan, a former employee of both Lewis Smith of Aberdeen and Forsyth and Young.[69] This library was open to all in 'respectable' employment and, with charges of 3s.6d. per annum for subscribers under twenty-one, and 4s.6d. for others, it undercut the Fergusons considerably.[70] Although the Literary Union Library does not appear to have been large, consisting of only eighty volumes when it was sold to the Mechanics' Institute in 1849 or 1850, this competition must have seemed threatening.[71]

The Fergusons did not survive in business for long, although it is not clear whether this was as a result of increasing competition, lack of patronage or personal circumstances. By mid-1846 Robert Ferguson was trading alone and in July 1846 he announced that he was giving up the business. He sold off his stock at thirty-three per cent discount, and offered the Elgin Circulating Library for sale as one lot.[72] Although he stated that this library was 'increasing in popularity every day', this seems highly unlikely. Very little stock appears to have been added since 1844 and when the library was sold it was said to contain only 2500 volumes.[73]

George Wilson 1846–1855

George Wilson was the son of Provost James Wilson and had trained as a bookbinder in Elgin before spending ten years working in America. On his return to Elgin Wilson set up in business as a bookseller, stationer and binder in a shop on the High Street in July 1846.[74] Just one week later Robert Ferguson announced that he was giving up his business. On 7 August 1846, having purchased the Elgin Circulating Library from Ferguson, George Wilson relocated his business to Ferguson's old shop in Roy Place, where he stayed for just a few months, moving to 121 High Street by the end of the year.[75]

At the outset Wilson undertook to add to the newly acquired library, 'selections of the best works in the language ... as they issue from the press'; however, his later newspaper advertisements suggest that after his initial

69 *Elgin Courant*, 1 November 1844, p. 1; 3 July 1846, p. 1.
70 *Elgin Courant*, 25 July 1845, p. 1.
71 *Elgin Courier*, 22 November 1850, p. 3.
72 *Elgin Courant*, 24 July 1846, p. 1.
73 *Elgin Courant*, 14 August 1846, p. 3.
74 *Elgin Courant*, 17 July 1846, p. 1.
75 *Moray Weekly News*, 3 July 1880, pp. 2, 3; *Elgin Courant*, 7 August 1846, p. 1, 14 August 1846, p. 3; *Elgin Courier*, 7 August 1846, p. 1; *Elgin Courier*, 21 December 1846, p. 1.

enthusiasm new titles were added in tens rather than hundreds.[76] The library's stock is stated to have consisted of 3000 volumes by late 1846 but remained at this level in 1852 and it is doubtful whether Wilson added much at all to the core collection he had purchased from Ferguson.[77] Although Wilson periodically placed advertisements in the local press for his bookselling and stationery concerns, there is no publicity for the library between 1846 and 1852 and he probably paid little attention to it.

Wilson's bookselling business was not unsuccessful initially but his library possibly stood little chance of success with its ageing stock in an increasingly competitive market. On the same day that Wilson announced his purchase of the Elgin Circulating Library, fellow bookseller, and former rival of the Fergusons, James Allan, also announced a change to his business. Allan proposed to open a 'new reading club and circulating library' at his shop in Elgin's High Street, the stock of which was to be supplied by 'an eminent London librarian' and would be made up of the newest and most up-to-date publications.[78] It seems likely that the London librarian in question was Charles Edward Mudie who had started his library business there in 1842. If James Allan's plans came to fruition, he must have been one of Mudie's earliest provincial customers as Guinevere Griest suggests that Mudie was not lending to provincial libraries in a major way until around 1860.[79] It is surprising that a bookseller based in the remote North-East of Scotland, in a town which was at that time unconnected to the rail network, should have contemplated, and perhaps established, such early links with a London library.

It is not known how successful James Allan's library was, or even whether it went beyond the planning stages, but Wilson could not escape competition. The newly formed Mechanics' Institute established a library in 1849 which by 1850 included, 'about 300 volumes of works of a lighter description, consisting of memoirs, novels, travels &c, all of the most unexceptionable character' alongside the 600 or so worthy tomes it had inherited from the Speculative Society and other libraries.[80] Wilson must have felt this competition keenly and any hopes he still entertained for his library must have been all but dashed when Francis Russell, having taken over James Allan's business in 1851, established his own circulating library in January 1852.[81] Russell was not alone in

---

76 *Elgin Courant*, 14 August 1846, p. 3; 14 May 1852, p. 3; 17 December 1852, p. 1.

77 *Russell's Morayshire Register and Elgin and Forres Directory for 1847* (Elgin: Courant Office/Alexander Russell, 1846) , p. 160; *Russell 1852*, p. 175.

78 *Elgin Courant*, 7 August 1846, p. 1.

79 Griest, *Mudie's Circulating Library and the Victorian Novel*, p. 22.

80 These books were 'procured for 1s 6d a volume' on credit from Mr Duncan Campbell, bookseller in Glasgow. *Elgin Courier*, 22 November 1850, p. 3.

81 See below. *Elgin Courant*, 6 June 1851, p. 1; *Elgin Courant*, 2 January 1852, p. 2.

wishing to capitalize on Elgin's enthusiasm for reading and it was probably later that same year that another Elgin bookseller, Thomas Smith, began a Reading Club, which seemed to cater for all age groups, at his shop (138 High Street), with an annual subscription of just 10s.6d.[82] Smith launched a further challenge in September 1854 when he established a Subscription Library and both Library and Reading Club continued until at least 1857.[83]

Wilson experienced competition not only from other libraries but also from the increasing number of booksellers in the area. In 1852 there were eleven booksellers in Elgin and its suburb New Elgin alone, undoubtedly too many for a town of its size, and competition was inevitably fierce.[84] In 1853 one of these booksellers, Robert Stewart, who had played host to the Mechanics' Library since 1852, boasted that the 'small profit and quick return system' which he had operated for three years, and which undercut the other booksellers in the town considerably, had been so successful that he had been forced to move to larger premises.[85] Another bookseller, Thomas Smith, was an extremely effective publicist, placing a single small advert on the front page of the *Elgin Courier* almost on a weekly basis. Even he excelled himself on 18 August 1854 when he placed a total of eight small advertisements on the front page of the *Courier* – two at the top of column one and one at the top of each of the other six columns.[86] In addition, Francis Russell enjoyed limitless free, or at least cheap, publicity in the *Elgin Courant* of which his brother, Alexander, was editor and proprietor. Wilson must have been concerned not only about the success of his business but also about its very survival.

Wilson was forced to respond to this aggressive competition and, during 1852 and 1853, he attempted to do this by buying in significant amounts of new stock for sale, selling off 'a considerable portion' of his existing stock 'at very reduced prices' and, apparently for the first time in years, adding some titles to the Elgin Circulating Library.[87] In spite of his efforts, however, Wilson was overwhelmed by the competition and his estate was sequestered in

82 *Elgin Courier*, 21 January 1853, p. 1, 23 September 1853, p. 1.

83 *Elgin Courier*, 18 August 1854, p. 1, 8 September 1854, p. 1, 9 January 1857, p. 1.

84 Namely George Anderson, A. C. Brander, James Campbell, David Christie, Alexander Edward, Peter McDonald, Thomas Smith, F. W. G Russell, Robert Stewart Sr, Robert Stewart Jr and George Wilson. Thomas, 'Printed Word', *Elgin Courier*, 24 December 1852; *Russell*, 1852.

85 *Russell 1852*, p. 189; *Elgin Courier*, 13 May 1853, p. 1.

86 *Elgin Courier*, 18 August 1854, p. 1.

87 *Elgin Courant*, 5 March 1852, p. 1, 14 May 1852, p. 3, 7 December 1852, p. 1; *Elgin Courier*, 5 March 1852, p. 1, 11 March 1852, p. 1, 14 May 1852, p. 1, 2 July 1852, p. 1, 10 December 1852, p. 1, 2 September 1853, p. 1, 9 December 1853, 13 January 1854, p. 1.

February 1855.[88] His property, furniture, book and stationery stock, and the Elgin Circulating Library, were put up for auction on 3 April 1855, but there must have been little interest initially as a further sale date was set for 8 May.[89] His stock was finally sold, probably very cheaply, to various booksellers, including Peter Macdonald and Francis Russell, with the latter also buying the Elgin Circulating Library as one lot.[90] Wilson, having failed as both bookseller and librarian, resumed work as a bookbinder at 127 High Street in late 1856, continuing until around 1878. Wilson made little money at this trade however and became a beneficiary of the Auchry Mortification 'for decayed merchants' in his later years and died in poverty in 1880.[91]

F. W. G. Russell 1852–1861, Russell and Watson 1859–1870

Francis, better known as 'FWG' Russell was born in Elgin in 1822 the son of John, a merchant and bailie in the burgh. His early career was in newspapers, and he was the founder and editor of both the *Banffshire Journal* and the *Banffshire Advertiser* in the 1840s. His brother Alexander also followed this path, being the editor and publisher of the *Elgin Courant* for many years. In March 1851 Russell purchased the bookselling and stationery business of the unfortunately insolvent James Allan, and by June of that year he had moved the business to very large premises under the town's Assembly Rooms at 157 and 159 High Street.[92] Russell had taken on responsibility for the libraries of the Morayshire Farmers' Club and the Elgin Literary Association when he purchased Allan's business and these moved with him, but from the outset he announced that he was also to open his own circulating library at his new premises.[93] This new library, which he promised would 'supply all the new important works of the day as soon as published', was opened during the first week of 1852 and from the outset it was run 'in connection with an extensive London library', which was, by 1857, clearly identified as Mudie's.[94] Russell may have got the idea for this library from James Allan's original plan, which may never have been put into effect, but it is also possible that he simply revived links already established by Allan which had fallen into abeyance when he gave up his business.

---

88 *Elgin Courier*, 9 February 1855, p. 1.
89 *Elgin Courier*, 9 March 1855, p. 3, et al, 27 April 1855, p. 1.
90 *Elgin Courant*, 6 April 1855, p. 3; *Elgin Courier*, 1 June 1855, p. 1.
91 *Elgin Courier*, 28 November 1856, p. 3; *Moray Weekly News*, 3 July 1880, pp. 2, 3.
92 *Elgin Courant*, 4 October 1850, p. 1, 7 March 1851, p. 1, 6 June 1851, p. 1; *Elgin Courier*, 11 October 1850, p. 3.
93 *Elgin Courant*, 6 June 1851, p. 1.
94 Ibid.; *Elgin Courant*, 2 January 1852, p. 2; *Russell 1852*, pp. 175, 226; *Russell 1852*, p. 175; *Elgin Courant*, 19 June 1857, p. 1.

HIGH STREET ELGIN.

Fig. 3. Elgin High Street looking east with Russell and Watson's shop in the left fore-
ground. J. & W. Watson, *Morayshire Described* (Elgin: Russell and Watson, 1868).
Facsimile edition Moray District Libraries, 1984, facing p. 157

It appears that Russell's library initially consisted of a permanent collection
of his own which was supplemented by books received each month from
Mudie's. By 1853 Russell was conducting both a 'First Class Library', which
attracted an annual subscription of thirty shillings and probably consisted of
the books from Mudie's, and a 'Popular Circulating Library', the subscription
for which was 12s.6d. a year.[95] Although expensive, the Mudie's section of the
library was undoubtedly popular but it was by no means large, consisting of
only 'one hundred new volumes', and it may be that only a proportion of

___

95 *Elgin Courant*, 14 October 1853, p. 3; 28 October 1853, p. 3.

these, rather than the entire collection, was changed each month.[96] In addition, it is known that the books which were delivered via Mudie's provincial service were inclined to be variable and these may not have included the most popular titles of the day. These collections were not selected by patrons but by librarians, who may have been tempted to circulate 'dead' stock to their more remote, and therefore less vocal, customers.[97] However, the arrival of new books from London on such a regular basis must have been a welcome change for the people of Elgin and this new library was undoubtedly well-used.

Through his link with Mudie's, Russell was able to offer the people of Elgin some of the newest and freshest material available and, when he took over the original Elgin Circulating Library in 1855, the range of other material he could offer was greatly increased. This new part of Russell's library retained its original title – The Elgin Circulating Library – and proud reference was made to its date of foundation of 1789 in publicity materials until at least 1867.[98] However, while the purchase of this library allowed Russell to offer a wider choice of books, it still contained no more than 3000 volumes, and many of these must have been part of Isaac Forsyth's original collection. Most of these volumes had probably already been read and re-read by many of Russell's customers. In recognition of this, and to allow 'all classes an opportunity of enjoying its choice selection', Russell introduced a new range of reduced subscription charges. Whilst the cost of subscription to 'Mudie's London Library' remained at thirty shillings, three classes of subscription to the remainder of the library were introduced, ranging from 10s.6d. per year for one set of books to 21s. per year for two sets plus magazines.[99]

The stock of the Elgin Circulating Library was probably never increased after Russell took it on as, in 1866, by which time it was termed the 'older library', it still consisted of only 3000 volumes, and by this time no separate subscription charge was made for access to it.[100] Russell continued to run the now tired and old Elgin Circulating Library, in connection with Mudie's, alongside his farming interests and his bookselling, binding and stationery businesses, until his tragic death from drowning in 1861.[101] He had taken a partner, his former apprentice James Watson, in 1858 and Watson continued to run

96 *Elgin Courant*, 5 January 1866, p. 4.

97 Griest, *Mudie's Circulating Library and the Victorian Novel*, p. 85.

98 *Black's Morayshire Directory Including the Upper District of Banffshire 1863* (Elgin: Courant Office/James Black, 1862), p. 25; J. and W. Watson, *Morayshire Described* (Elgin: Russell and Watson, 1868). Facsimile edition Moray District Libraries, 1984, advertising supplement p. 2; *Elgin Courant*, 16 August 1867, p. 4.

99 *Elgin Courant*, 19 June 1857, p. 1; 3 February 1860, p. 8.

100 *Elgin Courant*, 5 January 1866, p. 4.

101 *Forres Gazette*, 4 September 1861, p. 3.

the businesses along much the same lines after Russell's death and, possibly in partnership with Francis's brother Thomas, he continued to trade as Russell and Watson.[102] However, as with Forsyth and Russell before him, Watson had other interests and increasingly his preference was for publishing. With his son as his partner in this enterprise he wrote, and also published, several books on local subjects, including *Morayshire Described*, which rolled off his Elgin presses in 1868.[103] Watson also dabbled in newspaper publishing in the 1870s, producing a single sheet newspaper entitled the *Moray News*, to be re-titled by later proprietors the *Moray and Nairn Express*.[104] Watson acted as a safe pair of hands for the Elgin Circulating Library. He apparently did nothing to develop it and by 1870 the books received from Mudie's Select London Library had become the main element of the town's circulating library provision.

Isaac Forsyth had possessed a real interest in books, business, and the customers he served, and thus succeeded in creating what was, at its height, a very successful library. Forsyth's obituary credits him with 'forming the literary tastes and fostering the intelligence of the middle and higher classes of the population', and although these claims may seem a little too grand, he undoubtedly made a significant contribution to the intellectual life of the burgh through his bookshop and library.[105] In the early years Forsyth experienced little competition, with only one other bookseller known to have been active in the town until the 1820s.[106] The books chosen by Forsyth for his bookshop and library formed the bulk of the reading material available to the people of Elgin and district until the 1820s, and so it may be no exaggeration to say that he did play a major role in the formation of their literary tastes, at least in the early years.

However, the requirements of the people of Elgin changed, and it became obvious by the late 1820s that the large, static collection established by Forsyth in his library was no longer adequate to serve the needs of the avid readers of the town. The people of Elgin demanded new books, and since the library proprietors no longer enjoyed the monopoly on the supply of reading materials which Forsyth had possessed initially, they had to try to meet these demands. With limited funds available, the link established with Mudie's during the 1840s or 1850s appears to have been a very effective and practical solution to this problem, and it was possibly the only way to ensure the continuation of the Elgin Circulating Library.

---

102 *Elgin Courier*, 1 October 1858, p. 3; *Northern Scot*, 21 March 1908, p. 5.

103 J. & W. Watson, *Morayshire Described* (Elgin: Russell and Watson, 1868). Facsimile edition Moray District Libraries, 1984; *Northern Scot*, 21 March 1908, p. 5.

104 *Northern Scot*, 21 March 1908, p. 5.

105 *Elgin Courier*, 10 October 1828, p. 1; *Forres Gazette*, 25 May 1859, p. 3.

106 Thomas, 'Printed Word', p. 54.

David Steuart and Giambattista Bodoni: On the Fringes of the British Book Trade

BRIAN HILLYARD

WHEN WE DISCUSS the personnel of the book trade, because of the major resources that we now have in the British Book Trade Index and the Scottish Book Trade Index it is easy to allow ourselves to focus on those professionally involved in the book trade and so named in imprints, trade directories, apprentice lists, and so on.[1] But of course we know that with some persons the boundaries between collecting and bookselling or publishing could become quite blurred. David Steuart of Edinburgh was one such person: a late eighteenth- and early nineteenth-century collector and author who also ventured into bookselling and publishing.[2]

It is unnecessary for the purposes of this paper to outline in any detail the biography of this fascinating man of wide interests, but we do need to grasp his love of both books and business. Born in 1747 (he died in 1824), as a young man he went into commerce and spent time abroad, in both Spain and France. Returning to Edinburgh in 1776 he went into partnership with Robert Allan and formed Allan & Steuart, which started as a trading company and then moved into banking. S. G. Checkland's history of Scottish banking describes David Steuart as 'a man of great energy and initiative' and Allan & Steuart as the most important new private bank in the post-1772 period.[3] In 1785 it was Steuart who proposed the founding of a Chamber of Commerce in Edinburgh,

---

1   Online at <www.bbti.bham.ac.uk> and <www.nls.ac.uk/catalogue/resources/sbti>.

2   See my monograph *David Steuart Esquire: An Edinburgh Collector: The 1801 Sale Catalogue of Part of his Library Reproduced from the Unique Copy in New York Public Library with an Introductory Essay* (Edinburgh, 1993), and, more briefly, my article 'David Steuart' in *Pre-Nineteenth-Century British Book Collectors and Bibliographers*, ed. by W. Baker and K. Womack (Detroit, 1999), pp. 328–35. It is worth mentioning in this context that Steuart was also an author, though that is not central to this paper: see *David Steuart*, pp. 19–20. I believe him to be the David Steuart named on the title page as author of *The Historical Remembrancer* (Edinburgh, 1814). There is also a tantalizing reference in a letter of 30 November 1819 from Steuart to David Laing, Edinburgh University Library, MS.La.IV.5, fols 33–34, asking him to 'peruse the enclosed MS with attention & let me know if you think it would sell well at sixpence also the expence of printing 400 copies of it'. I think this is most likely to be his own manuscript, but have no more information about it.

3   S. G. Checkland, *Scottish Banking: A History, 1695–1973* (Glasgow, 1975), pp. 164–5.

of which he served as President in 1787 and 1790. He had also become prominent in local politics: in 1780–82 he served as Lord Provost of Edinburgh. He
was extremely wealthy, living in style in Queen Street and owning several
houses and many acres of land in Edinburgh's New Town.[4] His entrepreneurial
attitude is also something we need to appreciate: for example, in 1786 he wrote
to his nephew Charles

I sold an estate last week in Aberdeenshire for £5000 by which I clear above £400, Int.
& all other charges being previously paid & I shall clear above £300 by a small bit of
ground I bought lately and sold this day week on which I did not advance 20/–. I
mention these things to you privately with a view to shew you that much may be done
by industry & attention.[5]

Alongside this he could claim to be Edinburgh's leading bibliophile at that time.
When Steuart came to sell part of his library in 1801, Cornelius Elliot, the auctioneer, described it as 'the most uncommon, and certainly the most valuable
private library ever brought to the hammer on this side the Tweed.'[6] Admittedly there could be some salesmanship here, but he owned a number of early
Mainz books including the Gutenberg Bible; Durandus, *Rationale*, 1459, the
second book ever printed with a date; and the Mainz Bible of 1472, a copy
preserving a vellum leaf, rescued from a binding, of the much rarer 1462 Fust
& Schoeffer Bible. These alone would probably justify that description; in fact,
there were many more rare books, as can be appreciated from a reading of the
sale catalogue.[7] The status of this sale is also shown by the unusual (if not
unparalleled) auction report in the *Scots Magazine* for August 1801.[8] Most
usefully this lists twenty items sold, with their prices. The highest price was
£115 for the Durandus (12/47). The Gutenberg Bible and the 1472 Bible are
not listed. Although included in the sale catalogue (12/42 and 6/47), they were

4   A. J. Youngson, *The Making of Classical Edinburgh* (Edinburgh, 1966), pp. 205–8 (with
spelling 'Stewart').
5   National Archives of Scotland, GD 38/2/26, 29 November 1786.
6   This description comes from an advertisement (transcribed in *David Steuart*, p. 85)
contained in *Catalogue of the entire bound stock of Ross & Blackwood, Booksellers in Edinburgh*
(Edinburgh, 1803). This advertisement names thirty other collections Elliot has disposed of
in recent years.
7   Facsimile in *David Steuart*. Hereafter I refer to individual lots in this sale as 12/48 for
Day 12, Lot 48, and so on.
8   Transcribed in *David Steuart*, p. 87, with sale catalogue numbers added in square
brackets.

sold privately to the Advocates Library in 1806 for 150 guineas and 1810 for 50 guineas, respectively.[9]

These two sides of Steuart's life – bibliophile and businessman – came together most openly in that the wealth he accumulated enabled him to acquire great treasures but then his financial disasters caused the dispersal of those treasures, most notably in 1801, in the midst of bankruptcy proceedings. But his pursuit of fine books was also affected by his entrepreneurial inclination. The single best source for illustrating this is his exchange of letters with Giambattista Bodoni (1740–1813), the Italian typographer who set up a press in Parma and became known for his handsome type faces and fine printing.[10] There are seventeen letters, March 1791–January 1799, preserved in the Museo Bodoni, Biblioteca Palatina, Parma. Thirteen of these, in French, are Steuart's original letters to Bodoni, and the remaining four, in Italian, are Bodoni's drafts for his letters to Steuart. Internal references indicate that Bodoni wrote seven letters of which the Bodoni Archive may not preserve drafts; there is no evidence that any of Steuart's are missing. The extant texts have all been published in transcription.[11] The remainder of this paper explores some of the recurring themes in this correspondence that place Steuart on the fringes of the British book trade. I am not claiming that Steuart was Bodoni's sole or even main link with the British market. The important London book dealer James Edwards had met Bodoni in Parma in 1787, and they had subsequently corresponded, particularly about the edition of Horace Walpole's *The Castle of Otranto* which Bodoni printed for Edwards in 1790 and 1791.[12]

The earliest letter in the surviving Steuart–Bodoni correspondence is Steuart's dated 1 March 1791 and it is clear that this is the first letter that passed between them. Steuart says that by chance he has seen (at a guess in Edwards's shop, although there is no evidence known to me that the two men

---

9   Transferred to the National Library of Scotland on its foundation in 1925, they are now Inc.1 and Inc.2 respectively. For Steuart's Durandus, see H. P. Kraus, Catalogue 156 (1980), item 1, and Sotheby's New York, 12 December 1991, lot 21.

10   For his output see H. C. Brooks, *Compendiosa bibliografia di edizioni bodoniane* (Firenze: Tipografia Barbera, 1927). For a recent general appreciation in English see Colin Franklin, 'Giambattista Bodoni', *The Private Library*, 5th series, 6 (2003), 100–17.

11   In my article 'Parma and Edinburgh: Some Letters Relating to the European Book Trade at the End of the Eighteenth Century', *Bulletin du Bibliophile*, No. 2, 1992, 330–64. These transcriptions were made from photocopies (I have not seen the originals) generously supplied by Dott. Angelo Ciavarella, of the Museo Bodoni, and now forming National Library of Scotland, MS. Acc. 10525.

12   See Rosa Edwards, 'James Edwards, Giambattista Bodoni, and the Castle of Otranto: Some Unpublished Letters', *Publishing History*, 18 (1985), 5–48. 1790 is the date of the vellum edition, ESTCn885, and 1791 the date of the 'normal' edition, ESTCt131070.

were acquainted before September 1792; see next letter) three books printed by Bodoni: Torquato Tasso's *Aminta* (this has to be the quarto of 1789, Brooks 379; not in Steuart's 1801 sale), Theophrastus's *Characters* (1786, Brooks 315; 1801 sale 6/35) and Longus's *Daphnis and Chloe* (1786, Brooks 314; 1801 sale 6/35, in a single lot with Theophrastus), and he thinks them so superior to anything that has appeared to date that he would very much like to have two copies of everything that Bodoni prints as beautifully as these: if they include Homer, Virgil and Horace, he would be even more pleased, but any book at all, provided it is as beautiful as these three, will be welcome.

The next letter we have is Steuart's of about a year and a half later, 14 September 1792, when he writes that he has received several books (the titles we do not know) from Blanchon, a bookseller in Parma. More important, James Edwards has sent him a copy of Bodoni's folio Horace published in 1791, 'of the last beauty', and also told him about the forthcoming folio Virgil, 'in the same taste and of the same splendour as Horace', which was actually published in 1793. This prompts him to ask Bodoni for twelve copies of the Virgil edition, two on large paper and ten on ordinary paper.[13] He wrote again on 26 November 1792 to check up on this order and he comments that he would not mind if the order is duplicated – an indication of his keenness to have these books. On 8 February 1793, replying to a non-extant letter from Bodoni about the Virgil edition, Steuart amends his order, presumably because of the greater information available, and asks for three copies on Annonay paper[14] and twelve on fine Parma paper, making fifteen in all.[15] It might look like a revised order, but since on 6 April 1793 Steuart says that he will be pleased to have the twenty-four copies he has already ordered, that is not clear.

Steuart's obsession with Bodoni's books – and it seems particularly with the folio Virgil and Horace – is not in doubt. If we look at the 1801 sale catalogue, we find 35 Bodoni books there, and of the 24 lots in the catalogue

---

13 He also specifies that they should be 'demie [*sic*] reliés'. The point about the binding is clear enough: owners would want to arrange their own binding. We know that Steuart was a connoisseur of bindings, both of older bindings and of contemporary bindings: in the 1801 sale catalogue his copy of the four-volume 1780 edition of *Don Quixote* printed in Madrid by Ibarra is described as 'most superbly bound by Scott' (12/31), and although we cannot prove that Steuart commissioned this binding by James Scott of Edinburgh (which has not been traced), it does seem very likely.

14 Annonay was the home of French wove paper. R. F. Lane, *The Library*, 5th series, 17 (1962), 135, says that Bodoni's paper was manufactured in Parma: this requires further investigation.

15 This time he specifies that Bodoni should bind them in wrappers without cutting, 'en carton sans rogneure': large margins are also often mentioned in Steuart's 1801 sale catalogue (see *David Steuart*, p. 23).

that are marked with an asterisk indicating that application had to be made to the auctioneer to view them,[16] seven are Bodoni editions:

(quarto) 6/35 [2 items] Characterum Theophrasti; & Longus, printed by Bodoni, and are considered as among the finest specimens of his press – they are superbly bound in morocco, Parma 1786 [Brooks 315, 314]

(folio) 10/47 Thomas-a-Kempis de Imitatione Christi, large paper, printed by Bodoni, and most elegantly bound in red morocco, Parma 1793. N.B. Only twelve copies printed on large paper. [Brooks 484]

(folio) 10/48 [Tasso] Aminta, corresponding in every respect with the Kempis, Parma 1793 [Brooks 514]

(folio) 10/49 Longinus de Sublimi,　　ditto　　ditto　　Parma 1793 [Brooks 507]

(folio) 11/44 Publij Virgilij Opera, printed by Bodoni, large paper, of which only 25 copies were printed – superbly bound in red, blue, and yellow moro co, and ornamented with engravings from the antique, 2 vol. Parma 1793 [Brooks 406]

(folio) 11/45 Q. Horatij Opera, large paper, uniformly bound with the preceding article, and ornamented with the plates engraved for Gustavus III. King of Sweden, Parma 1791 [Brooks 417].[17] There were only 50 copies thrown off on large paper; and the printer wrote a friend here above three years ago, 'De Orazio e del Virgilio in Carta sopraffina levigata, non ne rimane piu esemplare vendibili.'[18]

It is evident that these books were very special to Steuart and that he was very proud of them. However his enthusiasm went further than this and on 12 September 1794 he is asking Bodoni for a price for supplying copies (one each) of Virgil and Horace on vellum. There followed a lengthy exchange about this. Only four vellum copies had been printed of the Horace and three of the Virgil and all were accounted for. Bodoni was willing to reset and reprint them for Steuart, but at a cost of £200 sterling for the two, and the final outcome was that Steuart thought them too dear.

16　This is stated in the conditions of sale set out at the beginning of the catalogue. As far as it is possible to tell, this relates to the fine condition of these books. It reflects, I think, Steuart's pride in the condition of his books.

17　In his letter to Bodoni of 20 September 1793 he says that he has a magnificent copy with the plates engraved for the late King of Sweden. As the wording implies, these plates were not a feature of the edition and may have been unique to this copy.

18　These words are not found in any of Bodoni's copies of his letters to Steuart, but one suspects that the 'friend' is Steuart (the reference preserves the anonymity of the sale catalogue which nowhere names Steuart as the owner of the books). The sale catalogue is so unlike any other Edinburgh catalogue of the period that the unusual amount of detail must have been provided by Steuart himself.

If we return to the letter of 8 February 1793 we read that in addition to revising his Virgil order, Steuart asks Bodoni to send two copies each, all on large paper, of

> Horace in quarto [printed 1793, Brooks 493; not in 1801 sale]
> Petrarch in folio [not printed until 1799, Brooks 733; not in 1801 sale]
> Dante in folio [printed 1795, Brooks 588; not in 1801 sale]
> Catullus &c in folio [printed 1794, Brooks 570; not in 1801 sale]
> Longinus in folio [printed 1793, Brooks 507; 1801 sale 10/49]

and moreover goes on to say that in the future he would like two copies of every classic author Bodoni prints whether in Latin, Italian, French, English or Spanish. At this point he introduces a totally new dimension to his relationship with Bodoni in suggesting books for Bodoni to print, but we will come back to that later.

On 6 April 1793, in addition to saying that he is happy to receive the twenty-four copies of Virgil he has already ordered, and would be pleased to have a couple of copies of Horace added (in the context of the Virgil this probably refers to the folio Horace[19] and not the quartos he had ordered on 8 February that year), he orders:

> 2 or 3 copies of Robert Trevor's *Britannia*, one on Annonay paper [1792, folio, Brooks 470; not in 1801 sale]
> 4 copies of Tacitus [1795, 3 vols, folio, Brooks 593; 3 vols, quarto, Brooks 594 and 595; none in 1801 sale]
> 4 copies of Thomson's *Seasons* [1794, folio, Brooks 531; quarto, Brooks 532; none in 1801 sale
> 4 copies of Thomas Gray [either *Poems*, 1793, Brooks 500/501; 1801 sale 6/37; or *Elegy*, 1793, Brooks 485; not in 1801 sale, but see below on sale of 20–21 December 1798]

On 20 September 1793, he orders a copy of the *De imitatione Christi* on Anonnay paper [1793, folio, Brooks 484; 1801 sale 10/47, one of twelve copies on large paper, in red morocco] and asks Bodoni to reserve for him twelve copies each, on the best paper, of the following authors if printed in quarto or octavo:

> Homer [none printed]
> Virgil [1795, 2 vols, 8vo, Brooks 620]
> Horace [1793, both 4to and 8vo, Brooks 493 and 494]

---

19 On 20 September 1793 he writes that the friend for whom he ordered the Horace finds it too dear. This – being followed by a reference to his own copy of the folio Horace – is most likely a reference to a folio edition.

Livy [none printed]
Tacitus [1795, quarto, Brooks 594/595; 1797, 2 vols, 8vo, Brooks 692]
Quintus Curtius [none printed]
Cicero [none printed]
Sallust [1799, 2 vols, 4to, Brooks 748]

Of those editions that were printed there is no evidence, at least not in the 1801 sale, that there were copies in Steuart's library.

Two months later, on 10 November 1793, Steuart is putting in the following order:

2 copies of Thomson [*Seasons*], folio, large paper
4 copies of Thomson [*Seasons*], folio, royal paper [additional to order of 6 April 1793?]
1 copy of Dante, folio, large paper [1795, Brooks 588; 1796, Brooks 653]
2 copies of Dante, folio, ordinary paper
1 copy of Dante, 4to, large paper [1796, Brooks 654]
1 copy of Dante, 4to, ordinary paper
1 copy of Petrarch, folio, large paper [1799, Brooks 733]
2 copies of Petrarch, folio, ordinary paper
1 copy of Petrarch, 4to, large paper [none printed; 1799, 8vo, Brooks 734]
1 copy of Petrarch, 4to, ordinary paper
2 copies of Ariosto [*Orlando furioso*], folio, large paper [none printed]
4 copies of Ariosto [*Orlando furioso*], folio, royal paper [none printed]
2 copies of Ariosto [*Orlando furioso*], 4to, large paper [none printed]
2 copies of Ariosto [*Orlando furioso*], 4to, ordinary paper [none printed]
2 copies of Tasso, [*Aminta*], folio, large paper [already printed, 1793, Brooks 514]
4 copies of Tasso [*Aminta*], folio, royal paper
2 copies of Tasso [*Aminta*], 4to, large paper [already printed, 1789, Brooks 379; false '1789' imprint, printed 1792, Brooks 380]
2 copies of Tasso [*Aminta*], 4to, ordinary paper

The problem with all these details is that it is uncertain what actually reached Steuart safely. There are references to some parcels arriving, but we do not know their contents. We also know that because of the international situation transport was very hazardous; in one letter (6 April 1793) Steuart made the suggestion of splitting his cargo into two separate parcels in order to spread the risk of losing books. What is difficult to explain is why at least one copy of each book ordered was not included in Steuart's 1801 sale, especially when we note that this sale did contain, in addition to the very special copies of the large paper folio Virgil and Horace (10/44–45), ordinary copies of each bound in a uniform blue morocco (5/46–47) and another ordinary copy of the folio Virgil (3/49). That Steuart did have yet other copies is shown by a letter James Edwards wrote to him on 29 November 1798 suggesting, in the context of a forthcoming Leigh & Sotheby's sale containing a copy of the 1462 Fust & Schoeffer Bible, that 'it would be a good opportunity to try a part of your Bodoni's books in the same sale – if you think so I will send one of each and desire Legh if there is still time to put em in'.[20] This was the sale of 20–21 December 1798 and there are some Bodoni books in it:

> quarto 43 Dissertazione intorno al Sublime del Girolamo Pradi. 4to.
> 1793 [Brooks 504]
> quarto 44 Elegia Inglese di Tomaso Gray, Lat. et Ital. da Torelli. 4to.
> 1793 [Brooks 485; perhaps the edition ordered on 6 April 1793]
> quarto 47 Museo Le Avanture D'Ero e di Leandro, Gr. et Ital. 4to. 1793
> [Brooks 499; 1801 sale 7/35]
> quarto 162 Horatii Opera. 4to. 1793 [Brooks 493; ordered on
> 8 February 1793 and 20 September 1793]
> quarto 172 Longinus de Sublimitate, Gr. et Lat. 4to. 1793 [Brooks 508]
> folio 69 Aminta di Tasso. fol. 1793 [Brooks 514; 1801 sale 10/48]
> folio 108 Britannia, Lathmon, Villa Bromhamensis, Eng. & Lat. fol.
> 1792 [Brooks 470; ordered on 6 April 1793]
> folio 209 Longinus de Sublimitate, Gr. et Lat. fol. 1793 [Brooks 507;
> 1801 sale 10/49; ordered 8 February 1793]
> folio 231 Virgilii Opera, 2 tom. fol. 1793 [Brooks 486; 1801 sale 5/47 &
> 11/44; ordered on 14 September 1792, 8 February 1793 and 6 April
> 1793]

Some or all of these might be Steuart's copies, but there is no proof. Some of them are books he ordered in his letters to Bodoni, and some are books of which copies are also included in the 1801 sale. They are all dated 1792 or 1793, and even those not specifically ordered might have been included in parcels from Bodoni.

When Steuart did buy multiple copies, would he himself try to sell them to collectors? That he did act sometimes as a middleman for collectors is shown by the reference in his letter of 20 September 1793 to a copy of Horace that a friend no longer wanted (above, with note 19). But it seems more likely that he

---

20 This letter is loosely inserted in National Library of Scotland, Inc.2, a copy of the 1472 Mainz Bible that has bound in at the appropriate place a vellum leaf (showing clear signs of earlier use as a binding) from the 1462 Fust & Schoeffer Bible (this is what links the letter to the 1472 Bible; Steuart did not succeed in buying the 1462 Bible, if in fact he even attempted to do so). For a full transcription of the letter see 'Parma and Edinburgh', p. 363.

passed them on to the trade. On 4 February 1794 Steuart acknowledges receipt of the bill for some books he has asked for and also for a crate of books that Bodoni is sending for which, wanting very much to help him, Steuart will try to get him the best prices possible. There seems to have been no prior discussion about this between Steuart and Bodoni but it is a clear case of Steuart acting as a distributor – or rather intending to do so, for, in fact, on 16 September 1794 Bodoni writes that because of the high cost of insurance it does not suit him to send the three packages of books he was going to send for Steuart to sell on his behalf. This provokes, on 3 November 1794, what is for us an extremely interesting response from Steuart: he is pleased with this decision because it would have been impossible for him to sell the books at present. The London booksellers (he is writing this letter from London) are little disposed to stocking Bodoni's editions in their shops: there are not twenty volumes for sale in London. He has been to James Edwards, Thomas Payne, James Robson, John & Thomas Egerton, Peter Elmsley, and others: they do not stock a single copy of the Virgil or the Horace. He comments that, undoubtedly inspired by Bodoni's editions, Edwards and Payne have published their own fine editions of Virgil and Horace, and although the beauty of their printing is not the equal of Bodoni's, the books are less expensive and on better paper.[21]

It would be interesting, I think, on another occasion to carry out a survey of booksellers' catalogues of this period to estimate what Bodoni editions were on sale. For example, Thomas Payne's 1794 catalogue contained at least sixteen Bodoni publications, including no fewer than six copies of Anacreon, 1791, two of them on large paper, and his 1795 catalogue at least twenty-two Bodoni publications.[22] Steuart might have formed an incorrect impression, or just possibly out of irritation because Bodoni had decided not to send the packages, he misrepresented what he had seen to make the packages seem less important. Although these packages were not sent, some of the Bodoni publications stocked by these booksellers may have been copies supplied by Steuart.

So much for Steuart as a purchaser of Bodoni's books and as a distributor of them, but potentially of greater significance is his role as a patron. In his fourth letter, 8 February 1793, in which he asked for two copies of every classic author that Bodoni printed, whether in Latin, Italian, French, English or Spanish, Steuart said that he very much wished Bodoni to print *Don Quixote* in

---

21 *P. Virgili Maronis opera.* 4 vols. Londini: typis T. Rickaby: impensis T. Payne, B. & J. White, R. Faulder, & J. Edwards, 1793; *Q. Horatii Flacci opera.* 2 vols. Londini: excudebant Gul. Browne, et Joh. Warren. Et prostant venales apud T. Payne et J. Edwards, 1792–1793. These editions are printed on wove paper.

22 These are minimum figures derived from using the truncated search term *bodon** in *Eighteenth Century Collections Online (ECCO).*

Spanish and *Gil Blas* in French, and that he would willingly take fifty copies of each to give as presents to his friends. He adds that, in English, Milton's *Paradise Lost* and Thomson's *Seasons* would also sell well. On 6 April 1793 Steuart orders four copies of Thomson, as well as making the further suggestion (in the event not taken up by Bodoni) that the *Castle of Indolence* should be included with the *Seasons*. On 20 September 1793 he counters the Bishop of Derry's preference for Ossian over Thomson, saying that Bodoni will sell ten copies of Thomson for every one of Ossian: therefore by then Bodoni may not have taken the decision to print the *Seasons*. However, by the time that Steuart wrote on 10 November 1793, it had been decided: Steuart corrects an English version of an announcement for this publication,[23] and orders two copies folio, large paper, and four copies folio, royal paper. Subsequently Bodoni had told Steuart that he was going to dedicate the Thomson edition to Steuart and his wife: in thanking him for this on 4 February 1794, Steuart orders four copies on Annonay paper and six on fine paper, apparently ignorant at this stage that folio and quarto editions were planned. The Thomson edition was published in 1794, and its fulsome dedication is worth consideration:[24]

To David Steuart Esquire of Cardneys[25] Late Lord Provost of the City of Edinburg [*sic*]

Sir, Convinced that the works of Fancy and Imagination have a peculiar claim to typographical beauty and elegance, I have of late almost entirely dedicated my labours to splendid editions of the most celebrated Poets of every age and in every language.

Amongst these your countryman James Thomson occupies a distinguish'd place, and in printing this Edition of the Seasons I avail myself with infinite satisfaction of the spontaneous offer of your patronage to introduce it to the Men of Taste and Letters in Britain.

If I particularly wish immortality to any of my works it is to this, that the testimony of my respect and gratitude for a person of so much worth and eminence may be handed down to future ages, and remain a monument of my ardent wish to extend the fame of my Press, and of your Liberality in not confining your protection to the Printers of your own country.

I have the honor to be, Sir, your most obliged and most humble Servant J. B. Bodoni

---

23 Brooks 516 is an example of an English-language 'Avviso' of 1793, but it does not advertise Thomson's *Seasons*.

24 This is quoted from the quarto edition, Brooks 532. Of the folio edition, Brooks 531, it is stated that 'in composizione è la stessa', but the copy I have seen (National Library of Scotland, BCL.B6832, on deposit) shows differences, e.g. the spelling 'Stewart' in the dedication).

25 Steuart had purchased the lands of Cardneys from John Menzies of Culdares in 1792 (National Archives of Scotland, GD 38/1/1119).

In his letter of 16 September 1794 Bodoni refers to this dedication and is more explicit about the protection provided by 'the plentiful commissions given to me for my books, thanks to which I have been able to undertake new editions which my reduced resources would not have allowed me to give to the cultured public [Pubblico Letterato].'

To return to Steuart's remark on 8 February 1793, when he had suggested that Milton's *Paradise Lost* and Thomson's *Seasons* would sell well, that he very much wished Bodoni to print *Don Quixote* in Spanish and *Gil Blas* in French, and that he would willingly take fifty copies of each to give as presents to his friends, we should look at how these suggestions developed. On 6 April 1793, responding to a non-extant letter from Bodoni, Steuart loses enthusiasm for *Paradise Lost* which Bodoni said was going to cost twelve guineas: he fears it will be too expensive for other Scots and probably even for the English, and he adds that it is a book that would sell only in England. However, he ends, he will speak to his friends about it and get back to Bodoni shortly. Are these friends collectors who might be expected to buy copies for themselves, or are they booksellers? *Don Quixote*, he says, is a different prospect because that is read all over Europe. If Bodoni can print that in two folio volumes at six 'zequins'[26] each and make it as beautiful as the Horace, he will take one hundred copies, although he would be more comfortable about taking fifty and not having to resell any. He also offers advice on the copy text Bodoni should use: the 1780 Madrid edition.[27] This both shows Steuart acting almost as co-publisher, and also confirms that when initially he said he was going to give fifty copies as presents to friends, he meant it: this intended generosity is quite striking. In this same letter he also offers to send a copy of *The Oeconomy of Human Life* for Bodoni to tell him the cost of printing one hundred copies in octavo in the latest fashion ('dans le dernier gout'), and he adds that he might be able, speaking to 'our booksellers' – Edinburgh and London, so Bodoni (see below) interpreted it – to get orders for a further two hundred copies. It is not known what Bodoni replied about *Don Quixote*, but on 20 September 1793 Steuart says that while he does not dispute Bodoni's calculations, the situation in Scotland does not allow him to take the number of copies proposed by Bodoni: instead he will happily take twenty copies, half of them on Annonay paper and half on fine paper. In a postscript to this letter Steuart makes a remarkable suggestion: 'It seems to me that you would not fail to make a great fortune in London if you were able to decide to set yourself up there. I will help you with my purse and my advice.' We know that Bodoni regarded this as

---

26 A zequin or sequin was a currency in use in a number of Italian city states in the eighteenth century. Its value varied, but very approximately it was worth half of a pound sterling at the time.

27 For Steuart's copy see above, note 13.

a serious and generous suggestion, for he wrote to the French bibliophile Auguste Renouard on 4 February 1794 saying that because last September Steuart had generously offered his purse and his advice if he, Bodoni, wished to move to London, he could not refuse to print one hundred copies of *The Oeconomy of Human Life* for him and three hundred copies for the booksellers of Edinburgh and London.[28]

In his letter to Steuart of 16 September 1794 Bodoni says that he is still waiting for a copy of the *The Oeconomy of Human Life*, to enable him to print an elegant edition of it, and is still thinking of going ahead with a magnificent Spanish *Don Quixote*, provided only that Steuart will commit to taking if not one hundred copies, at least seventy-five. In Bodoni's next letter, 8 October 1794, having had no answer to this previous suggestion, he refers to it as planned to be in four folio volumes, and compares it to the Horace and the Virgil. He says that it would be sufficient security for him if Steuart took fifty copies at ten pounds sterling each. He would print only one hundred copies (fifty copies for each of them), and so the edition would at once be scarce and people would pay any price for it. As both a bibliophile and a businessman, Steuart must have found this a powerful appeal. When Steuart wrote on 3 November 1794, he had not received Bodoni's October letter and was responding to his September letter, still saying that he will send *The Oeconomy of Human Life* when Bodoni can send him some printing costs, and commenting that the current European situation stops him thinking about the publication of *Don Quixote*, which would however be able to go forward successfully in due course. When Steuart writes on 10 December 1794, after receiving Bodoni's October letter, he says only that he will reflect on the *Don Quixote* proposition. On 13 January 1795 Bodoni says that he would like Steuart's support since his business is not flourishing as it was at the beginning of the war, and so he is keen for Steuart to make a decision about the *Don Quixote*, which he thinks will take at least most of the present year to print and is very reasonably priced at ten pounds sterling each for fifty copies of a four-volume folio edition. The final letter of Bodoni's that we know about, written at an uncertain date in 1795 (it is headed '6 del 1795'), tells Steuart that it is not necessary to think any more about *Don Quixote*, but he still values Steuart's 'protection'.

I am unaware of any evidence for subsequent business negotiations of this kind between Steuart and Bodoni. There is only the one last letter, 18 January 1799, in which Steuart says that it is a very long time since he has had news

---

28 This letter is quoted by A. Boselli, 'Quello che G. B. Bodoni non stampò (Spigolature dal carteggio bodoniano)', *Gutenberg Jahrbuch*, 1934, 231–247 (p. 245). In his final letter to Steuart, '6 del 1795', Bodoni again mentions the generosity of Steuart's offer.

from Bodoni. As he is sending a ship with a cargo of fish to Livorno,[29] he is taking the liberty of sending a request for one large paper and two ordinary paper copies of Thomson's *Seasons*, to be sent to either Edinburgh or London; in the case of London, addressed to James Edwards. Right at the end of the letter he says that if Bodoni can find him copies of Horace, Milan, 1470, and Virgil, Venice, 1470, and if they are in perfect condition, he will pay twenty-five guineas for each. Steuart's affairs were not good at this date[30] – and so probably his other business ventures with Bodoni had petered out – but he still wanted fine books to add to his library, and these were probably considered by him to be the first printings[31] of the two authors, Horace and Virgil, whose editions by Bodoni he most admired.

Steuart had the business drive, skills and contacts[32] that combined with his knowledge of books would have enabled him to enter fully into the book trade, and the evidence of his correspondence with Bodoni provides us with some glimpses how this could have developed.[33] However, the impression we are left with is that although he was always on the look-out for money-making ventures, perhaps ultimately the book trade had no appeal for him as a business opportunity pure and simple: it was, rather, the possession of fine books that motivated him.

---

29 See 'Parma and Edinburgh', p. 359, n. 145: probably salmon, but herring is also a possibility.

30 The debts were piling up and in June a Portuguese creditor, to whom he owed about £2,000, had him imprisoned: see *David Steuart*, pp. 18–19.

31 Details in 'Parma and Edinburgh', p. 359, n. 147.

32 In his letter of 14 September 1792, after ordering copies of the folio Virgil, Steuart says that reimbursement will be made by Messrs Otto Frank & Co., A. & D. Raguenau, and Simon Fraser, of Livorno, 'who are all in correspondence with my house at Leith', this referring to the trading company D. Steuart & Co. that Steuart set up in Leith after dissolving his banking partnership with Robert Allan. The letters contain other references showing how in his dealings with Bodoni he was able to utilize his existing business contacts.

33 Originally I had thought that by studying the provenance of copies of Bodoni's publications in present-day Scottish collections I might be able to show the effects of Steuart's importing of books from Parma into Scotland. In the event, I have carried out little of this research to date, but the lack of results might suggest, as does the correspondence, that London and not Edinburgh was the centre of this field of Steuart's activities.

A Scottish Imprint: George Robertson and The Australian Encyclopaedia

CAROLINE VIERA JONES

I N THE LAST DECADE Australian scholarly editors have resurrected colonial manuscripts and early editions from their unpublished state or from the 'corrupted' hands of copy editors. Their aim is to document each editorial stage so that scholars, students and critics may work confidently with an authenticated text.[1] The extent to which this literature mirrors authorial intention, however, is a contentious issue because the words 'authoritative' and 'authorial' are not synonymous. As Shillingsburg argues, the term 'authorial approval' hovers between manuscript transcripts on the one hand and the distinction between 'revisions undertaken for aesthetic reasons and those effected under duress from non-artistic influences'.[2]

Yet editorial changes, authorized or not, are themselves significant in analysing national cultural identity since not only do they reveal an editor's literary agenda they also contextualize contemporary society's fears, prejudices and value systems, especially if a manuscript has been subject to peer review. Whereas an author may imagine an ideal or a malevolent world vision, publishers are not as willing to alienate the book-buying public by publishing outside the middle ground. Readers are also consumers and, although publishers may challenge their customers' intellect or even shock them, they are generally less willing to offend their sensibilities. As Richard le Gallienne wrote, with tongue-in-cheek, more than a century ago: 'the publisher is a being slow to move, slow

---

1   For a discussion of the contemporary debate between scholarly and in-house editors, see Paul Eggert, 'Textual Product or Textual Process: Procedures and Assumptions of Critical Editing'; Peter Shillingsburg, 'The Autonomous Author: The Sociology of Texts and Polemics of Textual Criticism'; G. E. Bentley Jnr., 'Final Intention or Protean Performance: Classical Editing Theory and the Case of William Blake'; and Craig Munro, 'I've headed my Talk – "final working draft"' in Paul Eggert, ed., *Editing in Australia*, Occasional Paper No. 17 (Canberra, 1990). See also Paul Eggert, ed., *Manual for Editors* (Canberra, 1994).
2   Fredson Bowers cited in Peter L. Shillingsburg, *Scholarly Editing in the Computer Age: Theory and Practice* (Athens, 1986), pp. 4–5 and 13–14.

to take in changed conditions, always two generations, at least, behind his authors'.[3]

The Scottish-Australian publisher, George Robertson, did not fit le Gallienne's description. He was sometimes two generations ahead of his authors, especially those belonging to the Anglo-Australian elite. In *The Australian Encyclopaedia* he tried to include a variety of opinions which were sometimes outside those expressed by the colonial academy. Robertson was trained in the Scottish publishing and bookselling tradition by James MacLehose, publisher and bookseller to the University of Glasgow, while his fellow partner, David McKenzie Angus, was apprenticed to E. & S. Livingstone, booksellers to the University of Edinburgh. The methods inculcated in the young Scottish apprentices were employed half a world away, so much so that George Robertson confessed in 1895 that there was not much originality about them.

The Scottish links of many Angus & Robertson staff and authors did much to encourage the growing nationalism of the colonists, since the firm's gaze was not only pointed to London. Indeed, Robertson maintained his youthful contacts with Scottish publishers, booksellers and reviewers. For example, on 15 October 1898, Angus & Robertson wrote to W. and A. K. Johnston, map publishers of Edinburgh, asking them if they could produce a school wall map which would situate Australia in the middle of Mercator's Projection. Entitled 'The Australian Trades Route Maps of the World', such a chart would allow Australian school children to see their country visually and metaphorically as central to their education and as source of their knowledge.[4]

From ideas such as this, George Robertson established a tradition of supplying Australiana within the firm's non-fiction just as much as in Angus & Robertson novels and verse. The culmination of his dream was realized in the 1920s, however, when the firm published two volumes of *The Australian Encyclopaedia*.[5] First proposed in 1912, *The Australian Encyclopaedia* was

---

3   Richard le Gallienne, 'Poets and Publishers' in *Prose Fancies* (London, 1894), pp. 77–82; see also Teresa Pagliaro, 'Arthur Wilberforce Jose (1863–1934), an Anglo-Australian: A Study of his Contribution to Australian Literary Culture from the 1890s to the 1930s' (unpublished PhD thesis, University of Sydney, 1990).

4   W. & A. K. Johnston, Edinburgh, to Angus & Robertson (hereafter A & R), 30 November 1898, A & R papers, Mitchell Library State Library of New South Wales (ML) MSS 314/41/13; appended note written by George Robertson, 16 December 1916, ML MSS 314/41/13.

5   *The Australian Encyclopaedia*, ed. by Arthur Wilberforce Jose and Herbert James Carter, vol. I, 2nd edn (Australia: A & R, 1927), hereafter *A.E.*, vol. I, 2nd edn; *The Australian Encyclopaedia*, ed. by Jose, Carter and T. G. Tucker, vol. I, 3rd edn revised (Australia: A & R, 1927), hereafter *A.E.*, vol. I, 3rd edn; and, *The Australian Encyclopaedia*, ed. by Jose and

originally intended as a biographical and historical record under the editorship of the Sydney Municipal Librarian, Charles Bertie. The First World War stopped work on this venture until 1917, when it was decided to include material on scientific subjects under the editorship of Herbert Carter, president of the Linnean Society. Although he also worked on the encyclopaedia in 1917, Arthur Jose was only officially appointed general editor in 1920, a role he maintained until April 1926.[6] The first volume of *The Australian Encyclopaedia* was published in 1925 and revised twice in 1927, while the second volume was brought to press in 1926.

The idea behind *The Australian Encyclopaedia* was that it should be marketed alongside the ten volumes of *Chambers's Encyclopaedia*, which the firm distributed in Australia. Robertson sold the two Australian volumes at a cheaper unit price of fourteen shillings and sixpence net if they were bought in addition to the Chambers's volumes.[7] All twelve volumes were of the same size and colour (dark green) and had similar layout and captions.[8] Indentation, fonts and typefaces were the same with plates and line drawings of a comparable size and quality in most of the natural history items. However, the aims of *Chambers's* and *The Australian Encyclopaedia* were different – the one being to spread universal knowledge, the other to spread definitive knowledge about the Australian nation, such as its flora and fauna.[9] Angus & Robertson thus sought to complement rather than to override the Scottish editions and to add to that vast but specialized body of Australian scientific and historical knowledge already disseminated by the firm in its non-fiction texts.

Australian knowledge was not situated within the bigger picture. Factual knowledge had a regional focus while it was left to the Scots to present Australian readers with a world view. Indeed, so up to date was Chambers's understanding of the general Australian narrative, their 1923 edition described how contemporary Australian history was being rewritten and reconstructed:

So much study has been devoted to Australian subjects since the coming of the Commonwealth, and so much new material has been forthcoming, that all earlier

---

Carter, vol. II, 1st edn (Australia: A & R, 1926), hereafter *A.E.*, vol. II. In 1958 the firm published a new edition of *The Australian Encyclopaedia* in ten volumes. This was edited by Alec Chisholm.

6   Fred Shenstone to Jose, 2 December 1916, A & R papers, ML MSS 314/41/337.

7   George Robertson (hereafter GR) to Charles H. Peters, 21 August 1925, A & R papers, ML MSS 314/243/321.

8   David Patrick and William Geddie, eds., *The Illustrated Chambers's Encyclopaedia: A Dictionary of Universal Knowledge* (London, Edinburgh & Sydney, 1923–7).

9   Patrick & Geddie, eds., vol. I, *Chambers's Encyclopaedia* (1923), preface.

compilations dealing with those subjects must be read with caution, and many of them with profound distrust.[10]

Since most readers bought the Australian volumes alongside the Scottish ones because that was a cheaper option, general knowledge of the outer world therefore came to Australian households through Scottish eyes. The title page of *The Australian Encyclopaedia* even had an emblem combining the Scottish thistle with the Australian waratah as 'symbolic of the association of Scotland and Australia in the firm's establishment'.[11] Material within *The Australian Encyclopaedia* was also Scots-flavoured. Robertson corresponded with the Edinburgh office while many people written about in the Australian volumes were Scottish-born. Entries on land settlement and dairying, for example, even used the report from the 1910–1911 Scottish Agricultural Commission to Australia as basis for their research. A marketing decision about distribution over and above a nationalistic agenda thus drove how the Australian text was edited and written.[12]

Also significant in the Angus & Robertson encyclopaedia was the diversity of voices George Robertson allowed, although the conservative Anglo-colonial elite was better represented in the major articles. For example, the firm's literary editor, Professor Tucker, wrote a positive entry on convict history bathed in a contextual, measured and placating tone. 'The treatment of the first arrivals,' he argued, 'though expatriated as "the very dregs of society" was, relative to the times, unusually humane.' Indeed, Tucker's article quelled colonial establishment fears by emphasizing the minority of the country's convict forebears when contrasted with its burgeoning population. Firmly putting to rest this most delicate of subjects, Tucker attempted to bleach the nation's convict stain once and for all.[13] Acknowledging the importance of interpreting history from within 'the spirit of the age', the encyclopaedia's entry on 'transportation', moreover, even assured Australian readers that, much as the convicts were treated badly by their gaolers, contemporary prisoners in other countries fared much worse than those held under British law.[14]

---

10 'Australia' in *Chambers's Encyclopædia* ed. by Patrick & Geddie, vol. I (1923), pp. 600–2; and Arthur W. Jose, *History of Australia: From the Earliest Times to the Present Day with Chapters on Australian Literature and the Early History of New Zealand* (Australia, 1924).

11 *Fragment: The House Magazine of Angus & Robertson and Halstead Press*, No. 8, December 1956, p. 18.

12 James Dunlop, Member of the Scottish Agricultural Commission to Denmark 1904, Ireland 1906, Canada 1908, Australia 1910–11, *Farming in Australia, and Ayrshire Folks We Met When There* (Kilmarnock, 1912).

13 Thomas George Tucker, 'Convicts' in *A.E.*, vol. I, 3rd edn, p. 297.

14 'Transportation', no by-line, in *A.E.*, vol. II, pp. 581–2.

George Robertson did not favour one religious or political group over another, however, and he simultaneously allowed for a different interpretation of the Irish convict plight in entries on the 'Roman Catholic Church' and 'bushranging'.[15] Just as Angus & Robertson interestingly published two different children's history textbooks – one for the Catholic schools and one for the rest of the colonists – so we find an alternative convict narrative in Eris O'Brien's discussion of Australian Catholicism. Instead of praising the English for their handling of the colonies' convicts, this entry found fault with the colonial government's treatment of Irish Catholic prisoners:

A Protestant chaplain was appointed to the First Fleet, but no provision was made for the spiritual wants of Catholic convicts, although two priests had applied for permission to accompany it, and offered to pay their own expenses.

In the new penal settlement attendance at religious service was made compulsory for all; the Catholic convicts – including ... thousands of Irish 'rebels' of 1798 – were quite unprovided for spiritually, and even forced to attend services against the dictates of conscience.[16]

The Australian Encyclopaedia was criticized for not giving more space to Methodist education but that charge could certainly not be laid against the entry on Presbyterianism. Apart from a detailed history of its followers in the Australian colonies, the information on Dr John Dunmore Lang, Scottish minister, educationalist and political stirrer, is significant because of his impact upon the divided loyalties of the colonists. For example, *The Australian Encyclopaedia* stated that Lang objected to legislation which sought to regulate the Church's temporal affairs because it was 'against the spirit of a young and independent country'. Lang and other ministers formed the Synod of New South Wales on 11 December 1837, wrote the Reverend Anderson, 'with no appeal beyond the colony'. In recording Dr Lang's actions, George Robertson emphasized a rebellious voice outside an Irish Catholic one and set the Scottish Presbyterian influence as counterpoint to the Anglican-Australian elite in recording shades of political consciousness amongst the early settlers.[17]

George Robertson, however, was not above gently chiding his adopted country's readers. For example, in discussing ways in which Dr Lang enlarged the population of the fledgling city of Brisbane through organizing the immigration of six hundred 'virtuous Presbyterians', Robertson's encyclopaedia

---

15 Reverend Father Eris M. O'Brien, 'Roman Catholic Church' in *A.E.*, vol. II, pp. 395–9; and 'Bushranging' in *A.E.*, vol. I, 3rd edn, pp. 218–22.
16 Reverend Father Eris M. O'Brien, 'Roman Catholic Church' in *A.E.*, vol. II, pp. 395–6.
17 Reverend James Colwell, 'Methodist Church' and Reverend William Addison S. Anderson, 'Presbyterian Church' in *A.E.*, vol. II, p. 337.

emphasized just how sadly lacking in an educated citizenry Brisbane was before the 'industrious and capable Scots' ably rescued her: 'The population of Brisbane and Ipswich was about 1500, and a facetious chronicler has left it on record that it included six lawyers, six doctors, six clergymen, and a dozen other educated persons.'[18]

Whilst written from an anthropological perspective, the encyclopaedia's information on Australian Aborigines also quietly questioned contemporary educated thought. In a substantial section of forty and a half columns, in addition to twenty-six and a half columns devoted to Aboriginal languages and a section on the Tasmanian Aborigines, William Ramsay Smith, Sir Walter Baldwin Spencer and Sidney Herbert Ray documented Aboriginal culture, languages, belief systems and the effects of European disease, admitting honestly that 'a great many also die from our medical treatment'. At a time when phrenology was an accepted discourse, Robertson's encyclopaedia challenged perceived notions about the hierarchy of intelligence and, more importantly, puzzled over the comparative lack of a civilizing spirit in those Europeans who inhabited the Australian continent:

To one who knows how the blackfellow even in a single lifetime reacts to new influences – moral, intellectual and mechanical – the facts seem to upset all theories of cranial capacities, cerebral functioning and mental operations. They raise the question, indeed, whether ordinary anthropological investigations and tests supply the kind and amount of evidence with which we credit them for elucidating the evolution of races and the relations of peoples. It would appear that civilized man knows as little regarding the possibilities of the mind of his uncivilized brother as he does regarding the primitive savage instincts which he for a long time supposed to be dormant, dead or never existent in the civilization to which he belongs.[19]

Nevertheless, George Robertson went beyond supplying different voices in his encyclopaedia. He also set about articulating a uniquely Australian heritage. When his general editor, Arthur Jose, left for England mid-way through revising volume one, Robertson commissioned new and decidedly informal material which had been excluded from the earlier edition. He added a lengthy article on the game of 'two-up' and even entries on rabbits and septic tanks – unusual topics for a national encyclopaedia.[20] While criticized for not including 'coo-ee', 'larrikin', 'cornstalk', 'cattle duffing', 'bail up', 'damper' and 'jackeroo', George Robertson had his finger on the pulse of national

---

18 George Hendy-Pooley, 'Brisbane' in *A.E.*, vol. I, 3rd edn, p. 202; and 'Printing', no by-line, in *A.E.*, vol. II, p. 337.
19 William Ramsey Smith, 'Aborigines', in *A.E.*, vol. I, 3rd edn, p. 35.
20 *A.E.*, vol. I, 3rd edn, preface.

iconography and indeed delineated most of it. Importantly, he resurrected forgotten Australians who he believed had been unjustly left out of the national narrative and he readjusted misinformation about others in the public sphere.[21] Thus, the article on J. F. Archibald of the influential Sydney *Bulletin* originally depicted his ancestry as richly vibrant and multicultural in keeping with the cosmopolitan image Archibald invented about himself: 'Archibald's father was an Irishman of Scottish extraction, and his mother a Frenchwoman of partly Jewish descent, so that the qualities of many races blended in him.'[22]

George Robertson knew that Archibald's heritage was not nearly as exotic as he might have wished the general public to believe. Arthur Jose did not inform his readers of the truth even though his publisher outlined the details to him. When Jose went to England, Robertson took it upon himself to add in certain information which Jose excluded from the draft of the second volume and the third revision of the first.[23] As long as his changes fitted the pagination of the first volume's page proofs for its second edition, Robertson felt free to alter what he wished in the third edition. That is why he conjured up exactly twenty-seven words to replace the earlier second version of the Archibald entry: 'Archibald's father was born at Dublin, and his mother, Charlotte Jane Madden, at Cambridge, England. Early in life he exchanged the baptismal 'John Feltham' for 'Jules François'.[24]

The Australian Encyclopaedia provided a window on early Australia but also on George Robertson since whom he chose to celebrate in his encyclopaedia and how long an entry each luminary received was coloured by the beliefs and values he brought with him from Scotland. When the Anglophile Arthur Jose left the encyclopaedia unfinished, he also allowed George Robertson the chance to break free from conservative editing and to insert ideas outside the academy. The richness and breadth of the encyclopaedia's articles discouraged the Anglicization of Australia at a crucial time in her development. By extending the boundaries of allegiance just as surely as he widened the parameters of colonial knowledge, this Scottish Australian encouraged an idea of a strong national cultural identity. The encyclopaedia which George Robertson published, contributed to a quintessential Australianness in a way that might not have been possible had the firm bowed obsequiously to an Anglo-elitist tradition during this decisive period.

---

21 Ernest Whitfeld, '*The Australian Encyclopaedia*: A Purchaser's Criticism', ML MSS 314/243/615–27; and *A.E.*, vol. I, 3rd edn, preface.
22 'Jules François Archibald' in *A.E.*, vol. I, 2nd edn, p. 71.
23 GR to T. Dunbabin, 6 September 1927, A & R papers, ML MSS 314/242/369; and GR to H. L. White, 3 September 1925, A & R papers, ML MSS 314/243/605.
24 'John Feltham Archibald' in *A.E.*, vol. I, 3rd edn, p. 71.

William Somerville Orr, London Publisher and Printer: The Skeleton in W. & R. Chambers's Closet

SONDRA MILEY COONEY

C HAPTER THIRTEEN of the *Memoir of William and Robert Chambers* is entitled 'A Skeleton in the House, and other Matters'. In this chapter, William Chambers briefly describes problems the Chambers firm encountered during the more than twenty years that William Somerville Orr was their London agent.[1] The Chamberses had become associated with Orr almost as soon as they began publishing *Chambers's Edinburgh Journal* in February 1832. They discovered, as other Edinburgh publishing firms have before and since, that it is good business for a firm located in Edinburgh to have a London base as well. While both W. & R. Chambers and W. S. Orr undeniably benefited from their association, it came at a great cost to both. The hundreds of letters, contracts, inventories, and ledger pages in the Chambers deposit at the National Library of Scotland provide an enlightening picture of the economics of nineteenth-century cheap publishing.

We do not know much about Orr. Biographical information about him is sketchy. He was a Scot, probably born at the beginning of the nineteenth century. He had a well-established London bookselling business by 1832. He was married and had a family: a daughter and a son. During most of the twenty years between 1832 and 1852 he lived at Walthamstow in Essex.[2] We do know what he looked like. D. O. Hill took a joint portrait of him and Peter Scott Fraser; it appears in Sara Stevenson's catalogue of Hill and Adamson pictures at the Scottish National Portrait Gallery.[3]

Details of his business life are more readily available. Philip Brown's *London Publishers and Printers c.1800–1870* lists the addresses of Orr's various business premises. After first operating from 14 Paternoster Row between 1833 and 1834, he moved to 2 & 3 Amen Corner, which would be his principal address until 1859. Although Brown lists other addresses for Orr's businesses,

---

1 *Memoir of William and Robert Chambers*, 13th edition (Edinburgh: W. & R. Chambers, 1883, p. 310).

2 The 1871 census records the personal information; the birth date is approximate, 1801. The residence appears in the census and as an address on many of his letters.

3 Sara Stevenson, *David Octavius Hill and Robert Adamson, Catalogue of Their Calotypes Taken Between 1843 and 1847...* (Edinburgh, 1981).

they were never more than subsidiary locations added when he took in other associates. He also operated from North John's Street in Liverpool. At these various addresses, Orr conducted printing, bookselling, publishing and book wholesaling businesses.[4]

The National Library of Scotland has two catalogues for Orr's business, one from 1836 entitled 'Works Published by W. S. Orr and Co., London: and W. & R. Chambers, Edinburgh' and another from 1841 'Catalogue of Illustrated Works'. Works related to the Natural Sciences predominate in both. The catalogues list Paxton's *Magazine of Botany, The Kitchen Garden, The British Naturalist, Alphabets of the Science for the Use of Schools and Self-Instruction, Every Lady Her own Flower-Gardener* as well as *Drawing and Painting in Water Colours* by the author of *Drawing* in Chambers's Educational Course and the *Laws of Harmonious Colouring* by D. R. Hay. By the 1850s Orr had published *British Moths and Their Transformations*, Thomas Milner's *Gallery of Nature, The Poultry Book* (well known today as an outstanding example of nineteenth-century colour printing) and *The Theory and Practice of Landscape Painting in Water Colours*. In that same decade he was also advertising Orr's Circle of the Industrial Arts which was intended to complement Orr's Circle of the Sciences.

The Chambers-Orr association began when the Chamberses sent early copies of the *Journal* to Orr, who was acquainted with their brother James. By April of 1832, Orr had agreed to produce a separate impression of the *Journal* in London, not just sell from his shop copies sent down from Edinburgh. The agreement specified that he was to be able to print 6000 copies of each number and all profits from those 6000 were to be his. For each additional thousand he printed he was to pay W. & R. Chambers eighteen shillings, which was understood to be the half of his profit on each thousand. The Chamberses would supply, by post, a copy of each forthcoming number at least five days before it appeared. When reprinting the *Journal*, Orr was to preserve as nearly as possible the appearance of the numbers printed from, as regards typography and paper, and the subject matter was to be precisely the same. Finally, Orr could distribute the *Journal* in all of England except for the counties of Northumberland, Cumberland, and Durham, also Berwick-upon-Tweed and Belfast which were supplied by the Edinburgh office.[5] Soon thereafter he was sent stereotype

---

4 Philip A. H. Brown, *London Publishers and Printers c.1800–1870* (London, 1982) p. 142.

5 All documents relating to the dealings between W. & R. Chambers and W. S. Orr are in the W. & R. Chambers archive at the National Library of Scotland to whose North Reading Room staff I am indebted for years of gracious assistance. Most of the correspondence is filed in the yearly Literary Labour Files, slipcases with alphabetized sections. The individual papers within those sections are not numbered. Exceptions are so noted. The agreement between Orr and Chambers was dated 22 April 1832. National Library of Scotland, Dep. 341/312.

plates instead of proofs; he was then to pay fifteen shillings per thousand for every thousand over the initial 6000. Another revision was made to the agreement when Curry and Company of Dublin began receiving stereotype plates for printing an edition there. Consequently, Orr's price for plates was reduced from £5.7s.0d. to £3.0s.0d. He was still to pay, once a month, fifteen shillings per thousand for everything above 6,000 copies.[6] The agreement seemed to be benefiting both parties because the *Journal* was selling 20,000 copies in England.[7]

But by the beginning of 1833 – less than a year later – a problem developed which would establish an unfortunate pattern in Orr's business practices. Orr decided to take as a partner William Smith. He had done so, as he explained later to the Chamberses, because he was

contending against money difficulties, arising principally from a sudden and unexpected flow of business from the great success of the Journal and my own speculations which found me unprepared with other premises, or assistants so that for several months previous to this time I had not only to look after authors printing and money matters but I was compelled by the smallness of my warehouse which left no room for porters, to pack up with my own hands the Bales we had to send out. I mention these circumstances, because they are the only palliation I can console myself with, for the culpable manner in which I sacrificed the interests of myself and family in the arrangements I entered into at this time.[8]

Why Orr thought he could benefit from taking Smith as a partner is not clear because Smith was out of work and had no money. But because he presented himself as an acquaintance of Bradbury and Evans, Orr gave him a half interest in the business with the understanding that Smith was to travel through the country on a regular basis. Then, when he was able to do so, Smith was to pay £200 into the business. By late 1834, Smith announced that he did not want to travel anymore. He thought that he could be of more help in London and that they should employ another traveller. Orr would not agree to Smith's proposal and suggested that by Christmas 1835 they should terminate the agreement and begin a new one in January 1836. In the course of closing their affairs, Smith expressed the opinion that he was entitled to half of what he thought was Orr's interest in the *Journal*.[9]

This news was not received happily in Edinburgh. W. & R. Chambers sent a letter to Smith telling him that he had no claim on the *Journal*. Further-

---

6   NLS Dep. 341/312.
7   W. S. Orr letter to W. & R. Chambers, 3 October 1836, NLS Dep. 341/312.
8   WSO to W & RC, NLS Dep. 341/342.
9   WSO to W & RC, 3 October 1836, NLS Dep. 341/312.

more, because Orr had not fulfilled the terms of their agreement to the letter
for some time:

if we pleased we could at this moment take the agency of the work from him, at the
same time withdrawing the plates or interdicting their use. We beg, therefore, that you
will most distinctly understand that Mr. Orr has neither a copyright nor a permanent
interest in the publication.[10]

This explanation must have cowed Smith, because no more is heard from him.
Orr, on the other hand, was most apologetic. He told the Chamberses he did
not intend to take on another partner unless compelled to. 'I pledge myself to
you that I shall not do so without consulting you in the most confidential
manner before doing it.'[11]

Alarmed at the possibility of Orr's bad decisions harming their business,
the Chamberses drew up a new agreement with Orr in early 1837. They justified doing so on the grounds that a variety of changes had taken place which
made the 1832 agreement obsolete. First, their brother James, who had been a
party to the first agreement, was now dead. Second, the charge per thousand
was now fifteen shillings and not eighteen shillings. Third, plates, not proof
sheets, were now sent to London. Fourth, Edinburgh now supplied Ireland.
Fifth, payment was now to be made monthly, instead of bi-monthly. Sixth,
paper for the London printing was still not the same as that of the Edinburgh
edition. And finally, they said, 'We wish to be protected from you, and all who
may ever have to do with you or your business; and we would have you to
observe that we at the same time protect you from yourself.'[12]

Orr was not happy with the new agreement and insisted that the amended
1832 one was satisfactory. He thought that he was more than just an agency for
W. & R. Chambers. In protesting against the new agreement, he raised a point
on which the two parties never agreed:

I have spared no expence or pains to increase its circulation looking more to the future
than to the present for my remuneration:–in the same conviction I have entered into
extensive transactions:–I have engaged in machinery, solely for the purpose of printing
the Journal, and formed an Establishment about me, which would be [unsuited] were
the Journal removed but which is now requisite from the necessity of keeping up the
stock, which never averages less than from 250 to 300,000 Nos for which you have
already been paid:–Now, had my permission to issue the publication been all along a
common agency, subject, as all such are, to withdrawal at pleasure, is it likely that I
should have involved myself beyond what was necessary to meet the current demand.[13]

---

10 Draft letter dated 5 October 1836, NLS Dep. 341/312.
11 WSO to W & RC, 3 October 1836, NLS Dep. 341/312.
12 Agreement 15 April 1837, NLS Dep. 341/312.
13 WSO to W & RC, 14 February 1837, NLS Dep. 341/312.

Despite Orr's objections, the new agreement was signed on 15 April 1837. It contained a provision which, in the course of time, would be interpreted differently. It specified that the 'permission, right, power or liberty to print is only personal to the [aforesaid] Wm S. Orr himself, and can only remain in force during his Natural Life, or while he is Solvent, or able and willing to fulfill the terms of the present agreement.'[14] In time to come, Orr focused only on the second verb and ignored the adverbial clauses in that sentence.

The 1840s became a decade of crisis for W. & R. Chambers and their relationship with Orr. In 1841, the *Journal* was prospering. One hundred and sixty thousand sheets were distributed weekly – 8,000,000 a year, the greater part of which was prepared at Edinburgh. The five presses at Edinburgh printed 20,000 sheets a day. In London, Orr's two machines printed 'more than 40,000 per week of [the] sheets for English Circulation'.[15] By the middle of the 1840s, however, *Journal* sales were slipping. Writing to the Chamberses on 3 January 1845, Orr said that:

here as well as in Scotland rivals of a formidable character are springing up, who should be met with increased energy on all our parts . . . . a totally new class of minds have arrived at maturity who require a different pabulum to that of our younger days. The success of Punch, Dickens, Lever and others I think sufficiently prove that fact and I cannot help thinking that a gradual infusion of light sparkling articles addressed [to] the imagination as well as to contemporary events would give increased popularity to it... I cannot doubt but that there is a vast amount of talent both in Edinburgh, London and Dublin which is attainable if reasonable concessions were made and a liberal scale of remuneration adopted, and I think the Journal is in the state where an effort is worth making.[16]

To add insult to injury, on the business front Orr had again become involved with other people. This time the parties were none other than Bradbury and Evans. One thing is clear – Bradbury and Evans printed many of the works Orr published. I suspect that, as was usually the case, Orr was not paying Bradbury and Evans for their work in a timely fashion. To collect what Orr owed them, they thought that, since they were printing the *Journal* for Orr, they were entitled to a share of his *Journal* profits. They mistakenly thought, and Orr probably let them hold the impression, that he was a partner in the *Journal*, not merely its agent. William Chambers, writing from London to Robert reported that

---

14 Agreement 15 April 1837, NLS Dep. 341/312.

15 *Proceedings at Peebles. Wednesday, August 4, 1841, on Entertaining and Presenting the Freedom of the Burgh to Messrs William and Robert Chambers, of Edinburgh* (Edinburgh: [W. & R. Chambers], 1841), p. 10.

16 WSO to W & RC, 3 January 1845, NLS Dep. 341/312.

Having seen Evans by chance on the street, he told me that they did not claim upon us, but looked only to Orr who they consider has used them, very ill. I then saw Orr, who offers to give up the contract unconditionally at any time I like, and he seems utterly dispirited. I think I shall not have any serious difficulty, first in ridding Orr of B. and E. and then arranging with him in a new sense, the contract being destroyed.[17]

Bradbury and Evans, however, were not so easily managed. The very next day, William wrote again to Robert and was less sanguine:

The thing is no longer a question of our declaring the contract broken, or of Orr's relinquishment. It is this – what should we not do to avoid B. and E. dragging us into Chancery, on the plea that we have all along known of, or winked at, this partnership and therefore are liable to be bound just as much as Orr. I have some fear of this, and therefore watch the movements of B. and E. with all proper caution, ready to act promptly at a moments notice. Orr I repeat, will do anything we like. He is perfectly abject.[18]

Robert assessed the affair less generously. Writing to his friend Alexander Ireland, he reported that

William and I have lately had to make a stretch for our London agent Orr, to redeem him from the vampyre fangs of Bradbury and Evans – two most respectable men who live by sucking the blood of their fellow creatures, and who have been an incubus upon our journal for fourteen years, contrary to the very terms of our agreement with Orr and to the great detriment of the work.[19]

When the affair was finally resolved, it was at some cost to the Chamberses. Orr owed Bradbury and Evans approximately £2800 to get out of his agreement with them. He told the Chamberses that he could manage to pay £1750 of that himself, but that he would need to raise the rest of it from them or from other friends. They not only gave him what he needed but also assisted him in setting up premises for his independent business which would be located at 147 Strand. He told them he would retain his miscellaneous whole-sale business at Amen Corner and he planned to give more attention to what he referred to as a 'great School connection – and for this time that is favourable as besides your Educational Course is making daily progress... at the same time the movement gives you a very imposing London identity which had become a matter of some importance.'[20]

Nevertheless, because of Orr's careless business practices and the increasing competitive pressure on the *Journal*, relations between W. & R. Chambers and

---

17   WC to RC, 25 September 1846, NLS Dep. 341/314.
18   WC to RC, 26 September 1846, NLS Dep. 341/314.
19   RC to Alexander Ireland, n.d. [1846], NLS Dep. 341/110.
20   WSO to RC, 3 October 1846, NLS Dep. 341/314.

W. S. Orr continued to be unhappy. The Bradbury and Evans affair had hardly been concluded when letters were once again going from Edinburgh to London reminding Orr that he was delinquent in his monthly payments to the Chamberses. '[...] you are very strangely violating the terms of our mutual agreement as to settlements. This, I told you most distinctly in London was a thing we would not tolerate, and all things considered, it is what I never could have expected. I hold it to be no excuse that you are still engaged in clearing up partnership affairs [...].'[21] By 1847 Orr was asking them to be security for some of his bills. He had ordered some paper for printing Wordsworth's *Greece* and Carpenter's *Cyclopedia*.[22] The supplier refused the order because Orr still had outstanding bills. Then in 1849 the Chamberses gave Orr an additional £300 for the losses he had sustained from the shop in the Strand.[23] In the meantime, *Journal* sales and profits were declining. When the *Journal's* New Series began in 1844, weekly average sales were 86,750 copies with a profit of £3,422.16s.19d; when the Second Series appeared in 1847, its sales dropped to 74,653 copies with a profit of £2,824.13s.6d.[24] And most of this profit was going to Orr in London.

This decline greatly concerned the Chamberses because in the 1850s they were undertaking some new projects for which they would have to have substantial capital in hand. First, they were planning to expand and alter the firm's premises on Edinburgh's High Street. Second, they had purchased from F. A. Brockhaus of Leipzig the rights to publish a translation of the *Conversations Lexikon*. So by late 1851 they were exploring options for reinvigorating the *Journal* and making it more profitable. One suggestion was that the *Journal* be conducted from London and that they should set up some kind of operation to print it there. Orr discouraged them from doing so. He said that one of Robert Chambers's advantages as essayist for the *Journal* was that he did not get distracted by the turmoils of London society. Because of them, he would be poorly compensated for any small amount of 'information to be picked up in its coteries.' As for setting up a printing establishment, that would be out of the question because of the expense. The Chamberses also suggested that perhaps one of the brothers could come to London and establish a partnership with Orr. He did not like that idea either:

Partnerships except in a very large undertaking where each has his own department with unlimited power to carry out measures previously discussed and determined on, are the fruitful source of bickerings and heartburnings. I have for many years been a sort of

21 WC to WSO, 17 December 1846, NLS Dep. 341/314.
22 WSO to W & RC, 15 February 1847, NLS Dep. 341/314.
23 RC to WSO, 18 November 1849, NLS Dep. 341/315.
24 Publication ledger. NLS Dep. 341/275/2–4, 341/415/33.

dictator in a small way, and should dread of all things having to undergo even such discussions with a person I respect so much as your brother as have taken place between you and him occasionally.

Also, his was a small business, not large enough for two partners. If he were to join in a partnership with W. & R. Chambers, his operations would end up being simply a branch of theirs for 'all new projects would of course emanate from head quarters.'[25]

By early 1852 the Edinburgh office proposed that a new agreement between Chambers and Orr should be drawn up on the grounds that, since all literary labour costs were borne by the Edinburgh edition of the *Journal*, the London edition should pay more for the privilege of the *Journal* profits it derived. In June of 1852 William Chambers wrote to Orr that:

It seems surprising how at this late period we should make the discovery that we had hitherto gone upon an erroneous calculation. The explanation is, that, at the outset of the Journal, there was little or no paid literary labour, and that we reckoned our own services as nothing. Even at the change of arrangements in 1844 we did not go into this with proper care, and allowed the practice to go on of charging all the outlays for literary labour on the Scottish issue, merely looking at your issue as one of paper and print, with an inadequate sum in lieu of licence.[26]

Orr agreed that the English edition should bear more of the expenses; he would pay £3.5s.0d. for the *Journal* plates or £3.12s. subject to the ten per cent discount.[27] These terms were not agreeable to Edinburgh. Robert, writing on 13 July 1852, indicated that while they were disposed to continue their arrangement with Orr, they would need to be paid more. According to their calculations, he was making a profit of £1900 from the *Journal* while theirs was £894. They asked for £500 more per month.[28]

By April of 1853, they felt themselves almost driven to setting up a branch in London. In working papers they listed four reasons:

1. Two thirds of all our business passed through Mr Orr's hands. 2. The reasons of increase in England, not in Scotland. 3. If we go on publishing new and heavy undertakings, the addition to the agency in London will be enormous, and 4. ...we experience considerable difficulty in keeping Mr Orr to his payment schedule.

From 1 January 1852 to 27 January 1853, he failed to make his weekly and monthly payments on time 35 times. An additional concern, not spelled out in this memorandum of William's, was written out in a draft version of Robert's:

25 WSO to W & RC, 5 January 1852, NLS Dep. 341/319.
26 WC to WSO, 29 June 1852, NLS Dep. 341/319.
27 WSO to W & RC, 9 July 1852, NLS Dep. 341/319.
28 Draft letter RC to WSO, 13 July 1852, NLS Dep. 341/319.

'A crisis seems now to have arrived in our business as editors and publishers of popular literary works, there being now more competition than formerly, and consequently greater difficulty in maintaining our ground.'[29]

Along with these disadvantages the papers acknowledged the advantages of having Orr as their London agent. Because he handled numerous businesses he had a good knowledge of the technical and practical aspects of English booksellers. Second, there was an advantage to having a person between the trade and a publisher. Third, another advantage was that his business was not limited to Chambers's publications. Because trade was not favourable to cheap literature at the time, accounts and parcels limited to it were not large enough by themselves. Finally, small amounts were difficult to collect and there was a great risk of bad debts from ignorance of the individuals involved in the trade.[30]

These proposals took a much different turn later in 1853. Because of ill health, William Chambers decided to withdraw from active involvement in the firm, sell his shares to Robert, and retire to Peeblesshire as a country landowner. Without both brothers active in the firm, having a separate Chambers business in London would not be feasible. Thus Orr was to have a first chance at having it, if he did not take on projects or publications which would compete with theirs and if he maintained a sufficient capital to liquidate his obligations to them without difficulty.[31] But Orr was incorrigible. By May, Robert wrote to him saying that they had decided to revoke their proposal for his continuing as their agent in London. They had hoped that he would be more regular in making financial settlements with them and that he would devote his energies to their concerns.

We have now, however, to say that our hopes on these points have been clouded on finding reason to conclude that you are now to be engaged more extensively than ever in speculations calculated to engross time, energy, and capital, and also that some of these speculations are of the same nature with our own. We refer to your concern with the Home Companion, and your announced design of bringing out a new edition of Penny Cyclopedia. We attach particular consequence to the latter speculation, as coming into direct collision with our intended publication of a translation of the German Conversations Lexicon–a very large venture about which we are extremely anxious.[32]

Just a month later, on 17 June 1853, the Rubicon was crossed. The financial reality was that as of 30 April 1853, Orr owed W. & R. Chambers £10,929.18s.3d. By the end of June, that sum, plus goods received from W. &

29 Draft memorandum, [February] 1853, NLS Dep. 341/320.
30 Draft memorandum, [February] 1853, NLS Dep. 341/320.
31 Draft letter RC to WSO, April 1853, NLS Dep. 341/320.
32 RC to WSO, May 1853, NLS Dep. 341/320.

R. Chambers amounted to £14,346.14s.0d.[33] A memorandum of 20 June 1853 by William Chambers noted that the firm had bills from Orr to the amount of £6000 and an open account of £14,000. 'Discounting returns the open account will probably £10,000. Now if this sum is kept up, it will put us by and bye to a serious inconvenience, while all the time he may be using the money to our disadvantage.'[34] At the time when half-yearly accounts were to be paid, they had received only £2800 from Orr. A letter was written to W. S. Orr announcing that they had come to the 'painful resolution of withdrawing the agency of the Journal and other publications.' W. & R. Chambers would then open an establishment of their own, probably in July or August, 'our wish in this respect being to avoid all appearance of abruptness, and to put you to as little inconvenience as possible.'[35]

It took another month of letters and conversations before matters were settled. On Orr's part, there was always the claim that he had performed great service for them, a service he thought he was entitled to continue for his lifetime. On the Chambers's part, more and more evidence was provided regarding the extent to which the English edition was prospering over the Scottish and the problems of increasing competition.

From the first to last, your concern in London can hardly have realised less from our publications than from forty to fifty thousand pounds – a fortune in itself – independently of all other advantages. In 1852, it appeared that for the preceding [sic] years you had been profiting from the English sale of the Journal to the extent of 1900£ a year even taking its circulation at the lowest amount, while our remuneration had been at the rate of 391£ per annum. [...] In a word, you, in the period alluded to, realised between eleven and twelve thousand pounds, and weekly about 2300£. Even on the whole sales of the work (English & Scotch) your gains during those six years exceeded ours by 600£ a year.

Also of concern were the competitors, two of which Orr supported.

[We] assure you that nothing could have induced us to take the present step, with all its inconveniences, but the consciousness that, unless we vigorously interposed, the circulation of the Journal would inevitably dwindle into insignificance in the face of its many new competitors – some of them issued from your own establishment, and to which the poor Journal has been made as vehicle of publicity; one of them indeed, (The Leisure Hour) which we see in your invoices, being a publication which has been avowedly put forward by the Tract Society as an engine to destroy and rout out such papers as ours, while another, the Home Companion, belongs in the class which, from

---

33 WC memorandum, NLS Dep. 341/320.
34 NLS, Dep. 341/320.
35 W & RC to WSO, 17 June 1853, NLS Dep. 341/320.

comparative size and price, is by your own acknowledgement the most formidable that we have to contend with.[36]

Settling affairs after the dissolution was time-consuming and costly. The lawyers' ledgers go from 1852 up to March 1855. In attempting to cut their losses W. & R. Chambers took back all of their stock which Orr had on hand. In addition, they acquired from the printers Tyler and Manning, who were holding them as collateral, stereotype plates of several works which Orr intended to publish – the *Cabinet Shakespeare*, the *Pictorial History of England*, the *History of the Peace*, valued at £2500, the *Pictorial Bible*, valued at £1500, the *Pictorial Family Bible*, valued at £1000, and the *Penny Cyclopaedia*. W. & R. Chambers were to be the sole publishers of these works, to publish the works until completed, to revise them, and to have right of exclusive publication until the series of each was complete. In reality, when finally published these works brought nothing near their assessed value. By 1868 a profit of only £889 had been realized on the *Pictorial Bible*. Even after selling 5,360 copies of the *Family Bible* and selling the stock, copyright, and plates, the firm was still £645 in the red; and the *Pictorial History of England*, after 3584 copies were sold, as well as plates, stock, etc., was a £449.23s.0d loss. The *Penny Cyclopaedia*, which was the really valuable property, never made a penny. Charles Knight had not given Orr the rights to revise it – merely to reprint and correct errors. So the plates were shipped back to Tyler and Manning.[37] And finally, W. S. Orr gave the Chamberses a promissory note for the balance of his debt.[38] Robert Chambers's private diary notes that when everything balanced out, Orr was indebted to them for £3930.17s.2d.[39]

Despite the rosy projection from his lawyer that dividends would soon be forthcoming, Orr was not able to remain solvent much longer. In 1857, a year which saw sixty-three firms collapse, including the Western Bank of Glasgow, W. S. Orr in London and W. S. Orr & Co. of Liverpool went under because of having very heavy liabilities. Orr's situation at this point was reported by David Chambers, then the firm's London agent, in a letter to his nephew, Robert Chambers II:

I met Mr. Spalding of Drury Lane – and he informed me of Mr. Orr having suspended payment last week – this is number 2. A sheriff officer is in possession of his house – and he is dressed in the Footman's livery, as a ruse – and poor Mrs. Orr – thinks they are getting on so well to be enabled to keep two footmen isn't this a good joke. He has got three weeks to obtain security for a dividend to his Creditors – and if he is not

36 W & RC to WSO, 12 July 1853, NLS Dep. 341/320.
37 All the documents regarding these negotiations are in NLS, Dep. 341/321.
38 Papers regarding the Orr execution are in NLS Dep. 341/464.
39 This diary is in the possession of A. S. Chambers, Edinburgh.

successful – he will be turned out to be the streets – as the inspectors are determined to give him no question.[40]

This is not Orr's last appearance in Chambers's correspondence. In late 1864 he was working at their London office, preparing the Index for Thomas Milner's *Gallery of Geography*. William Somerville Orr died on 5 January 1873 at which time he was working for Chapman and Hall.[41]

Despite all the serious consequences W. & R. Chambers experienced during their association with Orr, there were undeniable advantages to it. He was the firm's primary presence in England, both in London and Liverpool. He was responsible, through advertising in newspapers and other periodicals and through hiring travellers, for distribution of Chambers's publications throughout England. As the Chamberses acknowledged in 1852 two-thirds of their business went through his hands. Moreover, he was something of a talent agent for them. Aspiring writers – Daniel Macmillan was one – would stop at Orr's office with manuscripts to be sent to Edinburgh. He introduced them to W. H. Wills, who helped edit the *Journal* and who would become their brother-in-law. Finally, he had a finger on the pulse of the British writing and reading publics, although his suggestions and advice were rarely heeded. For example, even in 1852 when relations between Orr and Chambers were undergoing great strain, he was analysing the scene for them. In once again trying to excuse the Bradbury and Evans affair, he claimed that without their connection with the *Journal* they would certainly have taken a part in the 'Cheap Literature' movement.

But in point of fact "The Household Words" is not the rival we have to fear. The real opposition which affects us is the mass of Penny Publications giving nearly half as much again as the Journal gives, some of them with costly illustrations, and otherwise well conducted. Some of them sell [word unclear] 220, & 230,000 weekly. A remedy for this I dare not propound, for to compete with them, you must surpass them, and it takes 100,000 copies to pay first expences. But in them, I assure you and not in Household Words selling at 2d. and circulating 35000, that we have to look for formidable rivalry.[42]

Was W. & R. Chambers responsible for W. S. Orr's bankruptcy? The weekly *Journal* income and the value which stock-in-hand gave him when he asked for credit were gone. But Orr had long engaged in poor business practices as these stories and letters have made clear. In the final estimation, he was a bad businessman. Why did the Chamberses continue to be associated with Orr for so long? I can only guess. They actually were friends. The Chambers's correspondence regularly refers to their kind feelings for him and

---

40 David N. Chambers to RC, Jr., 13 July 1857, NLS Dep. 341/324.

41 *Publisher's Circular*, 1 February 1873, p. 72.

42 WSO to WRC, 3 January 1845, NLS Dep. 341/314.

their friendship with him. Robert Chambers's son, Robert, had stayed with the Orr family. William Chambers's book *Fiddy*, printed by Orr for the Exhibition of 1851, refers warmly to Orr's children. Notwithstanding their friendship, whatever its degree and extent, the Chamberses had good reason to want out of their association with Orr. As William further comments in the *Memoir:*

About 1852, matters became critical. It was as clear as could be, that we were to incur a heavy loss. In nothing in his whole life did my brother manifest more vigour of character than in determining to get rid, at all hazards, of this source of disquietude. He thought of Scott and the Ballantynes, and how, by an extreme and misplaced confidence, arising from kindness of heart, a man may be irretrievably ruined. Without further periphrasis: taking all risks, we withdraw our agency in 1853, and established a branch business in London under charge of our youngest brother, David, on whose fidelity we thought we might rely.[43]

---

43 *Memoir of William and Robert Chambers*, p. 318.

William Dicey and the Networks and Places of Print Culture

GILES BERGEL

THE PRESSES OF WILLIAM DICEY are represented in several studies of the eighteenth-century book trade. The business is known to historians of newspapers for the *Northampton Mercury*, begun in Northampton in 1720; to scholars of ballads for supplying Thomas Percy with broadsides; to historians of chapbooks for the collection owned by James Boswell; and to art historians for the cheap prints in both copperplate and woodcut produced in Northampton and from presses in Aldermary and Bow Churchyards in London. Products such as Bateman's Pectoral Drops and Daffy's Cordial, which were produced, packaged and distributed from the firm's premises in Bow Churchyard in London and further distributed from Northampton, are prominent in the history of patent medicines. The firm is noted within literary history for its connections with Edward Cave and Samuel Richardson and for publishing a pamphlet by Daniel Defoe.[1]

---

1 For the *Northampton Mercury*, see Diana Dixon, 'Northamptonshire Newspapers, 1720–1900', in *Images and Texts: Their Production and Distribution in the 18th and 19th Centuries*, ed. by Peter Isaac and Barry McKay (Winchester, 1997), pp. 1–10; W. W. Hadley, *The Bicentenary Record of the Northampton Mercury* (Northampton, 1920) and 'The Northampton Mercury 1720 – ', *Mercury Extras*, 10 (1901). On Dicey ballad publishing, see Dianne Dugaw, 'The Popular Marketing of "Old Ballads": The Ballad Revival and Eighteenth Century Antiquarianism Reconsidered', *Eighteenth-Century Studies*, 21:1 (1987), pp. 71–90. On chapbooks, see Victor E. Neuburg, 'The Diceys and the Chapbook Trade', *The Library*, Fifth Series, 24:3 (1969), pp. 219–31. On prints, see Sheila O'Connell, *The Popular Print in England* (London, 1999). On patent medicines, see Juanita Burnby, 'A Note Concerning "Dr." Bateman and his Drops', *Pharmaceutical Historian*, 16 (1986), pp. 7–8 and 'Printers' Ink and Patent Medicines: The Story of the Diceys', *The Pharmaceutical Journal*, 229 (August 14, 1982), pp. 162–3, 169. For relations between Dicey and Edward Cave, see n. 10 and n. 14, below; the connection with Samuel Richardson is the apprenticing of William Dicey's son, Timothy, to Richardson; and the pamphlet attributed to Daniel Defoe is *The Evident Advantages to Great Britain and its Allies from the Approaching War: Especially in Matters of Trade* (Northampton: printed by William Dicey, and sold by the men that carry the news, 1727). See also Ian Jackson, 'The Geographies of Promotion: A Survey of Advertising in Two Eighteenth-Century English Newspapers', in *Printing Places: Locations of Book*

The fact that no individual press can be representative of the whole of the British book trade requires acknowledgment: the Dicey Press's breadth of publication and distribution does not so much typify the eighteenth-century trade's common features as mark some of its farther possibilities. Two models of book-trade history may help place the Dicey Press in relation to the trade as a whole; these can be introduced by referring to two titles from the series of papers to which the present essay is a contribution. The first model is that of charting 'the reach of print', the second, the collective inquiry into 'print networks'.[2] The first model, proposing that print is localized and therefore has limits, employs static geographical categories, typically such as 'province', 'region' and 'nation', which describe where the press is located and the extent of its market and sphere of influence. Print networks, contrastingly, are more suggestive of dynamic connections between the press and its variously located and often mobile suppliers and customers. The two models, jointly, describe the whole of the book trade's inputs and outputs.

The Dicey Press is generally considered to have been primarily localized at Northampton; however this location (adopted by William Dicey in 1720 in partnership with Robert Raikes) was preceded by a joint venture in St Ives in Huntingdonshire from 1719, and succeeded by another in Gloucester from 1720 until 1725. To these provincial localizations can be added a history of operations in the capital – in addition to the usual trade relations of subsidiary publishing and distribution on behalf of the London trade, there were two important presses owned by the business in London itself. From 1736 William Dicey's son Cluer managed a press in Bow Churchyard which had been acquired through the marriage of Elizabeth Dicey and John Cluer, after whom Cluer Dicey was named. Bow Churchyard produced patent medicines, rolling-press work (such as pictures and music from plates engraved by George Bickham) and cheap print in the formats collected by Thomas Percy in 1762 and James Boswell in 1763. A second press in London, at Aldermary Churchyard, was in operation from around 1760; from here John Marshall, the son of Cluer Dicey's partner Richard Marshall, produced the first of Hannah More's *Cheap Repository Tracts*.[3]

Production & Distribution Since 1500, ed. by John Hinks and Catherine Armstrong (Delaware and London: 2005), pp. 65–80.

2   *The Reach of Print: Making, Selling, and Using Books*, edited by Peter Isaac and Barry McKay (Winchester, 1998) is itself one of the series 'Print Networks'.

3   Information on the Diceys, their partners and presses can be found in the *Dictionary of National Biography* entry on 'The Dicey Family' by Timothy Clayton; Ian Jackson, 'Print in Provincial England: Reading and Northampton, 1720–1800' (unpublished doctoral thesis, Oxford University, 2003); and R. S. Thomson, 'The Development of the Broadside Ballad Trade and its Influence upon the Transmission of English Ballads' (unpublished doctoral

William Dicey's series of presses and partnerships was, then, both metropolitan and provincial. Clearly, metropolitan and provincial are relative terms; to question their relative fixity is to highlight the overall category to which they belong – that of the nation. An archaic model of book trade history fixated on London has been repeatedly raised and challenged by recent studies; the eighteenth century has been identified as the take-off point for an increasingly important history of provincial publishing, following the expiration of the Licensing Act in 1695.[4] The formation of the modern British state and its rise to prominence has also been the subject of much attention, of which the provincial press has been a rich source of evidence. News in print of foreign affairs, it has been argued, played an important part in building local interest in the nation's interests abroad.[5] The *Northampton Mercury* has been described as a local paper 'only in name'; this is an exaggeration, but certainly the overwhelming majority of its space in its first thirty years were devoted to the staple content of the eighteenth-century provincial press, which was news from abroad.[6] The preponderance of foreign news in the provincial newspaper should be seen as central to its appeal. The local newspaper, at least editorially, aspired to be a global newspaper. The placing of foreign news in the hands of provincial readers expanded outwards the rhetorical reach of print, beyond that of the area within which it was physically distributed, up to the edges of the territories in which Britain competed with other powers. Northampton, in the present instance, was localized as the centre of a sphere of news-gathering and reporting that broke local and national boundaries.[7]

Within this imaginative sphere there remained a material, political and economic sphere, a sphere of transaction and social relation. Within the transactional sphere and assisted by print, Dicey's patent medicines were particularly mobile, reaching the extremities of Great Britain and beyond. Bateman's Pectoral Drops were sold in North America accompanied by a local reprint of

---

thesis, University of Cambridge, 1974). For Hannah More's relations with the Aldermary Churchyard Press, see Anne Stott, *Hannah More: The First Victorian* (Oxford, 2003).

4   See John Feather, *The Provincial Book Trade in Eighteenth-Century England* (Cambridge, 1985) and Terry Belanger, 'Publishers and Writers in Eighteenth-Century England', in *Books and their Readers in Eighteenth-Century England*, ed. by Isabel Rivers (Leicester, 1982).

5   See Kathleen Wilson, *The Sense of the People: Politics, Culture and Imperialism in England, 1715–1785* (Cambridge, 1995); Linda Colley, *Britons: Forging the Nation, 1707–1837* (New Haven, CT, 1992).

6   Hadley, *The Bi-centenary Record*, p. 2.

7   See Karl W. Schweizer 'Foreign Policy and the Eighteenth-Century English Press: The case of Israel Mauduit's "Considerations of the Present German War"', *Publishing History*, 39 (1996), 45–53.

the book of testimonies.[8] In 1759, Cluer Dicey and company placed advertisements in the *Caledonian Mercury* revealing that they had won a case against counterfeiters of both Bateman's Pectoral Drops and an accompanying book of testimonials.[9] Provincial printer-apothecaries such as the Diceys, the Newberys in Reading and Benjamin Collins in Salisbury may in fact have been most profitable as dealers in drugs using the press and its networks as a platform for the packaging, marketing and distribution of these lucrative products.[10] The medicines' reach was subsequently an advertisement of the press network's potential as a general trading network through which other goods might be advertised, ordered and distributed.

Print's ability to cross boundaries argues for the importance of networks and point-to-point connections between the press and its suppliers, customers and partners in determining the overall shape of the book trade. Northampton's advantageous position on the roads to Sheffield, Manchester, Liverpool and further north, and on cross-country roads was the most tangible form of that network that the press celebrated.[11] However, the tendency of the press to exaggerate both its sense of localization and the extent of its reach and connectedness can be seen in an editorial in the *Northampton Mercury*:

If it is to be asked, How it comes to Pass that Dicey is so much more expeditious than any others of his Brethren? The plain and true Answer is this, That the extensive Circulation and great Demand for his Paper (not to mention his being within 6 Hours Reach of the Metropolis) has made it worth his while to be at very extraordinary Expences, one of which is his having no less than 4 Horses stationed on the Road every

---

8 William H. Helfand, *Quack, Quack, Quack* (New York, 2002), pp. 11–12. The printing history of the testimonial *Account* also shows the Diceys' connections to an important London printer – *The Bowyer Ledgers*, ed. by Keith Maslen and John Lancaster (London, New York, 1991) contain a ledger entry (3446 9 January 1748), for the printing of an 'Account of Bateman's drops'.

9 See Hamish Mathison, 'Tropes of Promotion: Advertisement and the Eighteenth-Century Scottish Periodical Press', in *News, Newspapers, and Society in Early Modern Britain*, ed. by Joad Raymond (London, 1999), 206–25, pp. 210–11. The patent for the remedy was prominently published by Raike's and Dicey's original partner, Benjamin Okell, *An Abstract of the Patent Granted by His Majesty King George to Benj. Okell, the Inventor of a Medicine, Call'd, Dr. Bateman's Pectoral Drops, and to J. Cluer, R. Raikes and W. Dicey, the Persons Concerned with the said Inventor, that They May Enjoy the Sole Benefit of the said Medicine* (London: Printed by J. Cluer in Bow Church-Yard, 1726) and reprinted in 1730.

10 For both the Diceys and Newberys see Ian Jackson, 'The Geographies of Promotion'; for Collins, see C. Y. Ferdinand, *Benjamin Collins and the Provincial Newspaper trade in the Eighteenth Century* (Oxford, 1997).

11 See 'L', The Early History of an Old Provincial Paper', *Antiquary*, 37 (1901), 84–8.

Saturday) for the quick Reception of News; for the extraordinary Dispatch in Printing it; and for the speedy Conveyance of it through so many different Counties.[12]

The relays of dispatch riders between London and Northampton and outwards from Northampton in a sequence of timed hand-overs shows a high degree of organization, perhaps arguing that the distance between the metropolis and the province was there to be closed and exploited, rather than to be asserted. However, simply to replace the distance between the two localities with a mechanism of connection risks taking the press's own account at face value. In the above example, the infrastructure of news-gathering and distribution is as much of a promotional tool, belonging to the editorial side of the operation, as well as a functional element on the production side. Some scepticism is therefore merited; this scepticism might take note of something of which the heroes and readers of eighteenth-century picaresque novels such as Henry Fielding's *Joseph Andrews* and *Tom Jones* are comically aware: that much else can happen on a road other than the predictable transit of people and goods.

Caution towards topological models of print argues, then, for the integration of the history of the book trade's connectedness with the larger histories of communication – the history of the post office, or of the turnpikes, canals and other highways and byways, each with their own constellation of governing public and private privileges, customs and discontents. The widespread practice of Members of Parliament distributing franked copies of newspapers in this period is a further demonstration of how communication networks enabled and channelled forms of political contest.[13] The dots and hairline threads of a topological history of the press are thus visible within and underpinned by other specialisms within legal, institutional and social history.[14]

Investigating the *Northampton Mercury*'s editorial claim also requires a level of analysis based on the opposite of scepticism, taking the claim on trust, which is to imagine the allure of connectedness to the press's users. Rapid retrieval of time-sensitive court, parliamentary, foreign and commercial news from London was an advertised strength of the *Northampton Mercury*. London was here acknowledged as the leading broker of such information, although its

---

12 *The Northampton Mercury*, 19 March 1759.

13 See G. A. Cranfield, *The Development of the Provincial Newspaper, 1700–1760* (Oxford, 1962), pp. 179–80.

14 See, for instance, Jeremy Greenwood, *Newspapers and the Post Office 1635–1834* (Reigate, 1971); Greg Laugero, 'Infrastructures of Enlightenment: Road-Making, The Public Sphere, and the Emergence of Literature', *Eighteenth-Century Studies*, 29:1 (1995), 45–67; and Nicolas Barker, "The Rise of the Provincial Book Trade in England and the Growth of a National Transport System", in *L'Europe et le Livre*, ed. by Frédéric Barbier, Sabine Juratic and Dominique Varry (Editions Klincksieck 1996), pp. 137–55.

appeal to provincial readers would depend on their degree of interestedness. In theory, the London news was dispatched to Northampton along the advertised route; the diffusion outwards of the finished goods of the *Northampton Mercury* through its own chain of agents and newsmen posited Northampton as a subsidiary relay of a metropolitan network. The boast of connectedness to the London information market, through the newspaper's private channels, provided a fixity of relation and a corrective distance, as well as a convenient proximity. The provincial newspaper claimed to compile London newspapers, newsletters and other sources into a more concise and locally nuanced form. This is evident in the newspaper's listing of its newspaper sources at the head of each issue; during 1745 running to fourteen titles, including the ministerial *London Journal,* since 1721, the historically-oppositional *Craftsman,* and official, authoritative in the literal sense *London Gazette* (subtitled 'printed by Authority').

Diverse attributions characterized the London newspaper market as a disorientating babble of competing voices. The provincial newspaper orchestrated and excerpted these voices in layered, mutually-supportive or contrasting patterns, often accompanied by editorial asides. The printer-owned and managed provincial newspaper was under commercial pressure to publicize itself as an active trader or mediator of information as well as being a disinterested agent or distributor. Its London counterparts could draw upon face-to-face networks to form profit- and risk-sharing cartels along the lines of the 'conger' model of copyright ownership.[15] Circumspection towards London sources, as well as being an expression of local loyalty, was thus directed towards maintaining the newspaper's position of being connected to London, while maintaining a local agency. Physical distance was moralized as critical distance.

In a networked sense, it was the newspaper's avowed *delocalization* of a mobility that happened to be centred around Northampton and connected to London and elsewhere, that was its most important characteristic. This mobility was advertised by the paper's title, as by the other *Mercuries, Couriers* and *Post-Boys* of the period; the *Mercury's* motto was *mobilitate viget* ('it flourishes by movement') or circulation, held aloft, to emphasize the point, on its front page by an angel resting on a cloud (Fig. 1).

The word *circulation* remains emblematic of the space through which print moves; a thoroughgoing image of circulation overcoming distance and boundary can be seen in the body of presswork relating to the 1743 foundation of the Northampton Infirmary, which includes printed sermons, statutes, accounts,

---

15   See Michael Harris, *London Newspapers in the Age of Walpole* (Rutherford, 1987).

VOL. I.   NUMB. I.

Northampton *Mercury,*

OR THE

MONDAY's POST.

BEING A

Collection of the most Material Occurrences,

Foreign & Domestick.

Together with

An Account of Trade.

MONDAY, May 2, 1720. ⌊ *To be continued weekly.* ⌋

NORTHAMPTON:

Printed by *R. Railes* and *W. Dicey,* near *All Saints Church* ; where
Advertisements and Letters of Correspondents are taken in, and all
manner of Books printed.

Fig. 1. The first edition of the *Northampton Mercury* (British Library)

newspaper reports and broadsides.[16] The printed subscription lists of the charity describe contributions from the Northamptonshire network of Anglican parishes that were remitted towards the network's hub and the charity's headquarters in Northampton.

Parish	By whom collected	£	s.	d.
Everton	Rev. Mr. Peter Layng	–	4	6
Barnwell	Rev. Mr. Braughton	–	13	7
Whilton	Rev. Mr. Spateman	–	10	11
Hinton	Rev. Dr. Grey	1	7	4
Dallington	Rev. Mr. Pasham	1	7	0
Floore	Rev. Mr. Warren	2	17	6
Gretworth	Rev. Mr. Winstanly	–	7	0
Harpole	Rev. Mr. Beet	2	3	9
Kingsthorpe	Rev. Mr. Patterson	1	10	8

Table 1. Contributions to the Northampton Infirmary by parish (1745)

Through this network, patients certified by local authority as being 'of the deserving poor' according to printed specifications would receive papers printed by the Dicey Press and would travel to Northampton for relief. This network, based on existing parish structures, somewhat resembles the hierarchical chain of agents and newsmen of the press itself, elsewhere used to distribute print for the Infirmary. There are, however, some limitations to these tables as markers of the circulation of print and its social grounding. Firstly, they do not include Dissenters, whose support for this and other infirmaries was fundamental.[17] Secondly, the distribution in print of appeals for support for the Infirmary was not confined to the vicinity. Another set of published

---

16 See F. F. Waddy *A History of Northampton General Hospital, 1743–1948* (Northampton, 1974).

17 At Northampton, the involvement of Philip Doddridge was vital; the extent of Doddridge's personal networks, which included nobility, royalty and clergy from across the denominations, can be seen particularly in his preaching and correspondence; see Alan Everitt, 'Springs of Sensibility: Philip Doddridge of Northampton and the Evangelical Tradition', in *Landscape and Community in England* (London, 1985), pp. 201–45; Malcolm Deacon, *Philip Doddridge of Northampton* (Northampton, 1980); and G. F. Nuttall, *Calendar of the Correspondence of Philip Doddridge DD* (London, 1979).

tables demonstrates this, containing as it does records of benefactions from Northamptonshire and from further afield:[18]

(Those who have increas'd their Subscriptions are distinguish'd by Italicks. Those marked with a Star, are the Twelve chosen, for the ensuing Year, (according to the tenth Statute) Members of the Standing Committee.)

Two Guineas

A

1743 John Ashley, Esq.; Ledgers-Abby
1743 * Mr. *William Atkins*, Northampton

B

1743 J. Blencowe, Esq; Marston St. Lawrence
1743 Rev. Mr. Baron, Pattishall
1744 Rev. Dr. Brown, Archdeacon of Northampton, and Master of University College, Oxon

1745 Robert Basket, Esq; Delapree

C

1743 Nathaniel Castleton, Esq; Pitchley
1743 Miss Cartwright, Aynho
1743 Rev. Dr. Crane, Hardingstone
1743 Rev. Mr. Cumberland, Stanwick
1746 George Cunningham, Esq; Northampton

D

1743 Sir John Dryden, Bart; Cannons-Abbey
1743 Mrs. Elizabeth Dolben, Thingdon
1743 Mr. William Dicey, Northampton
1744 Colonel Dejeant
1744 Lady D'Anvers, Culworth
1744 Sir Henry D'Anvers, Ditto

Table 2. Individual contributions to the Northampton Infirmary, including William Dicey (1745)

The Northampton Infirmary scheme was publicized in other newspapers, and in the *Gentleman's Magazine*, whose founder Edward Cave owned property in Northampton, was known to William Dicey through the town's Philosophical Society and was named as an agent or co-subscriber on several publishers'

---

18 *A List of the Annual Subscribers to the County Infirmary at Northampton, Established by a General and Very Great Meeting of the Nobility, Gentry and Clergy, on Sept. 20, 1743.*

imprints, as well as being a subscriber to the Infirmary.[19] If network theory is a game of 'six degrees of separation', the Cave-Dicey relation alone consists of at least four orders of connectedness. The networks of print were thus inter-penetrated by a number of other networks that intersected the Dicey network at many angles. These were made up of personal relationships, sometimes publicized in the *Northampton Mercury*, and including written correspondence and face-to-face contact; networks based on religious denomination; textual communities formed by the copying of sermons, from print and in shorthand and back to print; elite and mercantile networks, both glorified and goaded in the Infirmary sermons, based on inheritance and kinship, political faction or civic ambition. At the limits of these networks, the press rhetorically imagined a widening set of spaces: local and national political milieux, commercial and civic spheres overreached by space created by the proverbially boundless forces of charity and sympathy.[20]

The press, therefore, employed both the rhetoric of localization and of connectedness; as can be seen in several examples:

The Benefits of County Hospitals being universally Acknowledged, by the Estab-lishment of them at Winchester, Bath, Bristol, York, and Exeter, a Paper, containing the principal Reasons in their Favour, has been put into the Hands of several Gentlemen in this Town and County, and is very well received. It is entitled, Considerations offer'd to the Nobility, Gentry, Clergy, and all who have any Property in the County, with regard to the Establishment of a County Hospital at Northampton; and may be had gratis of the Printer hereof, and of the men that carry this News.[21]

In December of 1743 *The Northampton Mercury* printed a letter from 'Philanthropos', praising the nascent Northampton scheme and proposing one for Warwick and Coventry: 'The Noble Example set us in several Counties, and particularly in the Neighbouring One of Northampton, should stir US up to EMULATION.'[22]

Here, the press sets up locally-directed appeals within a larger and larger imagined community; the model of which is first implemented at the level of

---

19 C. L. Carlson, *The First Magazine. A History of the Gentleman's Magazine: with an Account of Dr. Johnson's Editorial Activity and of the Notice Given America in the Magazine* (Providence, RI, 1938).

20 On mid-eighteenth-century charity, see Donna T. Andrew, 'On Reading Charity Ser-mons: Eighteenth-Century Anglican Solicitation and Exhortation', *The Journal of Ecclesiastical History*, 43:1 (1992), 581–91; Rita Goldberg, 'Charity Sermons and the Poor: A Rhetoric of Compassion', *The Age of Johnson*, 4 (1991), 171–216; and Roy Porter, 'The Gift Relation: Philanthropy and Provincial Hospitals in Eighteenth-Century England', in *The Hospital in History*, ed. by Lindsay Granshaw and Roy Porter (London, 1989), pp. 149–78.

21 *The Northampton Mercury*, 18 July 1743.

22 *The Northampton Mercury*, 5 December 1743.

the parish and scaled up to that of the county. The following promotional statement seeks to show the possible development of these apparatuses on an even larger scale:

It is probable, that neighbouring Counties may quickly learn to imitate our Example, when they see in Fact it is no impracticable Design [...] Thus the remotest Regions of our Land may have Reason on this Account to call us Blessed.[23]

Comparison and competition between other county towns is directed both downwards and upwards, aiming both to secure consent from the parishes, also tabulated in comparison to each other and as members of the county, and a standing for Northamptonshire within a national patchwork of loyal and equal provinces. Local social networks are greatly enhanced as corresponding parts of a national network of charitable interest, publicized and connected through print.

The appeal, then, circulated outwards from the town's printing-office across the county and nation, through the networks of print to connect diverse communities. It was given imaginative substance by Charlotte Brereton in a poem distributed as a broadside and more widely distributed through reproduction in the *Northampton Mercury* and in the *Gentleman's Magazine.*[24] The poet employs a supernatural metaphor of circulation over-reaching distance through the personification of Charity as a goddess or muse:

> Mild Charity – blest Blessing of the Blest,
> Came down to Earth – a bright Celestial Guest;
> And as o'er Savage Lands she bent her Way,
> Regions that never felt her healing Ray!

The progress of Charity is traced across Europe; on arriving in Britain she finds it the most congenial:

> Here, could your Natives know my Value well,
> Here most delighted could I choose to dwell;

---

23 Philip Doddridge, *Compassion to the Sick recommended and urged, in a Sermon Preached at Northampton, September 4, 1743. In Favour of a Design then opening to erect a County Infirmary there for the Relief of the Poor Sick and Lame.* Published at the Request of several who heard it. By P. Doddridge, D.D. (London: Printed for M. Fenner, at the Turk's Head in Gracechurch-street; and W. Dicey, at Northampton. 1743), Price Six-pence.

24 *The Northampton Mercury,* 15 August 1743 and in *Gentleman's Magazine,* vol. 13, p. 377; Anthony Barker reveals that the poem was written at the request of Edward Cave – Anthony D. Barker, 'Poetry from the Provinces: Amateur Poets in the *Gentleman's Magazine* in the 1730s and 1740s', in *Tradition in Transition. Women Writers, Marginal Texts, and the Eighteenth-Century Canon,* ed. by Alvaro Ribeiro and James G. Basker (Oxford, 1996), pp. 241–58.

Charity visits in turn Winchester, Exeter, Bath, Bristol, York and Edinburgh; a footnote refers to texts printed in support of infirmaries in these towns. The goddess surveys Northampton and asks whether it alone will not be receptive:

> No, Britain's Peers who bless this Mercian Plain,
> The Lovely Goddess duteous shall sustain;
> For Generous MONTAGU the Goddess loves,
> She smiles in GRAFTON'S Breast – and HORTON'S Groves;
> To these (if these befriend her Just Design)
> Shall other Noble Names consenting join;
> NORTHAMPTON'S Self the Pleasing Task shall claim,
> To fix her in the Town that bears his Name;
> And Titl'd Pow'r its Noblest Use shall find,
> The Joy to bless and to relieve Mankind.

A footnote reveals that Northamptonshire 'abounds with the Nobility and Gentry' and gives the names of sixty-four (including those named in the poem), in order of precedence from dukes to 'antient families'. Some had already assented to the scheme, but few had done so in public: the next week's *Mercury* reports that Sir Edmund Isham, MP, had contributed

And we have great Reason to believe his Grace the Duke of Montagu, on his Return from Bath, and the Right Hon, the Earl of Northampton from Sussex, will honour us with their Favours. The Encouragement given by the High-Sheriff and Grand Jury (whose Example was followed by several Gentlemen, Clergy, Tradesmen, etc.) is known through the whole County.[25]

The progress of Charity from the celestial to the terrestrial sphere took an increasingly localized focus, from a vantage point above the continent of Europe, down to the nation, the county, parishes and to the houses of the powerful. Charity's sense of space is visualized as a hierarchy of nested localities, resting on top of an operative framework of print and social networks: a spectacular rhetorical extension of the reach of print that ultimately connected heaven and earth.

A history of print and place, then, during the explosive growth period of the early eighteenth century, might argue that the press's developing posture of disinterest and instrumentality tended to subsume and exploit factional

---

25 *The Northampton Mercury*, 23 August 1743. Amanda Berry reveals that the Northampton infirmary scheme commanded a very high degree of elite subscription or patronage – 'Of the twenty-four noblemen and gentlemen who had seats in the neighbourhood in the late eighteenth-century, twenty-two were listed as subscribers to Northampton's infirmary, as were two-thirds of the gentry resident in Northampton itself' – Amanda Berry, *Patronage, Funding and the Hospital Patient c.1750–1815: Three English Regional Case Studies* (unpublished doctoral thesis, University of Oxford), p. 44.

loyalties, except where that posture was threatened or where factionality could be seen to be instrumental beyond its immediate province. The tendency was to subordinate the factional and the local in favour of an interdependence that was based on intentional relation rather than geographical loyalty. However, any assumption that this social network's intermediary frameworks, of county or nation, were entirely fictional whereas the networks of print were purely functional is sharply rebuked by the leading domestic news-story of the Infirmary's foundational period – the 1745 Rebellion. The Infirmary's sermon of 1749 recalled the events:

Soon after the Commencement of this Design, an unnatural Rebellion breaking out in the Northern Part of our Island, threatened us with the dreadful prospect of an intestine War, wherein the Foundations both of our Civil and Religious Constitution might have been cast down [...] In this important, this perilous Juncture, let it be forever remembered, because the Remembrance of it will for ever reflect Honour upon this County, that our Nobles, our Rulers, and the Rest of our People, like truly Christian and truly English Patriots, Every One with one of his Hands wrought in the Work of raising our INFIRMARY, and with the other Hand held a Weapon for the Defence of his Religion and Liberties [...] May we not say, that the Alms of our People and the Prayers of the Distressed relieved by them in ours and the several other INFIRMARIES of this Kingdom [...] engaged him to refrain the Enemy from ravaging our Territories; and that the Blind and the Lame, even the Sick Poor (in effect) guarded our forts, and Capital-Towns.[26]

The crisis of 1745 was closely followed by the *Northampton Mercury*, which published private correspondence from Edinburgh and loyal petitions from the town to the monarch in London and publicized the formation of local militias. The Stuart army's progress south would have followed the road through Northampton (which passed within yards of the Dicey offices) where three Hanoverian armies under Cumberland planned to meet them: a convergence that has moved Christopher Duffy to argue that 'the crucial place was Northampton'.[27] Responding to the opportunity or threat, relay-networks were organized by Dicey facing both northwards and southwards.[28]

---

26 John Nixon *A Sermon Preach'd in the Parish-Church of All-Saints in Northampton, Before the President and Governors of the County Infirmary For Sick and Lame Poor, at the Anniversary Meeting on Friday, September 22, 1749. By John Nixon, A. M. Rector of Cold-Higham, and Fellow of the Royal Society* (Northampton: Printed by William Dicey; – and sold, for the Benefit of the Charity, By the Booksellers in Northampton; and by Benj. Dod, in Ave-Mary Lane, London. 1749), Price Six-pence.

27 Christopher Duffy, *The '45* (London, 2003), p. 302.

28 Coverage of the crisis – often contradictory or partial – can be seen in, for instance, *The Northampton Mercury* issues dated 2, 9, 16 and 23 September 1745. According to Hadley, news of the Jacobite army's turn northwards was acquired by couriers at Derby, who

Clearly a model of print and its authority as a concentric set of harmonized spheres, radiating outward from the capital to the provinces, would struggle to accommodate the events of 1745 and 1746. The return of the local and its discontents rebukes the press's rhetoric of having, for practical purposes, abolished both distance and division. The networks along which print was carried – soon to be upgraded and extended by General Wade – turned out to have been both two-way and multipurpose. From the Dicey Press, a better example of the inseparability of the connecting and localizing forces of the press could hardly be asked; nor, however, could a stronger illustration of their weaknesses.

'galloped southward, changed horses several times and brought the glad tidings to Northampton. It is a tradition in the office that the Mercury was the first paper in the country to publish this important news', Hadley p. 32. Bob Harris notes that 'The mayor of Northampton [...] appears to have sent expresses in the first week of December twice a day to Leicester, Derby and Nottingham. The information with which these expresses returned was printed in the *Northampton Mercury* of 9 December.' Bob Harris, 'England's Provincial Newspapers and the Jacobite Rebellion of 1745–1746', *History*, 80:258 (1995), 5–21, [p. 9].

Do the Dead Talk?: *The Daisy Bank Printing and Publishing Company of Manchester*

MICHAEL POWELL

O THE DEAD TALK? is the title of a work published by the Daisy Bank Printing and Publishing Company of Gorton, in Manchester sometime in the first two decades of the twentieth century. It is in many ways entirely typical of the press's output: a thirty-two page work, measuring eight-and-a-half by five-and-a-half inches, in paper wrappers. Whilst it lacks the title-page illustration common to many Daisy Bank works, its full title, *Do the Dead Talk?: Voices from the Great Beyond: Being the Authenticated Accounts of the Ghostly Experiences of Captain John Smith, U.S.A. Mercantile Marine, John Gale, Master Mariner, William Holt, Solicitor, Thomas Oxley, M.A., Miss Ethel Bell, Teacher of Music, Martha Higgs, Laundress, Compiled from Reliable Records and Written down by Tom Robinson*, indicates the characteristically quirky qualities of the press. Typically, like most Daisy Bank works, it is undated and is also extremely rare. As far as I have been able to tell, it survives in only two institutional collections, the National Library of Canada and in the McManus Young collection at the Library of Congress.

The reason for giving this paper the title 'Do the dead talk?' is partly to draw upon the title of a Daisy Bank book, but the main reason is to explore some issues about those minor provincial publishers that have left barely a footprint on the historical record. In particular, I want to see whether a printer/publisher of the last century, who produced no work of literary or typographical merit and who has left nothing in the way of a business archive, indeed virtually nothing other than some of the books he published, a press which has been dead for many years, can in any way talk to us. A recent ABE books listing for one Daisy Bank work describes the press as a publisher many years deceased[1] – a bit like the parrot in the Monty Python sketch "E's passed on! 'E is no more! He has ceased to be'. What then can we learn from the works of a press which is unknown even to students of the history of Manchester, still less to scholars of the provincial book trade? The purpose of

---

1   Description by Olde Musick & Cookery Books of Hobart, Tasmania of the Daisy Bank book, *Nine Patriotic War Songs*, <www.abebooks.co.uk> [accessed 19/7/2004].

this paper is first of all, an attempt to say something of the activities of the Daisy Bank Printing and Publishing Company of Manchester, to try to describe the range and content of its publications. Secondly, I hope at least to begin to show how the Daisy Bank press relates to other publishers of cheap 'penny dreadfuls' and 'how to' books. The Daisy Bank works were seldom original, and hopefully we can begin to see how a study of a minor press in Manchester can shed a little light on some wider questions of cheap printing in late Victorian and Edwardian society. Finally I want to look very briefly at the reception of Daisy Bank material and to look at the question of working-class reading, to gauge reaction to Daisy Bank titles and then to show how the Daisy Bank books relate to a number of studies on the Lancashire common reader that were published at the start of the last century.

Before we look at the output of the press we need to do a little demythologizing and deconstruct some of the stories that have arisen around the origins of the Daisy Bank press. By myths I mean those stories which have been preserved by descendants of the founder of the Daisy Bank Press, Jesse Pemberton, which have been brought into the public domain, in a number of articles by Jonathan Goodman and Steve Holland.[2] I use the term 'myth' to describe them not in a pejorative sense to claim that they are false but more in theological parlance where a story points to a deeper truth – in other words, they explain in the form of a narrative, a business undertaking and arrangement that is complicated and difficult to chart given the sheer lack of supporting documentation.

The first myth concerns the entry of Jesse Alfred Pemberton into the world of bookselling. Pemberton was born in Hoxton on 27 January 1863, the son of a journeyman boot-blocker. After a career as an actor and strolling player, Pemberton, a heavily-built man, settled in Gorton on the south-eastern outskirts of Manchester. Following a short period as the tenant of a pub, he set himself up as a greengrocer in premises on Wellington Street, a thriving suburban shopping street. Soon the greengrocery became a bookshop, when one of Pemberton's creditors offered payment in kind – a consignment of secondhand books – to settle a debt. Pemberton apparently used the books to separate potatoes from sprouts but found that they sold. In no time books replaced vegetables. Pemberton bought left-overs of editions, and sold them on at

---

2 Jonathan Goodman, 'A Shilling Life: Strolling the Story of Success', *Manchester Evening News*, 29 November 1984, p. 8, 'A Shilling Life: King of the Saucy Series', *Manchester Evening News*, 30 November 1984, p. 10, 'The Publications of Jesse Pemberton', *Antiquarian Book Monthly Review* (January 1985), 16–19, Steve Holland, 'Brave New World. The Origins of World Distributors Ltd. of Manchester', *PBO* (Newsletter of the British Association of Paperback Collectors), 1 (October 1995), 14–15.

Fig. 1. Jesse Pemberton and his first wife Alice at their wedding in 1893 (Photo: Donald Pemberton)

less than the published price but at a significantly higher price than he had paid for them.

The tale is attractive, not least because all of us can think of many books which could be happily condemned to trays of vegetables, but the evidence of Pemberton's activities from trade directories points to a more subtle process. In 1893 and 1894 Pemberton appears as a beer retailer at an address of 49 and 51 Cross Street, Gorton. His first wife Alice, whom he married in 1893 (see

Fig. 1), is listed at an address in the same street as a fruiterer. By 1898 Pember-ton had given up the beer trade and had acquired a newsagent's business at 85 Cross Street, a couple of houses away from his wife's shop. The two businesses were kept in separate names until his wife's death in 1904 when he inherited the fruit shop. By then he had acquired another trade, that of bookbinder, at an address of 107 Wellington Street, the major shopping street in the suburb. Jesse kept the fruit shop at least up to 1910 and put in one of his sons, Thomas, to run the premises. In 1908 the directories list Pemberton as a book-seller rather than as a bookbinder and throughout the second decade of the twentieth century Jesse operated as a newsagent at premises in Cross Street and as a bookseller, or wholesale bookseller, in Wellington Street. Thus, Jesse's experience in the book trade started alongside his wife's business as a green-grocer: he evolved into a bookseller after many years following a career as a newsagent and bookbinder and did not have a Damascus Road experience while standing in a shop full of sprouts.

The second myth is Pemberton's evolution from bookseller into publisher, in other words, the creation of the Daisy Bank Press. The story goes that Pemberton was having a conversation in the bookshop with a Mr Miller of the Manchester printing firm of Miller and Fazackerly. Miller happened to men-tion to Pemberton that he had been caught by a customer who had ordered the printing of a sixty-four page work but who had run out of money just when the third of the four sixteen-page sections was coming off the press. Pemberton struck a deal: if the printers would wrap covers round the forty-eight page work, he would pay a quarter less than what the printers were out of pocket. A couple of months later the books arrived at the bookshop. Only at this stage did Jesse realize that the book, entitled *From Mill Girl to Millionairess: a Romance*,[3] was somewhat truncated and that the narrative, as it stood, asked rather a lot of its readers. (In point of fact it asked them to write the last quarter of the book!) Undeterred, Pemberton purchased a dozen 'John Bull' Printing sets and enlisted local children, at the rate of a halfpenny per thou-sand, to stamp beneath the last printed line on page 48: 'And then they got married and lived happily ever after. THE END'. Surprisingly the book sold and

---

3   No copy of this book has survived, if indeed it was ever published, although the tale of upwardly mobile cotton workers was a surprisingly popular genre of popular fiction. See for example the works *The Princess of the Loom, A Daughter of the Loom, or Go Marry Your Millgirl* (1922), *Only a Mill Girl, Madge o' the Mill*, or *The Story of Jenny: A Mill Girl's Diary.* Victor E. Neuberg, *The Batsford Companion to Popular Literature* (London, 1982), p. 21, Patrick Joyce, *Visions of the People: Industrial England and the Question of Class 1848–1914* (Cambridge, 1991), p. 225.

from this beginning, which can only charitably be described as inauspicious, the Daisy Bank Printing and Publishing Company was born.

I will return to this second myth later. The name Daisy Bank was taken from a more prosperous, and certainly more scenic part of Manchester than Gorton. The Press's works are all undated and are impossible to list in the order in which they appeared.[4] The occasional title was brought out after some specific event – a boxing match, or a celebrated criminal trial – and these can be approximately dated. But we do not know when the Press actually started business and there is no supporting evidence from trade directories to indicate when the bookseller turned publisher. The company was certainly up and running some time before 1912 when Pemberton drafted his will.[5] It survived as a family business, employing the children from Pemberton's first marriage and possibly his nephew and his nephew's sons, until his death in 1922. His second wife, Sarah Alice Thomstone, whom Pemberton married in 1905 was pregnant with their eighth child when Pemberton died.[6]

Pemberton's will of 1912 provides some insight into the business. The will appointed Alfred Miller, printer of the firm Miller and Fazackerly, and Pemberton's second wife, Sarah Alice, as executors. Pemberton's three eldest sons from his first marriage, Jesse Edwin, Thomas Abel, and Edwin, were not allowed to inherit the business but were expected to carry on the trade or business of a publisher and remainder dealer, known as the Daisy Bank Publishing Company and Remainder Dealers, at the salary of thirty-five shillings per week. The three sons were all illegitimate and were born before their father's marriage in 1893 to their mother Alice Ann Carr, and the sons were identified in the will as Carr, or Pemberton. Their salaries would come out of the profits of the business, but, in the event of a shortfall, would be paid out of Pemberton's residuary estate. In addition, Pemberton's widow would receive a payment of thirty-five shillings a week and his daughter from the first marriage would receive ten shillings a week up until Sarah Alice's death or remarriage or until the youngest child reached the age of twenty-one. If Sarah Alice died or remarried after Pemberton's death, the eldest surviving son, Jesse Edwin would take over as executor. The executors were given the power to increase the salary

---

4   The Bibliothèque Nationale du Québec, for example, gives a date span of between 1836 and 1900 for the work *The History of Maria Monk* (Call no. 260580 CON). Even this guess is incorrect.

5   Dated 6 July 1912, codicil 12 October 1922, proved 19 February 1923. I am grateful to Pam Hawkins for a copy of the will.

6   Jesse's children were as follows: from his first wife, Jesse Edwin, Thomas Abel and Edwin, Alice and Victoria; from his second wife: Mary, Sydney, Harriet, Alfred, Edith, John, James, Jesse.

of the three sons to two pounds per week, and the same increase would go to the widow.

When the widow remarried or died, or when the youngest child reached majority, the business was to be valued and was to be offered for sale to such of the three eldest sons who had survived. If any or all of the sons refused to purchase the business, it was to be sold and the proceeds added to the residuary estate, comprised of his insurance policies and real property. Curiously, the sole condition about the actual operation of the business was that the sons were prohibited from publishing any new title under the series of Daisy Bank for twelve months after their father's death.

In essence, Pemberton was doing no more than attempting to provide for all of his children from both of his marriages, but the way that he tried to do this inevitably caused problems. The three sons, who worked with him to develop the business, were expected to continue as employees, effectively of the trustees, in the persons of their step-mother and Alfred Miller, who controlled the business and who allocated the proceeds. Profits from the Daisy Bank Press and from the remainder book business were to be built up and eventually divided between all of the children in equal shares. The problem was exacerbated by the fact that the number of beneficiaries increased as Pemberton's second family continued to increase. The sons, therefore, were given an incentive to develop the business for the benefit of the eight children from Jesse's second marriage, their step-mother and their own sister. Furthermore, this situation could be expected to continue for a maximum of twenty-one years, until the youngest child, who was in fact not born until after Pemberton's death, reached the age of maturity. In short, Pemberton's hope that the children of his first marriage would run the business for the benefit of their step-mother and stepbrothers and sisters was simply untenable. Shortly before his death a short codicil to the will, dated 12 October 1922, acknowledged that the business would not continue and that the two surviving illegitimate sons would trade not as the Daisy Bank Printing and Publishing Company but under their own name as T. A. and E. Pemberton and Sons.[7] Whether the Daisy Bank business was sold off, as anticipated in the 1912 will, is not known, but Jesse's fourth son, Sydney, born in 1907, ran a separate firm, which became known as Pembertons of Manchester Ltd.[8] In other words, the Daisy

---

7   The eldest son, Jesse Edwin, died in 1918. The surviving sons were now to receive a weekly salary of £4 out of the residuary estate.

8   For the later history of the two firms, T. A. & E. Pemberton and Pembertons of Manchester Ltd, see Steve Holland, 'Pembertons: the Case of the Canadian Connection', *British Association of Paperback Collectors Newsletter* (1994), and *The Mushroom Jungle: a History of Postwar Paperback Publishing* (Westbury, 1993), pp. 51–2.

Bank Press spawned two rival firms representing Pemberton's two families. To all intents and purposes the Daisy Bank Printing and Publishing Company died with its founder in 1922.

In the ten to twenty years during which the press operated about 110 titles have been identified bearing the Daisy Bank imprint.[9] Whether this represents all or nearly all of the press's output is difficult to say: Daisy Bank books were flimsy works, to be bought and not borrowed and were not intended for public libraries. We suspect that there may be more titles, certainly of the most ephemeral publications – children's books, drawing books and toy books – that bear their imprint. The books are easily identified: the name and postal address, and later the telephone number, of the press appears prominently at the end of the text and on advertisements printed on the wrappers. Indeed most titles contain advertisements for other Daisy Bank works. These advertisements appear in different forms and in different parts of the book, occasionally on the inside covers but mainly on the back cover. At first Pemberton simply listed the titles, but towards the end of the press's life titles were numbered, up to fifty-nine titles in total.[10]

Analysis of the press by subject or genre indicates that the largest category of material published under the Daisy Bank imprint was magic and popular entertainment, a broad category that encompasses books on conjuring but also works on spiritualism, as well as recitations, joke and dream books. This accounts for thirty-five titles, a little under forty percent of the press's entire output.[11] Next comes the story – mainly true crime stories but also editions of popular myths, dramas, biography and autobiography. These account for just under thirty-five percent (twenty-eight titles) of the press's work. The next category is music with eighteen titles (sixteen percent), whilst the rest of the output is as follows: twelve children's books, eight sport, and four cookery, gardening or miscellaneous titles.

Of these smaller categories of material little can be said. No copy of a toybook or drawing book has so far been located, perhaps no surprise with titles such as *Fireside stories for young folks entitled prince Peter Fearless of*

---

9   A checklist of Daisy Bank publications will be published in 2006 in *Quadrat* (a periodical bulletin of research in progress on the history of the British book trade, ISSN 1357–6666).

10   The numbered sequence of advertisements includes the work, *The Crumbles Crime*, which was not published until 1922 and as a result must have been one of the last works to have issued from the press.

11   Patrick Joyce points out that superstition and magic were a powerful hidden presence in late nineteenth-century Lancashire, illustrated by the work of the Lancashire folklorists, and the persistence of beliefs in ghosts, divination and astrology. *Visions of the People*, p. 161.

Fagoland by Uncle Jonathon Jollyboy. This work sold for one penny and was described as a complete story, full of interesting and instructive reading, well illustrated. Pemberton's cookery books were more expensive; *Hints for the Housewife*, a thirty-two page work, costing sixpence. For the same price one could buy *Monster Book of Recipes: Valuable Hints for the Young and the old*, compiled by one of Daisy Bank's stock writers, Reginald B. Jones. These were published in a large foolscap format, with red, green and white coloured covers. Sporting books followed the same instructive tone of the cookery books and included manuals on Association Football, Indian clubs and dumb-bells, roller skating, swimming and boxing. One work, *Wrestling and Ju Jitsu Fully Explained*, appears to have been penned by Pemberton himself, and his photograph appeared opposite the introduction. The picture, in so far as it portrayed the publisher as a fit and healthy specimen, was essential in a work which advocated exercise and sport as essential to national well-being:

This physical deterioration of ours as a nation is no bogey, but as every man knows, is an actual and deadly peril… Every student of history has learnt from the records of time that loss of virility and physical decay in the individuals of a nation have invariably been the preludes to the fall of that nation, irrespective of the position it may hold in the world's history.

As countries prepared for conflict, the work attempted to explain the rise of the Japanese nation as the result of the cleanliness and simplicity of living of its people and of the careful development of the body as an article of religion. The book is significant in that it is the nearest we have to an expression of the publisher's personal philosophy, a philosophy that includes physical exercise, moderation and temperance.[12]

Musical items consist of three main types: patriotic songs produced during World War I – national anthems of the allies, and songs full of the mawkish sentimentality of the period: *God Bless my Sailor Daddy, God Keep my Daddy Safe, I Want to go to my Daddy*, and *The Soldier's Widow*.[13] Most of these were penned by Tom Robinson, author of a number of popular songs usually arranged by J. Vane.[14] Alongside these were popular editions of hymns, the usual suspects: 'The Old Rugged Cross', 'Abide With Me', and standard piano

---

12   Temperance seems an unusual choice for an ex-publican but Pemberton also brought out a temperance reciter.

13   This last work came with a the picture of a child consoling its mother with the words 'Mummy dear you have [still] got me'.

14   I have been unable to find any biographical information on Robinson. Andy Aliffe claims that he was a journalist working on the Ripper case. http://www.casebook.org/authors/interviews/int-aa.html> [accessed 17/10/04].

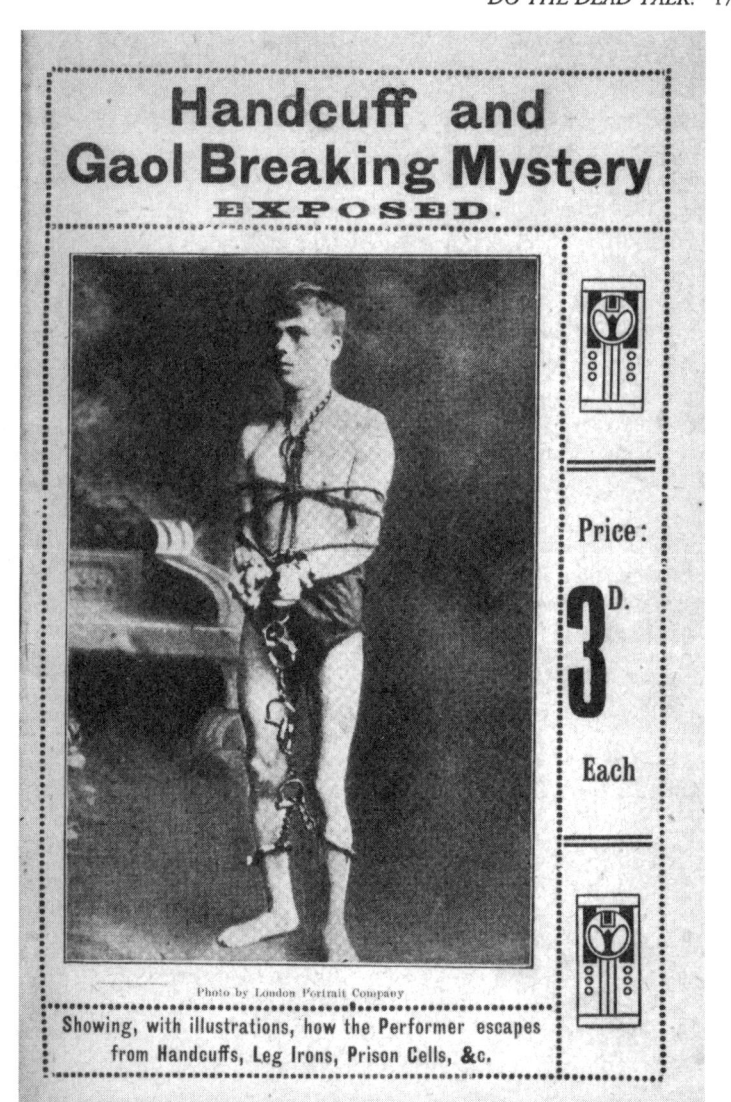

Fig. 2. Handcuff and Gaol Breaking Mystery Exposed, title-page. © Chetham's Library, Manchester

pieces, such as Handel's 'Largo' and 'La Sympathie'. A third category consisted of original pieces for the piano composed by Gladys Adamson, a local self-taught prodigy from Stockport.[15] Pemberton published half a dozen pieces by Adamson, pieces very much typical of the day: *A Forest Idyl, Whistling Plough-boy, Motor Spin, Golden Daydreams*. These musical items were advertised in a different way from Pemberton's usual fare. Whereas a printed book could be promoted just by its title – *How to Tell Your Fortune With a Pack of Cards*, for example, doing exactly what it says, the musical pieces were printed in part and in miniature on the back covers of some Daisy Bank works. It would be poss-ible for those in the know to just about manage the melody, but one would need the score to play the tune properly. The works of Gladys Adamson were available from the publishers but were also obtainable from the composer, whose address was given in significantly smaller type than Pemberton's at the foot of the page. Possibly in an attempt to facilitate sales of music, Pemberton brought out a manual for the piano entitled *How to Play the Piano Without a Tutor*.

The two largest categories of publication, the magic books and the story – fictional or factual narratives – are the most interesting works that the press brought out. The magic books covered subjects such as ventriloquism, stage-craft and thought reading as well as books of tricks, many of which involved the use of electricity, conjuring and cards. Some of the authors of these Daisy Bank titles were well known, established practitioners of magic, such as Albert Morrow, 'Karlyn' (J. F. Burrows – see Fig. 3), and Horace Goldin, but other titles seem to have been assembled by Jesse Pemberton himself, notably *How to Tell Your Fortune With Dice and Dominoes, By An Old Gipsie, The Cup of Destiny: How to Tell Fortunes With Tea Leaves*, by 'Mistress Zodiah', and the same author's *Dreams and their Interpretation*. The last title, which testifies to the continuing importance of the dream book in to the twentieth century, has the splendid cover illustration of a man in military uniform holding a gun complete with a bayonet standing over a woman asleep on a chaise-longue, a questionable image for a book devoted to the interpretation of dreams.[16] One title, *Handcuff and Gaol Breaking Mystery Exposed* (see Fig. 2), a manual of escapology, was translated into Swedish and published in 1921 in Stockholm; this is the only example of a Daisy Bank title being translated or indeed

---

15 Adamson wrote a number of pieces for other publishers but seems to have lost her way as a published writer of piano music possibly once her days as a prodigy were over. She died in 1974 aged 85. 'Miss G. Adamson Obituary', *Stockport Advertiser*, 3 October, 1974, p. 14.
16 Joyce, *Visions of the People*, p. 162.

Fig. 3. Karlyn, *The Stage Artist*, title-page. © Chetham's Library, Manchester

reprinted during Pemberton's lifetime.[17] Another title, *Conjuring Tricks: Making an Omelette and Other Tricks*, has an identical text to an edition published in the 1890s by Milner and Company of Halifax. The caption title has been reset in a different typeface but the text is otherwise identical, clear proof that Pemberton had access to Milner's original type, and confirms that the Daisy Bank press must have had a business relationship with Milner's, who had premises in Manchester at this time.[18] It is interesting to note that Milner's edition was itself lifted entirely from pages 17 to 48 of *A Boy's Own Conjuring Book*, which had appeared in numerous editions from the late 1850s.[19] Because tricks, jokes and recitations are not the property of individual magicians, comedians or story tellers, this type of material is easy to copy, usually in part, but occasionally, as in this instance, in entirety.

This is confirmed by an advertisement for some of Milner's publications which appears on the back cover of their edition of *Six Months in a Convent*,[20] a work that was constantly reprinted during the nineteenth and early twentieth century, and a title that was also published by Pemberton. Of the sixteen titles listed, no fewer than thirteen were brought out by the Daisy Bank Press, evidence of a trade in cheap reprinting, where one publisher of cheap reprints brought out the very same titles as another. This had enormous advantages for a small publisher over original publishing in that many of the risks involved in bringing books out into the market had been removed. By taking books published previously by Milner's, Pemberton presumably drew on titles which had already met with some success. The risk of a complete flop was not exactly

17 *The Whitechapel Horrors – being an Account of the Jack the Ripper Murders*, has been reprinted more recently by the Ripper scholar, Andy Aliffe, see. n. 14.

18 The firm of Milner's is crying out for a detailed history. For its early history, see H. E. Wroot, 'A Pioneer in Cheap Literature. William Milner of Halifax', *The Bookman* (March, 1897), D. Bridge, 'William Milner: Printer and Bookseller', *Transactions of the Halifax Antiquarian Society* (1989), 75–83, Victor E. Neuberg, *Popular literature: a History and Guide From the Beginning of Printing to the Year 1897* (Gainsborough, 1977), pp. 177–85.

19 James B. Findlay, 'The Daisy Banks', *The Magic Cauldron*, 20 (1966), 79–82, also available at
<http://www.illusionata.com/mpt/view.php?id=151&type=mc> [accessed 17/9/04].
A further piece by Findlay entitled 'The Daisy Bank Series – Extra', was published in no. 21 of *The Magic Cauldron* (1966), 91–2, at
<http://www.illusionata.com/mpt/view.php?id=152&type=mc> [accessed 17/9/04].

20 *The Thrilling Story of Six Months in a Convent* (London: Milner & Co,[190–?]). Copy in Chetham's Library (Call. no. 10.B.2.61(8)). Pemberton went in for popular anti-Catholicism with three titles: *The History of Maria Monk.: What I Have Written is True, Thrilling Story of Six Months in a Convent*, and *Revelations of the Confessional. The Problem of the Twentieth Century?*

removed but it was significantly reduced. It is important to remind ourselves that Pemberton described himself as a wholesale bookseller in the trade directories, and that he bought from publishers such as Milner left-overs of editions, before selling them on. In order then to explore more closely the workings of his business, one would have to look at other cheap publishers of the period, such as Nicholson of Halifax (later Wakefield) or some of the eighty or more publishers active in Manchester at this time. Analysis of the publishing activities of Manchester's most important publisher, the firm of Abel Heywood and Son Ltd, one of the most prolific publishers of the entire nineteenth century, would also be instructive. The firm brought out over 500 popular dramas, operettas, recitations, monologues, duologues, and children's plays, and included works similar to those published by Pemberton – recitations, joke books, and even a temperance reciter.[21] We know that Pemberton got some of the titles for his publications from Milner but we have no idea where he obtained the books that he bought and sold. What does appear clear, however, is that Pemberton approached publishing as an extension of his book wholesale business. By bringing the books out himself he took on some of the risk, but at the same time greatly increased the rewards.[22]

Because the magic books are more collectable and accordingly survive in larger numbers than other works, an examination of these works gives us more insight into the workings of the press.[23] What emerges is that many individual titles were published with significant variations, which are always concerned with the covers and not the text. Four variants have been noticed for *The Daisy Bank Book of Magic*, for example: one with pictorial brick red covers, one with

---

21 For Heywood, see Brian Maidment, 'The Manchester Common Reader – Abel Heywood's 'Evidence' and the early Victorian Reading Public', in *Printing and the Book in Manchester 1700–1850*, ed. Eddie Cass and Morris Garratt (Manchester, 2001), 99–120, and G. B. Heywood, *Abel Heywood 1832–1913* (Manchester, 1932). Heywood's works, like those of Pemberton, were listed as advertisements in other publications.

22 On the publishing boom in reprints in late Victorian England see Peter Keating, *The Haunted Study: A Social History of the English Novel 1875–1914*, Fontana edition (London, 1991), pp. 433–4.

23 For magic books, S. W. Clarke and A. Blind, *The Bibliography of Conjuring and Kindred Deceptions* (London, 1920) and *Short-Title Catalogue of Works on Psychical Research, Spiritualism, Magic, Psychology, Legerdemain and other Methods of Deception, Charlatanism, Witchcraft, and Technical Works for the Scientific Investigation of Alleged Abnormal Phenomena, from Circa 1450 A.D. to 1929 A.D.* compiled by Harry Price (London: National Laboratory of Psychical Research, 1929) and supplement (1935) remain indispensable. Daisy Bank books are briefly referred to on pp. 22 and 77 of Clarke and Blind's *Bibliography*, while references to Price's catalogue are listed in the relevant entries in the checklist; see note 9.

the same coloured cover but with different text on the back, one with pale pink covers, priced two pence and one with the same coloured cover priced three pence. Four variants have been identified for the works *Conjuring up to Date* and *The Book of Tricks*, while two have been noted for other titles such as *The Book of Electrical and Mechanical Tricks*. One work, *The Daisy Bank Book of Recitations and Elocutions*, has on the top left hand corner of the cover the statement '3rd issue'.[24] Thus the variants consist essentially of different coloured wrappers and of changes to the price of a particular title. A possible explanation of this is that Pemberton simply wrapped the books in the same coloured paper until that paper ran out and then chose whatever was available. Possibly, he increased the price when he chose to reprint the book, and if so, here we see the advantage of not putting a date on books, enabling them to be reprinted whenever there was a demand.[25] In all probability Pemberton's bookshop was used as a warehouse for the Press's output and the limitations of storage space may have determined the number of copies printed. If so, print runs would be kept low but could be continually reprinted.

Turning to Pemberton's stories, specially his true crime works, we see a combination of reprints of old cases whose notoriety remained strong in the early part of the twentieth century – Burke and Hare, Charles Peace, Palmer the poisoner, the Babbicombe tragedy, and Maria Marten (the Red Barn murder)[26] – and new or recent cases still lodged in the popular imagination – the Whitechapel horrors (Jack the Ripper), the Crippen murder and the flight with Ethel Le Neve (two titles), and the trial of Mrs Maybrick.[27] One work, *The Crumbles Crime* (the murder of Irene Munro) was published almost immediately after the crime in 1920, and the trial and execution of her murderers the following year. A few items, notably *Charles Peace: Authentic Account*

---

24 Findlay, 'The Daisy Banks', 79–82, and 'The Daisy Bank Series – Extra'.

25 It is equally possible, however, that an increase in price may indicate where the book was to be sold, an extra penny being added to books that were sold by travelling vendors. After 1867 no books appearing under Milner's imprint were dated. Neuberg, *Batsford Companion*, p. 133.

26 It is believed that Pemberton was acting in a touring performance of a play of the Red Barn murder immediately before arriving in Manchester. Goodman, 'The Publications of Jesse Pemberton', pp. 16–17. A Catnach sheet of the report of the trial of William Corder for the murder of Maria Marten sold over one and a half million copies. Neuberg, *Popular Literature*, p. 139.

27 The two seminal studies by Richard Altick remain essential for an account of the popularity of this material in Victorian and Edwardian England: *The English Common Reader: A Social History of the Mass Reading Public, 1800–1900* (Chicago, 1957), and *Victorian Studies in Scarlet* (London, 1972).

of the Life, Trial, & Execution of the Notorious Burglar and Murderer and *A Famous Conspiracy: Attack on Prison Van in Hyde Road, Manchester* (1867) were of local interest, as was the autobiography of the former Manchester policeman Charles Bloomfield, with the marvellous title, *Dredging a City's Filth.*[28] Pemberton's crime books were similar to many works published in London and in the provinces, brought out by publishers such as Catnach's successor, W.S. Fortey, and J. H. Evans, the Emmetts, Charles Fox, Edwin Brett, and Nicholson; indeed most were possibly derived from them, although more as precis or paraphrases than as copies.[29] For the most part Pemberton employed writers to produce new versions in order to condense them into a thirty-two page book. *The Babbicombe Tragedy: John Lee the Man They Tried to Hang Three Times, Burke and Hare the Body Snatchers,* and *Palmer the Rugeley Poisoner* were all edited by Reginald B. Jones, author of one of Pemberton's cookery books, while *Charles Peace: Authentic Account of the Life, Trial, & Execution of the Notorious Burglar and Murderer, The Bride in the Bath, The Ghoul of Gamblais* and the account of *Jack the Ripper,* were penned by Tom Robinson, author of a number of Daisy Bank's popular patriotic songs. As always with Daisy Bank works, the back cover advertisements claim that all of the Press's titles were carefully compiled by an expert and that they were the best and most reliable ever published. This is not entirely a piece of advertising puff. A number of works contain prefaces and introductions which emphasized that what the reader had before them was the truth and a more trustworthy account than any other published version, the Daisy Bank edition having separated the fictional from the true. In the case of works such as *Jack Sheppard,* or *Dick Turpin,* Pemberton attempted to give them a gloss of respectability, not by sanitizing the text or by adding the moral lesson so common at this time, but by creating the impression that what was put before the reader was more reliable than its competitors.[30] The texts remained derivative but were being transformed into something more sophisticated than the usual offerings. Similarly the covers of Daisy Bank crime books show a

---

28 Bloomfield came to Manchester in 1890 aged 26 and was involved in the 1897 investigation into police corruption in the city. He died on 29 April 1906.

29 Neuberg's, *Popular Literature,* ch. 4 remains essential for the publications of this material. See also John Springhall "'Disseminating Impure Literature': The "Penny Dreadful" Publishing Business since 1860', *Economic History Review,* 47 (1994), 567–84. For an informative, up-to-date discussion of this subject see the Yahoo Group: Bloods and Dime Novels A forum for collectors to discuss Bloods, Penny Dreadfuls and Dime Novels, <http://groups.yahoo.com/group/BloodsandDimeNovels [accessed 21.9.2004].

30 For examples of this, see James Sharpe, *Dick Turpin: the Myth of the English Highwayman* (London, 2004), pp. 183–4.

Fig. 4a. Palmer the Rugeley poisoner, printed by Pemberton.
© Chetham's Library, Manchester

Fig. 4b. Palmer the Rugeley poisoner, printed by Evans of London.
© Chetham's Library, Manchester

degree of flair and artistic ability that make them stand out. A comparison of the Daisy Bank edition of *Palmer the Rugeley Poisoner* with the London version of J. H. Evans bears this out (see Figs. 4a and 4b).

It is interesting to note that Daisy Bank published 'penny dreadful' material almost at the tail end of that trade and that Pemberton moved on from the cheapest type of publication to threepenny or even sixpenny works, produced with attractive, even artistic covers. Surprisingly no earlier publishers of 'penny dreadful' books in Manchester have been identified, Pemberton's press occupying a lonely and not insignificant place in the publication of cheap crime material in what at this time was the country's second city certainly at least for printing and publishing. In addition to crime, Pemberton went in for the sensational, with versions of Mrs Henry Wood's *East Lynn*, and a translation by Reginald Jones of Alphonse Daudet's 1884 novel *Sapho*, alongside three of the more controversial of Tolstoy's works, *The Kreutzer Sonata, Ivan the Fool* and *The Relations of the Sexes*.[31]

What then can we say about Pemberton's business? What exactly is the printing of the Daisy Bank Printing and Publishing Company? Was there a printing press occupying a room of the bookshop or rather a covered piece of the backyard? Did Pemberton acquire the skills of a printer to add to those of binder and bookseller? The answer, I suspect, to all these questions is 'no' and the reasons for this are as follows. The press was advertised, as far as we can tell, only on the back covers of its publications. It was not listed in any trade directories, or newspapers and the address given on its publications was the same as the bookshop on Wellington Road. In a twenty-year period it brought out perhaps only a hundred or so titles, at a rate almost equivalent to that of a private press. Daisy Bank did not do any jobbing work, indeed it did not print anything other than its own titles. One suspects that the actual printing was carried out by Albert Miller, of whom we heard, when discussing the myth of the bookseller turned publisher, of Miller & Fazackerly, printers, engravers, bookbinders and stationers of 15 Palace Street, Manchester.[32] Indeed the story

---

31   Tolstoy's works were reasonably popular at the turn of the twentieth century. Between 1880 and 1920 at least four editions of *The Kretuzer Sonata* were brought out in England, and two editions each for *Ivan the Fool*, and *The Relations of the Sexes*. See A. Yassukovitch, *Tolstoi in English, 1878–1929: A List of Works by and about Tolstoi Available in the New York Public Library* (New York, 1929). For the reception of Tolstoy see Donald Davie, "Mr Tolstoy, I presume?' The Russian Novel through Victorian Spectacles', in *Slavic Excursions: Essays on Russian and Polish Literature*, (Manchester, 1990), pp. 271–312.

32   Miller is even more elusive than Pemberton and I have only been able to find one example of a work of Miller and Fazackerley in COPAC: *Handy Guide for Pork Butchers,*

whereby Pemberton takes on three-quarters of a book printed by Miller, seems to allude to the start of a business relationship that continued right up to Pemberton's death. Pemberton's will appointed Albert Miller as executor and trustee and Miller was closely involved with the family and its finances for years to come.

The Daisy Bank Printing and Publishing Company was then a firm set up by Pemberton and the printer Alfred Miller, the purpose of which was to publish a small number of paper-covered books, specifically written or often rewritten for the Press. Pemberton seems to be the driving force but it is nonetheless a partnership – if it were not then we would expect to find the identity of the printer in the form 'Printed by Miller and Fazackerly for the Daisy Bank Publishing Company', but there is no evidence that Pemberton owned printing equipment. The publishing firm thus supplemented Pemberton's other business as a newsagent and a wholesale bookseller, a business of which virtually nothing is known.

Some idea of the attraction and appeal of the press's books is indicated in an account given by the Scottish-born historian and collector of magic books, James Findlay. Writing in the 1960s in the journal *The Magic Cauldron*, Findlay reminisced of his encounters with Daisy Bank books:

The writer's first acquaintance with this particular series of conjuring booklets goes back more than fifty years. I was a very small boy and then it was a popular jaunt on Sunday morning to pay a visit to Glasgow Green. On a corner of this famous park where both Prof. Anderson and David Prince Miller had their theatres, soap box orators practised their "arts", entertaining and enlightening their audiences with colourful views on religion, politics, racehorse tipping, the Bible, miracle medicines, and there was also a blind man who used to relate biographical details of Robert Burns, our National Poet.

Throughout this conglomeration of speechifying people wandered to and fro, always on the look out for the most popular 'act'. If the weather was good there was always on the scene a vender of the intriguing Daisy Bank publications. Many and varied are the tiles and, of course, some of these such as 'Paris by Night', 'East Lynne', 'Sapho', 'Life of Dick Turpin' did not have the same appeal as, for instance, 'Thought reading Exposed', 'Book of Magic', 'Electrical and Mechanical Tricks' and so on. Those last titles had an ardent appeal and with the odd copper at one's disposal one had to have time ere the great choice was made.[33]

Findlay's account is of interest for a number of reasons, not least because it confirms that the Daisy Bank books were sold well outside Manchester and that they appear to have been sold not in bookshops, or on railway stations, but

---

Bacon Curers, Sausage & Brawn Manufacturers, Provision Merchants, &c., by Thomas B. Finney, published in three editions before 1915.

33 Findley, 'Daisy Banks', p. 79.

by travelling vendors. What we have here is almost a vestige of the chapbook trade, the pamphlet, complete with the coloured paper cover, being sold by travellers at popular gathering grounds. One suspects, however, that the travelling bookseller, equipped with a case full of Daisy Bank titles, was only one, and by no means the most important, way that Daisy Bank books were distributed. Pemberton was a wholesale bookseller and his own titles may have been sold on to the retail trade. Magic books, in all probability, were sold in those shops concerned with the sale of magic or theatrical equipment.[34] A number of Daisy Bank titles invited the reader to send off for a catalogue of the Press's publications, and the published catalogue was an important means of advertising even cheap material.[35] But clearly the main vehicle for the sale of Daisy Bank books was the newsagent of whom after all Pemberton was one. All of the advertisements for Daisy Bank books point out that 'For a full list of all our publications ask your newsagent or send direct to us'. In 1912 the directory for Manchester and Salford identifies over 500 newsagents although, as with pubs, we suspect that the real figure is possibly far greater. If we look at neighbouring towns – Oldham, Rochdale, Bolton, and the rest – all of which were reachable by tram, the numbers of possible outlets for these books was enormous. Sale through newsagents necessitated that the cover of a work had to be striking because it was to appear in the shop window. At the same time the physical size of a work was important in a window display where space is of a premium. In spite of a number of recent studies of the corner shop, the newsagent is still something of a blind spot and studies have tended to focus on the way that the newspaper quickly become a staple commodity of the working classes in the late Victorian period. There is, however, much scope here for a study of the role of the book or pamphlet.

Findlay's story is of extra value because it is the only account of anyone buying a Daisy Bank book to read.[36] For the period in which the Daisy Bank books appear, there are a number of reports and investigations available, most of which expressed long-established middle-class concerns about what working-class readers were reading: the first by John Leigh appeared in the *Economic*

---

34 The Brown University copy of *The Stage Artist*, for example has the following label pasted onto the title-page: 'Munro's Experts in Everything Magical, 9 Duke Street, Adephi, London, W.C. Where all the tricks and puzzles come from'.

35 An example from one of Milner's catalogues, probably dating from the 1880s, is reproduced in Neuberg, *Popular Literature*, p. 187.

36 Findlay's collection was sold by Sotheby's in London on the 5th and 6th July 1979. See *Catalogue of the J.B. Findlay Collection of Books and Periodicals on Conjuring and the Allied Arts* (London, 1979). The Daisy Bank books were sold in lots 75, 243, 393, 419.

History Review in 1904,[37] and the second by James Haslam appeared in articles in the *Manchester City News* in 1906.[38] Leigh acknowledged the central role of the newspaper and magazine, and especially the sporting papers rather than the book, in working class homes.[39] Women were depicted as enthusiastic readers of penny novelettes as well as keen followers of the serialized novels.[40] Haslam also emphasized the extraordinary importance of the sporting press and the appeal of newspapers and magazines baited with prizes, but acknowledged that different areas within the city revealed different reading habits. In the poorer areas of Ancoats, Hulme and lower Salford the book was almost extinct, whereas in more prosperous areas such as Harpurhey, book buying among working men took in the purchase of self-educators and encyclopaedias in weekly, fortnightly, and monthly parts, and the paperbacked sixpenny novels. The newsagent according to Haslam was the labourers' bookseller: for the bulk of the working classes, the newsagent is the only bookseller they patronize. For Leigh, his experience of purveyors of second-hand books led him to the conviction that the *Life and Times of Charles Peace* (see Figs. 5a and 5b) is far more attractive than bound volumes of magazines or indeed any other class of literature.

Pemberton's paper-wrapped crime tales and stories, were then the very sort of material that was being sold in newsagents in the better parts of the city's working-class districts. His works, on the one hand, look back to the 'bloods' and 'penny dreadfuls' of Victorian England, and also look back to an earlier form altogether, the chapbook, but at the same time they were very much part of their own time. With their emphasis on reliability, they made a direct appeal to the more sophisticated elements of working-class society at a time, in Manchester and elsewhere, when greater disposable income among the working classes meant that sixpenny paper covered books would sell. Their use of cover illustrations also anticipated the paperback book of the inter-war years. Pemberton peddled both escapist fantasy and practical advice – indeed the

---

37 'What do the Masses Read?', *Economic History Review*, 14 (1904), 166–77.

38 23 June, 30 June, 7 July, 14 July, 1906. For a good account of the debate see Terry Wyke, 'Publishing and Reading Books etc in Nineteenth-Century Manchester', in *Printing and the Book in Manchester*, pp. 29–49 (pp. 38–49).

39 The enormous popularity of betting helped to create and sustain another important type of popular publication, the ready reckoner, examples of which were issued by Milner's and by Heywood.

40 A good example of this for Manchester is the journal *Thrilling Stories* published by the Thrilling Stories Committee, active in Holmes Chapel and Manchester between 1896 and 1903. See Frederick Leary, 'History of the Manchester Periodical Press', (Manchester Local Studies Library, MS 052 L161), pp. 524–5.

Figs. 5a and 5b.
Charles Peace, two variant Daisy Bank issues. © Chetham's Library, Manchester

Fig. 5b

'how to' book was almost his staple work.[41] With the Daisy Bank Press Pemberton established a business based on a relatively low number of titles, but probably very high print-runs, that sought to provide his two families with a decent, if not a prosperous life.[42] Publishing appears to have provided him with much of his wealth, but it is important to note that he continued his other trades and that he diversified and invested the proceeds of his business not in more publishing or in additional retail outlets but in property.[43] It is significant that the businesses that were run by his children moved things on, and looked less to the age of the 'penny dreadful' and 'blood' and more to the American market and the import of American 'pulps' and science fiction.[44]

Pemberton's activities admittedly tell us only a little about the work of a publisher-bookseller-newsagent at a time when we know almost nothing about the trade in books in Manchester. It is interesting to note that Pemberton was active at a time when local societies, historians and antiquarians in Manchester began to take note of its printed heritage and compiled lists of books printed and sold in Manchester.[45] Not surprisingly this interest did not extend to their own day and no copy of a Daisy Bank book appears to have found its way into any public library in the region. Our knowledge of late nineteenth- and early twentieth-century publishers in the town is skeletal at best, and one suspects that there may have been dozens of other publishers active like Pemberton who made a living out of the trade in books but about whom we know next to nothing. We are fortunate that the Daisy Bank books, especially those concerned with crime, music and magic, were collected by people such as the young James Findlay and later preserved in private collections and libraries,

---

41   Recent post-modernist criticism of sensational fiction emphasises that fiction narratives should not be read as development sequences but as allegories or metaphor. Working-girl fictions, where the working girl becomes a lady, should not be interpreted as wish fulfilling, escapist fantasy but involve the reader in affirming the daily life of the working girl and exploring the relations between the poor and the rich. M Denning, *Mechanic Accents: Dime Novels and Working-Class Culture in America* (1987), pp. 146–7, cited in Joyce, *Visions of the People*, p. 224.

42   The only evidence of a print run of a Daisy Bank book is, of course, the myth of the bookseller turned publisher, where it is reported that Pemberton employed children at a rate of a halfpenny per thousand to amend the work *From Mill Girl to Millionairess*. If this were true, clearly the print run would be enormous. Goodman, 'The Publications of Jesse Pemberton', p. 18.

43   Jesse bought quite a number of the cheap terraced houses, typical of property in Gorton, some of which were intended for his children and their families.

44   Holland, *The Mushroom Jungle*, pp. 51–2.

45   See for example C. W. Sutton, *Special Collections of Books in Lancashire and Cheshire* (Aberdeen, 1900).

and still later catalogued and the records made available on-line. Each of these processes is essential in allowing us to recreate some of the press's activities. In the case of the Daisy Bank Printing and Publishing Company, the dead may not exactly talk, but their silences can be eloquent if we pay attention in the right way.

Acknowledgements

I am grateful to a large number of individuals and colleagues for their help in the course of my research into the Daisy Bank Printing and Publishing Company. This work could not have been undertaken without the assistance of a number of collectors, librarians and booksellers who copied and digitized Daisy Bank works and who answered queries that went well beyond the call of duty. Special thanks to John H. Stanley of Brown University Library, Margaret Wilde of Stockport Local Heritage Library, John Billingsley of Halifax Central Library, Duncan Broady of the Greater Manchester Police Museum, and Marie Elmer of Clifford Elmer Rare Books. Trefor Thomas, Jonathan Goodman and Steve Holland clarified my enquiries arising out of their own considerable researches into the Press. Terry Wyke provided me with a wealth of information on reading books in late nineteenth-century England and Graham Moss helped to correct my inadequate understanding of printing practices. Donald Goodman, a descendant of Jesse Pemberton, provided me with helpful information, and gave me the copy of the wedding photograph of Jesse. My main debt, however, is to another of Jesse's descendants, Pam Hawkins, his granddaughter, who has carried out extensive research into Jesse's family and who generously made material concerning the family available. Without her this work could not have been written.

Changing Perspectives in a Journey through Personal, Parochial and Schoolmasters' Libraries: 1600–1750

JANE FRANCIS

THERE WAS PROBABLY much wider and more substantial book ownership beyond that of the wealthy landed classes in the period between 1600 and 1750; Peter Clark has written about the period 1560–1640 but he has very little evidence of specific titles.[1] The end point of the period discussed in this paper is dictated by the book collections of two schoolmasters who died in the 1740s. Books, especially the smaller ones, are fragile commodities; they fall to pieces, they go out of fashion, they are lost or dispersed on death. It is only rarely that books are listed and even rarer for the books themselves to survive. I was especially lucky, over 40 years ago, that my very first encounter with a seventeenth-century library was with a very large one of approximately 7400 titles still extant and in the room built for it by its donor Thomas Plume.[2] The library was Plume's gift to his native town of Maldon in Essex on his death in 1704 after a life as a parson who, in addition to holding the living of Greenwich, was Archdeacon of Rochester Cathedral. Little is known of Plume, but the greatest influence so far as his book collecting is concerned was probably Bishop Hacket of Lichfield. Hacket, a royalist, was deprived of his livings during the Civil War but allowed to keep his rectory at Cheam. Plume seems to have been under Hacket's patronage in his early years and later assistant and buyer of books for Hacket who, after the murder, as he saw it, of Charles I refused to set foot in London which he regarded as having been polluted by the sacrilegious act.[3]

Plume's library was a large personal working library; theology and religious controversy were, not surprisingly, well represented and in view of his donation

---

1 Peter Clark, 'The ownership of books in England 1560–1640: the example of some Kentish townsfolk' in *Schooling and Society* ed. by L. Stone (Baltimore, MD, and London, 1976, repr. 1978).

2 S. G. Deed, compiler, with the assistance of Jane Francis, *Catalogue of the Plume Library at Maldon: Essex* (Maldon, 1959); Oxford DNB, Thomas Plume, http://www.oxforddnb.com [7 June 2005].

3 W. J. Petchey, *The Intentions of Thomas Plume* (Maldon, 1985), p. 8.

of £1902 to 'erect an observatory and to maintain a professor of astronomy and experimental philosophy at Cambridge' (known today as the Plumian professorship) these subjects are also well represented.[4] In spite of the wide range of subjects covered by the books there are some gaps such as the scarcity of plays and the lack of any of the works of Plato but this is probably a reflection of personal interests and preferences and is also demonstrated by the books owned by the schoolmasters whose collections I have recorded. This extremely large and catholic collection must have been of great value to the gentlemen, scholars and clergy of the town for whose use the library was donated. Plume's will also specified that there was to be a librarian who would be paid £40 per annum and provided with rent-free accommodation; he was to be 'a scholar that knows books' and was expected to have another income as a clergyman or schoolmaster.[5] Libraries were by no means unusual in churches or towns by this date but Plume's donation must have been one of the larger ones.

This might have been my only brush with a seventeenth-century library had it not been for another chance. I had retired from a working life as a librarian in industry when I came across some notes my father had made in the 1930s relating to the Kedermister Library at Langley Marish, now on the outskirts of Slough. In my efforts to give the papers to the library I found myself recruited as its honorary librarian. Curiously, in view of the paucity of libraries still in their original homes, especially purpose-built ones like that of Dr Thomas Plume, Sir John Kedermister's library also remains in the room built and furnished by him.[6] It was donated in his will of 1631 for the use of the local clergy. In contrast with Plume, Kedermister was collecting books at a time when the possession of proscribed books could lead to imprisonment or worse; indeed it is almost certain that a visitation by Archbishop Laud's Commissioners in 1637 resulted in the catalogue dated April 1638 which hangs on the wall of the library today.[7]

This catalogue was the starting point of my paper in *Records of Bucks*. A transcription of the catalogue has been published; in addition, using what appeared to be contemporary shelf numbers shown against each entry, it was

---

4   Deed, *Catalogue of the Plume Library*, p. vii.

5   Ibid., pp. xiii–xiv.

6   My father was F. C. (later Sir Frank) Francis of the British Museum; in the 1930s he had been asked by the Pilgrim Trust to advise them on the state of the books in the Kedermister Library and the notes were made then. My involvement came in the 1990s after his death and has led to my later interests. It should also be said that my work on the Plume Library catalogue owed much to him and provided important experience. Jane Francis, 'The Kedermister Library: an account of its origins and a reconstruction of its contents and arrangement', *Records of Bucks*, 36, 1994, issued 1996, 62–85.

7   Ibid., 65–7.

also possible to suggest the original arrangement of the books and to demonstrate that the number of shelves in the library today exactly matched the number required for the books listed in the 1638 catalogue. The transcript also made it possible to establish which books had been lost over the centuries since its foundation.[8] The 1638 catalogue records a library of 'safe' books which might have been found in a college or university; they were mainly in Latin and consisted of the work of the Church Fathers.[9] The Reformation is represented by the works of Calvin, Luther and Erasmus although religious controversy is largely eschewed.

After working on the Kedermister Library I was interested to follow up a slightly mysterious entry in the 1959 directory of parochial libraries.[10] This was a library at Mentmore which had been left to that parish by William Beasley who had been vicar of the neighbouring parish of Cheddington. I found a list of the books left to Mentmore in the parish records held in the Buckinghamshire Record Office, it was a very abbreviated list of some six hundred titles.[11] The Buckinghamshire Record Office also has a list of books belonging to Benjamin Robertshaw, an almost exact contemporary of Beasley; they both died in the 1740s.[12] Robertshaw was vicar of Amersham and master of the grammar school and his list of books included date, place of publication and size. There is a predominance of textbooks – grammars, lexicons and classical texts – but Robertshaw clearly had an interest in the law and it is the only one of four collections I have recorded which includes Shakespeare.[13] Beasley's collection reflected not only his schoolmastering at Eton but also his role as tutor to the son of the patron of his living, the Duke of Bridgewater.[14] His duties as tutor to the Duke's son might account for his books on horsemanship, Boyer's *The Complete French Master for Ladies and Gentlemen* and the works of the statesman William Temple as well as Dallington's *Aphorisms Military and Civil.*

---

8 Ibid., 72–9.
9 Ibid., 64.
10 Neil Ker, *The parochial libraries of the Church of England* (London, 1959); this has now been updated by Michael Perkin, *A Directory of the Parochial Libraries of the Church of England* (London, 2004).
11 Buckinghamshire Record Office (BRO), PR146/3/1, 'Mentmore Com: Book, A catalogue of books left by Mr Beasley to ye vicarage of Mentmore 1744'.
12 BRO, PR4/28/4, 'Catalog book', consisting of odd sheets of paper sewn together in a brown cover.
13 Unpublished.
14 Wasey Sterry, *The Eton College Register 1441–1698* (Eton, 1943), p. 27.

Tanya Schmoller has noted an auction catalogue of the library of a Sheffield schoolmaster,[15] Thomas Balguy, which was not listed in Munby and Coral's list of book auction catalogues in spite of being in the British Library.[16] Checking Munby and Coral from 1676 to 1750 produced only one auction catalogue devoted solely to the library of a schoolmaster: that of a Mr Hodgson.[17] Both the Balguy and Hodgson catalogues are from the 1690s and demonstrate the contrasting content of catalogues; the Balguy list of some 1500 titles consists of a single line of a two-column page while, that of Hodgson includes date and place of publication for the larger-format books, while octavo and smaller books are listed in as abbreviated a form as those of Balguy. These two collections contained many of the classical texts found in the other libraries and like them demonstrated the personal interest of their owners. However, it is the Balguy collection that presented two types of material that are particularly interesting. These are maps and 'effigies' or portraits. While there is nothing particularly unusual about either group of material, they are interesting as being listed alongside the books. Does their separate listing and, indeed, survival to be listed suggest they were quite large? Beyond the name of the map and picture there is no indication of size or origin except in the case of many of the maps which are attributed to Nicolas Sanson (1600–67, the founder of a French cartographic dynasty).[18] Were these maps and pictures printed on the largest paper size of the period, approximately 40 x 56 cms?[19] Could the maps have been wall maps? There is no answer to either question. It is even impossible to know whether the pictures were woodcuts or engravings.

In attempting to investigate the portraits it became apparent that there are no indexes such as those for books in the *English Short Title Catalogue* (*ESTC*); Malcolm Jones suggests survival rates could be as low as 25 per cent but that is

---

15 *Catalogue of excellent books ... being the library of the learned Mr Baulgy ... for sale by way of auction ... Sheffield ... May 1697.* British Library, Press mark 1482.d.8 (catalogued under Baulgy; the name is recorded elsewhere as Thomas Balguy.

16 A. N. L. Munby and Lenore Coral, *British Book Sale Catalogues 1676–1800, a union list* (London, 1977).

17 *A catalogue of valuable books ... the library of Mr Hodgson ... will be sold by retail ... April, 1698 at Little-britain, by John Nicholson,* British Library, Press mark S.-C. 922 (9); MIC.B.619/216.

18 Alan G. Hodgkiss, *Discovering Antique Maps,* 5th rev. ed. (Princes Risborough, 1996), p. 38; Nicolas Sanson was succeeded by his sons Adrien and Guillaume.

19 Ronald B. McKerrow, *An Introduction to Bibliography for Literary Students* (Oxford, 1928), pp. 103–4; McKerrow notes that hand-made paper is now manufactured up to 56 x 76 cms and suggests workmen in the sixteenth and seventeenth centuries could have made paper of 41 x 61 cms, double the normal small size.

an estimate.[20] The case of the maps is equally difficult and the possibility that any of the maps are wall maps is even more uncertain but a reference to an article about 'a rare seventeenth century wall map' had led to my flight of fancy.[21] However, as wall maps usually consisted of more than one sheet, and there is no evidence for that, the idea should perhaps be abandoned. Although the twenty maps listed under Sanson's name have English titles it seems possible that they came from various atlases produced by him; these have been indexed by Mireille Pastoureau in *Les Atlas Français xvi–xvii siecles.*[22] It is also possible to speculate that four other maps without attribution could have come from atlases.

The problems encountered in estimating the survival of single-sheet publications may well be similar to the difficulties of estimating the printed material distributed by chapmen; much of this material may have been chapbooks but they would have been slim volumes and often read to destruction. But the chapbooks of the seventeenth century helped to spread literacy, as the Bible, Prayer Book and Catechism in English had started to do in the previous century; English-language printing overtook Latin and other languages from 1620 and especially after 1640.[23] There was a considerable growth in the ability to read through these informal channels even by the least privileged in society, Margaret Spufford has recorded some examples in her *Small Books and Pleasant Histories.*[24]

In the grammar schools reading was taught quite independently of writing which was the responsibility of the writing master. Locke considered that a child should be able to read English well before he was taught to write.[25] It is possible that this separation of skills has contributed to the underestimation of literacy, many people being able to read but unable to sign their name; it is also

---

20 Malcolm Jones, 'Engraved works recorded in the Stationers' Registers 1562–1656, a listing and commentary', in *The 64th Volume of the Walpole Society*, 2002; see also Antony Griffiths, *The Print in Stuart Britain 1603–1689* (London, 1998); and Sheila O'Connell, *The Popular Print in England 1550–1850* (London, 1999).

21 Gunter Schilder, 'Rare Seventeenth Century Wall Map of British Isles Found', *Map Collector*, 43 (1988), 12–15.

22 Mireille Pastoureau, *Les Atlas Francais XVI–XVII Siecles* (Paris, 1984).

23 Project LOC, Report, July 1972, typescript, p. xv (The Frank Francis Collection, British Library Deposit 10001); this was one of the reports produced preparatory to proposals for the automation of library procedures, the acronym derives from London (the British Museum/Library), Oxford and Cambridge.

24 Margaret Spufford, *Small Books and Pleasant Histories: Popular Fiction and its Readership in Seventeenth-Century England* (London, 1981) especially Ch. 2: Elementary education and the acquisition of reading skills.

25 John Locke, *Some Thoughts on Education, 1693*, new edition with introduction and notes by the Rev. Canon Daniel (London, n.d.), p. 280, para. 160.

suggested by Clanchy in *From Memory to Written Record* that the use of a cross to mark a document was associated with its religious significance and hence preferred to a signature as being of greater symbolic meaning in the same way as swearing on a Bible would have done.[26]

The question of literacy is important in understanding the extent of book ownership. Today there is a great deal of information, especially in the ESTC, about what books were published and even some idea of the popularity of individual titles but who actually owned what remains difficult to discover.[27] The small number of libraries belonging to schoolmasters which I have unearthed demonstrates that our knowledge of them is entirely due to the chance survival of lists and the even greater chance of finding them. It is clear that the survival of the books themselves is an even rarer occurrence. Mark Purcell has provided a fascinating story of the Brownes at Townend, Westmorland and their library and in cataloguing their collection has found some remarkable survivals.[28]

There are other interesting records like those of William Drake (1603–69) of Amersham whose commonplace books have been written about by Stuart Clark[29] and subsequently by Kevin Sharpe but Drake does not really fit into my profile of the book owners I looked at.[30] My subjects are not the wealthy and especially not the landed classes but those of lesser degree. By comparison with the exuberance of the subject matter in the libraries of Plume and the schoolmasters, Drake's commonplace books seem to reveal a man whose mindset was a throwback to the age even before Kedermister when books were less available.

In my continuing quest to explore book ownership I looked at those school libraries which were based on the gift of their founders; I have produced a database for several of these for the period 1600–1750.[31] However, it was

26 M. T. Clanchy, *From Memory to Written Record: England 1066–1307*, 2nd edn (Oxford and Cambridge, MA, 1993), p. 8.

27 Ian Green, *Print and Protestantism in Early Modern England* (Oxford, 2000), investigates the extent to which popular texts were reprinted.

28 Mark Purcell, 'Books and readers in eighteenth century Westmorland: the Brownes of Townend', *Library History*, 17 (2) July 2001, 91–106.

29 Stuart Clark, 'Wisdom literature of the seventeenth century: a guide to the contents of the 'Bacon-Tottel' commonplace books', *Transactions of the Cambridge Bibliographical Society*, 6, 1976, 291–305 and 7, 1977, 46–73.

30 Kevin Sharpe, *Reading Revolutions: the Politics of Reading in Early Modern England* (New Haven, CT, and London, 2000).

31 Unpublished database recording the books in four school libraries: Hull Archives M361 and M347D Hull Grammar School (list of 1676); The King's School Canterbury, MS list of 1740s; Mary A. Fleming, *Witney Grammar School 1660–1960* (Oxford, 1960) includes list of books dated 1767; University of Newcastle upon Tyne, Library Publications, Extra Series, no. 11, *Short-title list of the Sandes Library (Kendal Grammar School)* compiled by Alistair

impossible to be certain how many and which titles were owned by the founding schoolmaster. Also, unlike the libraries of the four schoolmasters, most were primarily collections of standard textbooks. The joy of the books owned by the four schoolmasters I have recorded is that they suggest wide interests and that all grammar schools may not have been as hidebound in their curriculum as has been generally thought.

Many criticisms of the grammar schools were made, from the rather extreme view of Thomas Hobbes, who blamed the classical curriculum for the Civil War, to more practical ones.[32] During Pepys's time at the Navy Office in the 1670s the need for naval officers to learn mathematics was recognized and this led to a number of coastal schools such as Dartmouth Grammar School taking up mathematics in the 1670s.[33] This need was also recognized and recorded in a memorial tablet of 1702, in Chichester Cathedral cloister, to the founder of a school which was to teach, among more orthodox subjects, 'mathematical learning as may fitt [the pupils] for honest and useful employment with a particular regard for **Navigation**'.[34]

John Locke in *Some Thoughts on Education*, of 1693 had a rather more root and branch criticism:

Can there be anything more ridiculous than that a father should waste his own money and his son's time in setting him to learn the Roman language, when at the same time he designs him for a trade ... while the writing of a good hand [is neglected, as is] casting accounts.... But these qualifications, requisite to trade and commerce, and the business of the world are seldom to be had at grammar-schools... Custom serves for reason ... as if their children had scarce an orthodox education, unless they learned Lilly's grammar.[35]

Interestingly this might be the specification for the curriculum of the dissenting academies set up outside the city, as exemplified in the London area by that in Stoke Newington but found all over England from Taunton to Warrington and Whitehaven.[36] So far I have not found any library of a dissenting minister or schoolmaster.

Elliot and John Bagnall (Newcastle upon Tyne: typescript, 1969), most of the books date from the seventeenth century, later books have not been included.

32 Thomas Hobbes, *Leviathan*, edited and abridged by J. Plamenatz (London, 1962, repr. 1983), p. 209.

33 W. A. L. Vincent, *The Grammar Schools: Their Continuing Tradition, 1660–1714* (London, 1969), pp. 98–9.

34 Recorded through personal observation on visit to Chichester Cathedral (navigation is emphasized in the original).

35 Locke, *Education*, pp. 287–9, para. 164.

36 W. Kenneth Richmond, *Education in England* (Harmondsworth, 1945), pp. 55–6; Roy Porter, *English Society in the Eighteenth Century* (London, 1982), p. 179.

Examples of wills providing useful information about specific titles are rare[37] as Peter Clark found;[38] however, they can be tantalizing. A complete list of books owned may be found with the exception of those bequeathed to a female relative, such as Beasley's 1743 bequest of 'such English books as my wife shall choose for her use'[39] or Thomas Hickman, founder of an Aylesbury charity whose will of 1698 excluded from his main bequest 'any good books that [my] cousin Faith may like to read'.[40] Archbishop Sancroft left all his books to Emmanuel College, Cambridge in 1693 but we have no idea what books his widow had selected to keep for herself.[41]

I have only scratched the surface during my chance journey through books owned by individuals, whether extant collections or those only in lists, but I hope I have been able to provide a flavour of the times and suggest the potential wealth of information on the world of the seventeenth- and early eighteenth-century book owners which may be buried in the records; maybe even providing a less London-centric bias.

---

37 The wills of John Croft (1714), Hertfordshire County Record Office 158 AW 8, and Lewis Atterbury (1730), Public Record Office, PROB 11 728, are examples, see Michael Perkin, *A Directory of the Parochial Libraries of the Church of England* (London, 2004), pp. 301, 394.

38 Peter Clark, 'The Ownership of Books in England 1560–1640'.

39 Public Record Office PROB 11 728, fol. 115, William Beasley's will dated 12 May 1739.

40 Hugh Hanley, *Thomas Hickman's Charity, Aylesbury: a Tercentenary History 1698–1998* (Oxford, 2000), p. 101.

41 Visit to Sancroft Library at Emmanuel College.

Retail Distribution Networks in East Kent in the Eighteenth Century

DAVID SHAW

A T EARLIER MEETINGS of the British Book Trade History conference, Sarah Gray and I have looked at some aspects of the activities of
Canterbury printers and publishers in the eighteenth century.[1] Canterbury's first printer (excluding the ephemeral press of John Mychell in the mid-
sixteenth century) was James Abree who established himself in the city in 1717
after completing his apprenticeship under Ichabod Dawkes in London between
1705 and 1712.[2] His activity as a book producer was documented in my earlier
article.[3] Abree's surviving output of books and pamphlets between 1717 and
his death in 1768 amounts to just over one hundred books and pamphlets (a
number of them being single-sheet ephemeral items such as the annual
bellman's verses). It is clear that he cannot have hoped to make a living in
Canterbury solely as a book printer. No doubt he also did jobbing printing
which either does not survive or which cannot be recognized as Abree's work.
His advertisements show that his bookshop sold titles from London producers
and also the usual range of goods including stationery and patent medicines. As
with printers in other provincial towns in the early eighteenth century, Abree
no doubt intended from the start that his business plan was centred on the
regular income to be had from the production of a newspaper.

Another factor in Abree's business plan would seem to be the establishment of retail opportunities beyond the city of Canterbury itself, whose
population was probably insufficiently large to support his activities. We shall

---

1   David J. Shaw and Sarah Gray, 'James Abree (1691?–1768): Canterbury's first "modern"
printer', in *The Reach of Print: Making, Selling and Reading Books*, ed. P. Isaac and B. McKay
(Winchester, 1998) pp. 21–36; David J. Shaw, 'Canterbury's external links: book-trade
relations at the regional and national level in the eighteenth century', in *The Mighty Engine:
the Printing Press and its Impact*, ed. P. Isaac and B. McKay (Winchester, 2000) pp. 107–19;
Sarah Gray, 'William Flackton, 1709–1798, Canterbury bookseller and musician', in *The
Mighty Engine*, pp. 121–30.
2   D. F. McKenzie, *Stationers' Company Apprentices 1701–1800* (Oxford, 1978), p. 104
(record 2421).
3   Shaw and Gray, 'James Abree', pp. 29–36.

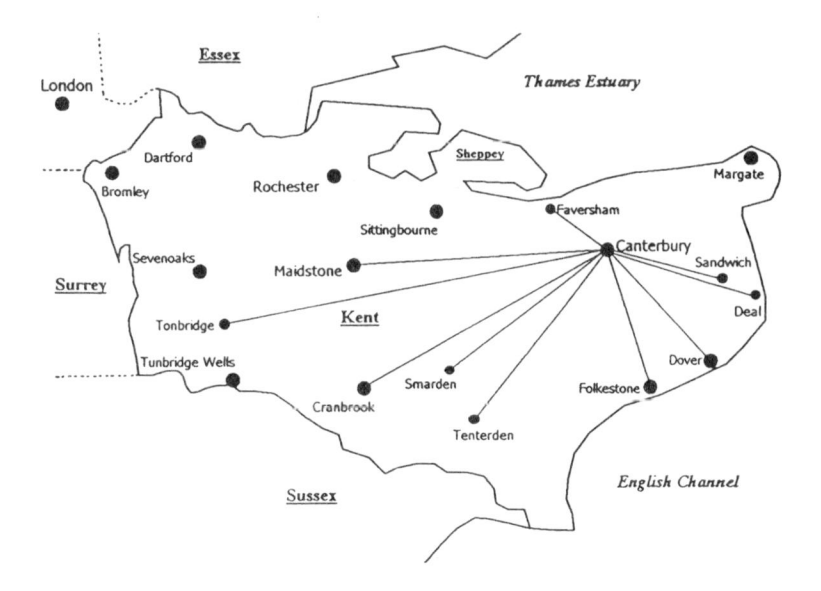

Fig. 1. Distribution of books printed by James Abree by other booksellers in East Kent

look later at the distribution networks for the newspaper. For books printed in his workshop, Abree from time to time arranged distribution deals with other booksellers in the region (in addition to trade connections with London booksellers). The imprints of his books show a variety of such co-publication arrangements during his career:[4]

> 1722: Sandwich
> 1739: Cranbrook, Smarden, Tenterden
> 1744 and 1745: Cranbrook
> 1748: Maidstone
> 1762: Deal, Dover, Faversham, Folkestone, Maidstone, Sandwich, Smarden, Tonbridge.

The second half of the eighteenth century saw this pattern of regional co-publishing and distribution continue, though most co-publishing ventures by

---

4   For further discussion, see Shaw and Gray, 'James Abree', 23.

Fig. 2. Masthead of the *Kentish Post*, 19–22 December 1722
(Canterbury Cathedral Library)

Canterbury printers are with London tradesmen.[5] Within Kent, Canterbury printers shared imprints with tradesmen in the following towns:

> Chatham (2), Cranbrook (1), Dover (6), Faversham (4), Folkestone (2), Maidstone (4), Margate (17), Ramsgate (10), Rochester (6), Sandwich (3)

This pattern is not essentially different from Abree's, though it now extends to the Medway towns.

As indicated above, newspaper production also required a larger distribution than could be found within Canterbury itself. The first newspaper was *The Kentish Post and Canterbury Newsletter*, printed in Canterbury by James Abree, and produced bi-weekly from 1717 to 1768 when it merged with James Simmons's newly founded rival, *The Kentish Gazette*. The merged paper,

---

5   For a fuller discussion, see Shaw, 'Canterbury's external links', 108–9 (Canterbury and Kent) and 110–12 (London); see also Tables 2 and 3.

called *The Kentish Gazette, or Canterbury Chronicle*, started in July 1768 and is still in business today, appearing every Thursday.[6]

In order to sell the newspaper twice a week in the towns and villages in Kent, a distribution system was needed. This was no doubt a typical situation for newspaper proprietors in the provincial towns. The solution was to employ newsmen who carried the newspaper twice a week on a circuit of the county, selling the paper, collecting advertisements for the next issue and delivering goods such as patent medicines. Early issues of *The Kentish Gazette* carry lists of the towns visited by the newsmen and I had hoped to study the patterns of distribution throughout the century. Unfortunately, Abree did not list his distribution rounds in the *Kentish Post* in the surviving copies produced between 1726 and 1767. However, the existence of the newsmen is clearly indicated in some of his book imprints and in advertisements in the newspaper. For example, the colophon for issue no. 795 reads

Canterbury, Printed and Sold by J. Abree in St. Margaret's. Where Advertisements are taken in. And all sorts of ALMANACKS Sold for the Year 1726. To be had also by the News-men. Likewise several sorts of MUSICAL as well as Playing Cards.[7]

There is an advertisement in another issue in 1726 for 'Dr. Daffey's Original and Famous Elixir ... NB. The said Elixir is brought, Carriage free, by speaking to the Men who carry the Canterbury Newsletter'.[8] Another advertisement for a patent medicine in 1729 announces 'Dr Richard Rock's Famed Stomach Plaister, Sold at the Printing Office in Canterbury, and by the men who carry the Canterbury News Paper'.[9]

Some advertisements give details of the other Kentish bookshops where goods can be purchased; these almost certainly indicate part of the route travelled by the newsmen. For example, a book advertisement lists trade partners in Sandwich, Ashford, New Romney, Dover and London:

Subscriptions for Mr De Gols's Book, Entitled, A Vindication of the Worship of the Lord Jesus Christ. ... Will be sold under five Shillings in Sheets. Subscriptions are taken in by Mr. Silver at Sandwich, Mr. John Smith Junior at Ashford, Mr. Hammond at New Rumney, Mr. Gill at Dover, Mr. Bettesworth in Pater-noster Row London, and at the Printing-office Canterbury.[10]

---

6   The take-over battle is further documented in Shaw and Gray, 'James Abree', 26–8.
7   *Kentish Post* no. 795, 1–5 January, 1725/26.
8   *Kentish Post* no. 801, 22–26 January, 1725/26, p. 3.
9   *Kentish Post* no. 1184, 7–10 January 1729/30, p. 3.
10 *Kentish Post* no. 801, 22–26 January 1725–6, p. 4.

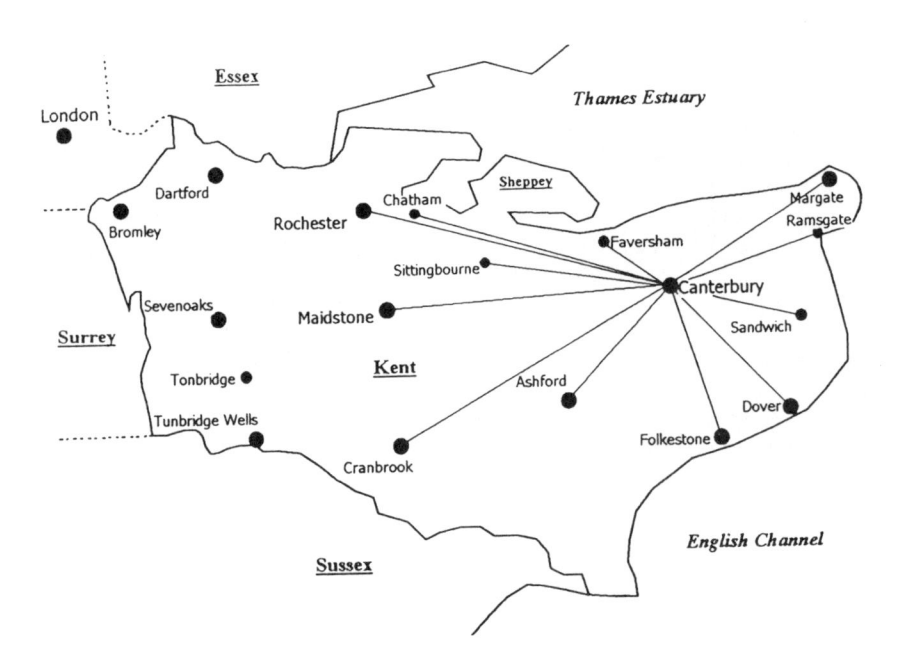

Fig. 3. The probable extent of distribution of Abree's *Kentish Post* in 1767

Another advertisement for Daffey's Elixir gives a long list of tradesmen in the region to whom Abree had sub-contracted the sale of the brew:

Dr Daffey's Original and famous Cordial Elixir Salutis ... Truly prepared at London, and appointed to be sold at no other place in Canterbury, but at Mr. James Abree's ... Printing Office. Price 2s.6d. The large Half Pint

Also appointed to be sold at ...

> Mrs Hickels by the Market Place in Deal
> Mr Bayleys *Shopkeeper* at Folkstone
> Mr Richard Harrys in St Peter's in the Isle of Thanet
> Mr John Atkinsons *Grocer* in Ashford
> Mr Rigden's, *Grocer* in Faversham
> Mr Robinson's *at the Bull* in Newington
> Mr Samson Price's, *Grocer* in Dover
> Mr Boys's at Charing
> Mr Goodwin's *Grocer* at Pluckley
> Mr Richard Oliver's *Grocer* in Sandwich

Fig. 4. Masthead of the *Kentish Post*, 16–20 July 1768 (Canterbury Cathedral Library)

       Mr Armstrong's *at the Rose and Crown* in Margate
       Mr Stonestree's *Gardener* at Sittingborn
       Mr Hopwood's near the Little Conduit, Maidstone
       Mr Thatcher's *Grocer* at Wye
       Mr Nicholas Peckers *Butcher* near Ramsgate.[11]

Interestingly, none of these are book-trade personnel: they are a mixture of publicans and shopkeepers. It can be assumed that the newspaper would also be sold in these towns and probably by the same people.

    Towards the end of Abree's career, the newspaper still gives no indication of the routes of the newsmen, but once again the location of advertisers indicates distribution to the following towns:

Littlebourne, Petham, Elham, Birchington, Broadstairs, Deal, Dover, Sandwich, Wye, Ashford, Ivychurch, Faversham, Sittingbourne, Charing, Biddenden.

    By the middle of 1768, the elderly James Abree was preparing to hand over his business to his former assistant George Kirkby, who immediately set to

---

11 *Kentish Post*, no. 1183, 3–7 January 1729/30, p. 4.

work to modernize the paper. He purchased new type and redesigned the masthead.

Another innovation was the introduction (at last) of a colophon carrying a list of the towns visited by the newsmen. Almost all of the outlets mentioned are public houses, with the addition of two London coffee houses:

The Fountain in Dover; the Five Bells in Deal; the Old Bell in Sandwich; the Spread Eagle in Ramsgate; the Fountain and Old Crown in Margate; the Three Kings at Sittingbourne; the Bull at Newington; the Haunch of Venison at Maidstone; the Windmill at Hollingbourne; the Bell at Harrietsham; the Dog and Bear at Lenham; the George at Newnham; the Woolpack at Chilham; the Flying Horse at Wye; the Saracen's Head at Ashford; the George at Bethersden; the White Lyon at Tenterden; the George at Cranbrook; the Red Lyon at Biddenden; the Chequer at Smarden; the King's Head at Charing; the Rose at Elham; the White Hart at Folkestone; the White Swan at Hythe; at Mr Mate's, Saddler, at New Romney; the George at Lydd; the Royal Oak at Newing Green; the Drum at Stanford; and at Tom's Coffee-house in Cornhill, and St. Paul's Coffee-house in St. Paul's Churchyard, London.[12]

This set of routes shows a well-defined circulation area in East Kent and out to the Medway Valley and Romney Marsh.

The rival *Kentish Gazette* appeared on 25–28 May 1768 before Kirkby's plans were complete. Its imprint announced an intention to distribute far more widely than Abree's paper had:

Printed by James Simmons, at the King's Arms Printing Office, in Christ-Church-yard, Canterbury

This paper will be published in Canterbury every Wednesday and Saturday Morning, and circulated not only to those parts of the County where the News Paper has been usually sent, but to many more distant towns, a Correspondence for that purpose being already established.[13]

Simmons seems to have set out to establish links with other members of the book trade in Kent. His announcement that 'Advertisements, Letters and Orders are taken in' listed booksellers in Sittingbourne, Rochester, Maidstone, Tonbridge, Ashford, Tenterden, Deal, Sandwich, Margate, and 'Mr. G. Pearch, Bookseller, London'. He also listed a shopkeeper in Hythe, and the postmaster in Romney and in Folkestone. Issue no. 2 added 'Mr. Newport, Bookseller, Dover; Mr Walter, Bookseller, Faversham' and issue no. 4 added 'Mr Ingram, Shopkeeper, Cranbrook'.

---

12 *Kentish Post*, no. 5274, 22–25 June 1768.
13 *Kentish Gazette*, 25–28 May 1768.

Simmons made Kirkby an offer of a merger of the two newspaper but in early July he announced Kirkby's rejection of the merger and boasted that

Many improvements have already been made in the different circuits throughout the County ... The Kentish Gazette is now sent to Tunbridge the very day it is published, making a circuit between forty and fifty miles beyond Maidstone, where a Canterbury paper was never sent before. ... It is also circulated through Stroud, Rochester, Chatham, and Brumpton, early each day, and in London every Wednesday and Saturday evening. I have certain sale for upwards of SEVENTEEN HUNDRED papers every week, besides the accidental papers sold on the different roads, and the demand at my own office.[14]

It is clear that James Simmons was a vigorous and ambitious businessman and within two weeks, Kirkby had capitulated. Issue no. 16 of the *Kentish Gazette* (16–20 July 1768) announced a partnership between Simmons and Kirkby to produce *The Kentish Gazette and Canterbury Chronicle*. The partnership proved to be longlasting: it remained in existence until the end of the century. Distribution of the *Gazette* continued to expand. In 1775 it covered:

Rochester, Chatham, Strood, Brompton, Rainham, Newington, Milton, Sittingbourne, Faversham, Maidstone, Lenham, Newnham, Ospringe, Boughton, Charing, Ashford, Tenterden, Wye, Cranbrook, Biddenden, Smarden, Margate, Ramsgate, Sandwich, Dover, Deal, Wingham, Folkestone, Hythe, Elham, Romney, Lydd, Appledore, Rye, Winchelsea, Brookland, Tonbridge, Tunbridge Wells, Sevenoaks, Sandhurst, Goudhurst, Seale, Northfleet, Gravesend, and London coffee houses.

There can be no doubt from the attention which both Kirkby and Simmons gave to developing their distribution circuits that Canterbury on its own could not assure the economic viability of a bi-weekly newspaper. It is well known that the regional newspapers of the time had surprisingly little local news and drew extensively on the London papers for their content. Provincial booksellers of course had of necessity to have good links to London if they were to satisfy their customers' needs for books (not to mention patent medicines and fire insurance). Both Kirkby and his rival had London coffee houses as the final stop in their list of places served by their newsmen. It is difficult to be sure what sales a Canterbury paper might have had in the capital but clearly a London presence was thought to be an important element in the sales strategy, possibly for reasons of prestige. In 1772–1775 the new *Kentish Gazette* listed its London outlets as the Surrey, Sussex, Chapter, London, Peele's and Guildhall coffee houses and also listed one or more wholesale booksellers as distributors, no doubt the same wholesalers who were used for book supply:

---

14 *Kentish Gazette*, no. 12, 2–6 July 1768.

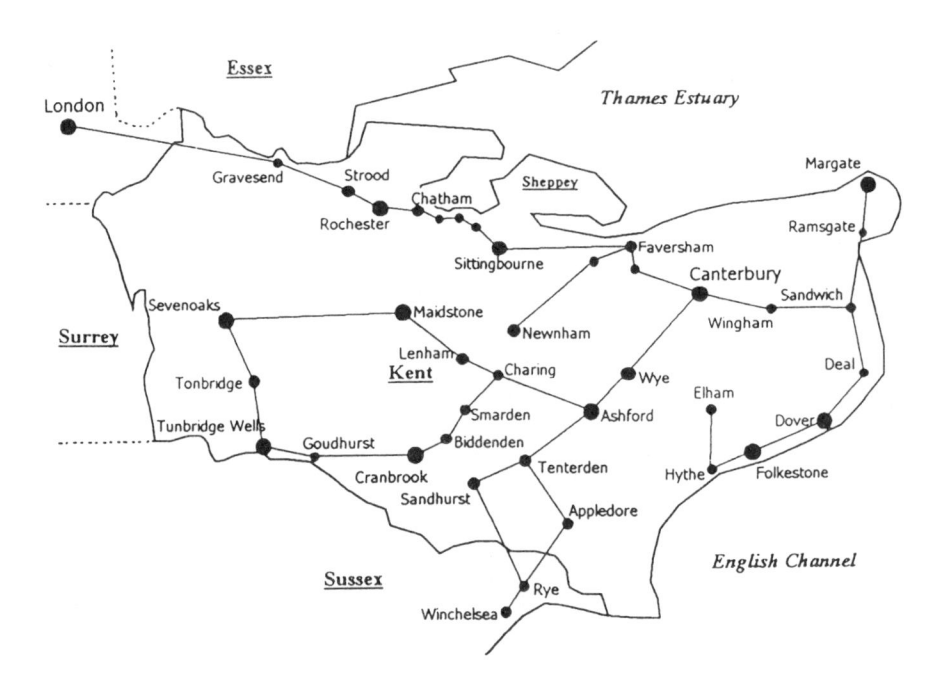

Fig. 5. Reconstruction of the circuits of the *Kentish Gazette*'s newsmen in 1775

G. Pearch to April 1771
R. Baldwin from April 1771
J. Johnson from April 1775

In conclusion, we have seen that book publishing was merely sideline for a typical provincial printer like James Abree. The regular income from printing a newspaper was much more lucrative. However, Canterbury was not big enough to support a bi-weekly newspaper on its own and from the start it seems to have been an essential part of the strategy to secure advertisements and sales by means of newsmen who carried the newspapers throughout East Kent. Regional distribution must always have been vital to the economics of the newspaper. Extending this distribution network seems to have been an essential part of George Kirkby's plan to modernize the paper and also the key to James Simmons's aggressive takeover of the old *Kentish Post*.

Smith, Elder & Co.
and the Realities of New Grub Street

FREDERICK NESTA

GEORGE GISSING (1857–1903) is best known today as the author of *New Grub Street*, the quintessential novel of authorship and publishing in the nineteenth century. In *New Grub Street* the career of the struggling but artistically dedicated author Edwin Reardon is contrasted with that of Jasper Milvain, a writer who saw literature as more commerce than art. Gissing, like Reardon, was an author of much talent but little commercial success. Like Reardon, he would sell the entire copyright of his current novel to a publisher and live on the proceeds until he had another novel ready for sale. After selling *New Grub Street* to Smith, Elder and Co., Gissing of necessity began to think more like Milvain, looking for royalties, foreign sales, and serialization to increase his income. Gissing's life as an author is well documented in the nine published volumes of his letters, his diaries, and in the archives of his publishers and agents, providing us with a detailed dossier of the economics of late Victorian publishing. His period with Smith, Elder is illustrative of the lot of young writers of literary merit but no popular market, who wrote novels that were just profitable enough to remain in print for decades. Those years also saw the end of the three-volume novel, the growth of international rights sales, the rise of the literary agent, and the beginning of modern publishing.

Smith, Elder and Co., founded in 1816, was one of the leading publishers of the nineteenth century. Over a period of five years, Smith, Elder published five of Gissing's novels: *Demos: A Story of English Socialism* (1886), published anonymously, established Gissing's reputation. It was followed by *Thyrza* (1887), *A Life's Morning* (1888), *The Nether World* (1889), and *New Grub Street* (1891). Gissing sent the manuscript of his first novel, *Workers in the Dawn*, to Smith, Elder in January 1880, following with the manuscript of *Mrs Grundy's Enemies* in 1882, both of which they declined. Gissing became a Smith, Elder author when they accepted *A Life's Morning* at the end of 1885. Gissing's primary contact with Smith, Elder was through James Payn (1830–98), who was Smith's reader from 1874, editor of the *Cornhill Magazine* from 1883 to 1896, and author of over 160 books, including 46 novels. At sixteen he wrote a sketch of life at Woolwich Academy that was published in Dickens's journal *Household Words* and brought him into an acquaintance with Dickens. With his early publishing success and family contacts, Payn had an easy entry into a literary career. Payn could have been Gissing's model for Milvain in that Payn saw himself as 'a businessman engaged in turning out saleable articles according to a successful formula'.[1] George Smith, in his unpublished memoirs, described Payn as:

... a model of literary industry. Literature was his 'business', exactly as shares are the business of the stockbroker and teas and sugars the "business" of the merchant. He set himself to earn an income for his family by his pen, and he did it with a method and a diligence altogether admirable. He wrote novels, reviewed books, contributed leading articles to 'The Times', 'Notes of the Week', to 'the Illustrated London News', and charming letters of literary and social gossip to half a hundred newspapers in every part of the empire. I think Payn could have written very much better books if he had been content to write one novel a year instead of three. He would probably have agreed with that judgment quite frankly but would have added, 'My object is to earn an income; and I should not get so much for one first-rate book as I do for three second-rate ones'.

As a reader for Smith, Elder, Payn was unappreciative of Gissing's works. As George Smith said, 'Payn had an acute judgment for literature of the lighter order; but he soon got out of his depth and he lacked what may be called intellectual courage.'[2]

Smith, Elder's normal practice with Gissing's books, as with most novels published in the period, was to print from 450 to 750 copies of a three-volume first edition. Five of those copies went to the copyright deposit libraries, six to the author and 50 to 70 for gifts and review. Almost all of the remaining copies were sold to the circulating libraries at fifteen shillings. Circulating libraries and booksellers were also given additional discounts by the practice of counting every thirteen copies sold as twelve. A few copies would be sold to trade booksellers at 22s.6d. – to sell at the retail price of 31s.6d. If a second printing were made after the initial printing, the publisher would designate it as a second edition. For Gissing's works only *New Grub Street* had a 'second edition' (i.e. issue) in the three-volume format.

The next true edition was a one-volume crown octavo edition, which would usually be printed seven to nine months after the three-volume edition appeared. The text of this edition might be revised by the author, as Gissing did for *Thyrza*, or simply reset from the three-volume edition. For Gissing's novels the print run would be from 750 to 2500 copies, half or more of which Smith, Elder usually sold in quires at one shilling to Petherick, an Australian publisher and bookseller, for resale in the colonies. The crown octavo edition

---

1   R. C. Terry, *Victorian Popular Fiction, 1860–80*. (London, 1983), p. 146.
2   George Murray Smith, 'The Recollections of a Long and Busy Life'. Typescript. National Library of Scotland MS23191, p. 6.

retailed at six shillings, but was generally sold to the trade at either four shillings or 4*s*.2*d*., again with the thirteen as twelve discount. For *Demos*, *Thryza*, and *New Grub Street* the higher price on the six-shilling edition helped to offset the costs of resetting the text and preparing stereotypes for printing this edition and the cheaper issues, a 2*s*.6*d*. foolscap issue, bound in limp red cloth, and a two shilling 'yellowback' issue. The foolscap issue also required the engraving of blocks for stamping the cloth covers and the drawing and engraving of illustrations for the yellowback cover. The cheap issues sold to the trade at several price points, with effective discount rates of 30 per cent to 46 per cent. The two-shilling issue was sold to the trade at 1*s*.1*d*., 1*s*.3*d*., 1*s*.4*d*. and 1*s*.5*d*. The cloth-bound 2*s*.6*d*. issue trade prices were 1*s*.5*d*., 1*s*.8*d*., and 1*s*.9*d*. The thirteen as twelve discount was only given to those who purchased above 1*s*.1*d*. The potential profit to booksellers could range from seven pence to thirteen pence without the thirteen as twelve discount and from eight to fourteen pence with it.

Production costs remained fairly fixed during the period. The cost for binding the three-volume edition was constant at £1.14*s*.6*d*. per hundred copies. Binding the crown octavo in cloth varied between £1.13*s*.6*d*. to £1.17*s*.6*d*. per hundred copies, a little over four pence a copy. The foolscap issue generally cost from six pounds to £6.17*s*.7*d*. to bind in boards while the cost for binding the 2*s*.6*d*. issue in cloth varied from £1.11*s*.6*d*. to £1.14*s*.4*d*. The cost of drawings and engravings for the yellowback covers was consistent at £6 10*s*, as was the eight shillings cost of engraving blocks for the cloth covers.

Gissing remarked that Smith, Elder never skimped on advertising his books. They would spend between sixty and seventy pounds on the initial appearance of a new novel, from seventeen to thirty-six pounds on advertising the crown octavo and between sixteen and thirty pounds on the announcement of the cheap issues. In addition to sales of book stock, Smith, Elder sold reprint and translation rights. They would print copies for sales in cheap editions in the colonies and, in the case of Gissing's *A Life's Morning* they sold stereotype plates and printed sheets to J. B. Lippincott to publish an American edition. Selling advertising in the volumes could also bring in small sums: Smith, Elder did this on occasion with Sell's Advertising Agency. When a particular edition had no further sales value it could be remaindered for a small sum, recovering perhaps half the cost of producing a volume. Finally, the copyrights, remaining stock, and the stereotypes had a value in themselves and could be sold or transferred as John Murray, Smith's successors did with all of their Gissing titles in 1927. Gissing had sold all of his rights to Smith, Elder and never received any payments beyond the copyright sale. From his correspondence with Payn, Gissing only knew that the sales of the three-volume novels were poor, which, considering the limited nature of the three-volume novel, did not necessarily mean that the novels were unprofitable. *Demos: A Story of English Socialism* was published in three volumes by Smith, Elder in 1886 during a time of social unrest in England and while there was an interest in socialism and fear of an uprising of 'the mob'. Gissing received one hundred pounds for the sale of the copyright, 'at home and abroad' on 8 March 1886 and the novel went to the press on 23 March.

Reviews collected in *George Gissing: The Critical Heritage*, pp. 79–93, agreed that the timing was right for *Demos* and reviewers generally found it an important and well-written novel. The reviews helped the sales but did not make it a best-seller in the circulating libraries, despite an advertising commitment of almost seventy pounds by Smith, Elder. They printed 750 copies of the three-volume edition and sold 477 copies, with 200 copies sold to Mudie's, an equal number to the other circulating libraries, and sixty-three to subscribers. Seventeen, an unusually high number, were sold to the trade. Seventy-one copies were sent out as author's, deposit, and review copies and the balance of 202 were remaindered to T. Miles in 1887. Continental rights were sold to Tauchnitz in May 1886 for twenty pounds and reprint rights were sold to the *Manchester Weekly Times* on 12 July 1889 for twenty-five pounds. There was also a Harper Brothers 1886 edition published in America. No payment for it was recorded in the ledgers or translation book, but Gissing was informed by Harpers in 1891 that they had paid ten pounds for the copyright (*Diary* 251). Not counting the Harper payment, Smith, Elder made a £47.2s.5d. profit on the three-volume edition on total sales of £378.13s.4d.

On 22 November 1886 Smith, Elder printed 1000 copies of the one-volume, six-shilling edition. In 1886 and 1887 Smith, Elder sold 508 to the trade at four shillings and 4s.2d. In 1888 they sold 422 as 390 at 1s.3d. to W. H. Smith, printing a cancel title page with W. H. Smith's imprint, an 1888 date, and adding Gissing's name as author. W. H. Smith retailed this edition for 3s.6d. Despite the reviews and interest in the novel, and Smith, Elder spending thirty pounds initially on advertising, sales were poor. After the first two years' sales the remainder of the edition sold one or two copies a year, leaving three unsold at the end of 1901, 15 years after publication. Smith lost £69 13s.6d. during the first year of sales but made small profits of £18.17s.3d. and £23.8s.2d. in 1887 and 1888. The foolscap issue was printed on 16 May 1888 in two printings, one of 2000 copies and one of 1000; 2250 were bound in boards at the initial printing. This issue was much more successful, earning Smith, Elder £135.11s.9d. on sales of £385.9s.6d. to the end of 1903. The net profit on all of the editions of *Demos* amounted to £147.2s.4d. over the fifteen-year period.

Gissing had sold *Demos* outright and he knew that reprints of his novel were selling not only in England but in Germany and America as well. While Gissing was in the middle of writing volume one of *Thyrza*, he wrote to his sister Margaret in June of 1886 complaining, 'Ah, if I had some of the money they have made out of "Demos." I sold them the rights both for at home & abroad. I expect it is already pubd. in America.'[3] He resolved to earn more on *Thyrza* and wrote to Payn on 16 January 1887, that he would bring them the completed manuscript of *Thyrza* the next day and that he wanted 'sell the first Edn. for a stipulated sum & and to receive a Royalty on each copy sold after the first Edition is exhausted'.[4]

Five hundred copies of the three-volume edition of *Thyrza* were printed on 26 April 1887. A total of 444 were sold, including thirty remaindered to T. Miles & Co. at 2s.3d. per copy, well below the 6s.6d. cost. There were no attempts to print a second three-volume edition or to print a cheap edition until after Gissing had sold his entire copyright to Smith, Elder four years later, on 9 January 1891. This was quite contrary to their normal practice with Gissing's novels, in which a cheap edition was issued within eight or nine months of the three-volume edition.[5]

Three years after the publication of *Thyrza*, and considering its sales a failure, Gissing asked Smith, Elder if they would consider buying the copyright. They made their first offer in August 1890, but Gissing declined to take their initial offer, 'as the prospect of a cheap edition is so little encouraging' and he preferred to complete *New Grub Street*.[6] In 1891, Gissing accepted

---

3   George Gissing, *The Collected Letters of George Gissing*, ed. by Paul F. Mattheisen, Arthur C. Young, and Pierre Coustillas (Athens, OH, 1990–1997), III, 40 (hereafter referred to as *Letters*).

4   *Letters*, III, 73–4.

5   On 23 March 1886 Smith, Elder printed 750 copies of *Demos*, selling 480 by the end of the year and printing 1000 copies of the 6s crown octavo edition on 22 November 1886. On 12 November 1888 Smith, Elder printed 500 copies of *A Life's Morning* and had sold only 332 by the end of the year. In August 1889, they printed 2000 copies of the one-volume, two shilling and 2s. 6d. edition. On 1 April 1889 Smith, Elder printed 500 copies of *The Nether World* and sold 371 by the end of the year. On 3 December 1889 they printed 750 copies of the six-shilling crown octavo edition. *New Grub Street* had a first printing on 3 April 1891 of 500 copies, followed on 15 May by a second printing of 250 more copies. The first edition sold 447 copies, with further sales of the three-volume edition effectively killed by the printing of 750 copies of the one-volume edition on 30 October 1891, six months after the first edition appeared. None of Gissing's books *sold* 500 copies in their first edition, but few novels would induce the circulating libraries to take more than 400, in part because of the quick re-issue of them in 6s formats.

6   *Letters*, III, 229.

Smith, Elder's offer of £150 for *New Grub Street* and their offer of ten pounds for *Thyrza*, asking that:

When you think of a cheap edition, kindly let me have notice, for I should wish thoroughly to revise the book, & to shorten it somewhat. It *ought* to have something like a popular sale in a cheap edition, when a few superfluities have been cut away.[7]

Gissing did make extensive revisions to the text, remarking in his diary that he 'knew the cheap edn. would not be long delayed after the copyright came into their hands'.[8] Six months after acquiring the entire copyright to *Thyrza*, and with Gissing's revisions, Smith, Elder printed 750 copies of the six-shilling crown octavo edition and 1000 copies of a colonial edition. The one-volume edition of *Thyrza* was printed only two months after the April publication of *New Grub Street* and sold poorly, losing money for Smith, Elder. They would make up for it on the two shilling and 2s.6d. issues issued a year later. They also sold translation rights in August 1891 for five pounds to 'D. Steinhoff, Baden-Baden' but, as far as is known, this translation did not appear.

Had Gissing been entitled to his 10 per cent, his own earnings through 1904 would have brought him £14.18s.6d. on the crown octavo and £25.0s.6d. on the cheap issues, or almost forty pounds for the novel, with most of the income coming during the first printings of the novels in their cheap format. Smith, Elder made over eighty-two pounds on *Thyrza*. Had Gissing accepted their initial one hundred pound offer, or had he been paid a royalty, their bottom line would not have changed substantially but by deliberately withholding publication until they could secure the entire copyright, Smith, Elder enjoyed the modest profit that would have gone to Gissing.

The next Gissing novel published by Smith, Elder, *A Life's Morning*, was sent to them in November 1885, while *Demos* was still unwritten. Gissing received fifty pounds for the entire copyright 'at home and abroad', with the understanding that he would receive a further fifty pounds if it were to be published in the *Cornhill Magazine*. It would be three years before *A Life's Morning* would be published, appearing first as a serial in the *Cornhill*, running from January to December 1888. The three-volume edition was advertised for publication on 15 November 1888.Gissing was in Paris when he saw the advertisement and was surprised as he had written it to be in two volumes.[9] Five hundred copies were printed and 450 bound. Of the three-volume edition, 337 were sold, 117 remaindered and £60 earned from the Lippincott sale. *A Life's*

---

7   *Letters*, III, 293.
8   George Gissing, *London and The Life of Literature in Late Victorian England: The Diary of George Gissing, Novelist*, ed. by Pierre Coustillas (Hassocks, 1978), p. 238 (hereafter *Diary*).
9   *Diary*, p. 58.

Morning bypassed the crown octavo format and appeared directly in cheap editions in August 1889. Two thousand copies were printed on 12 August and bound in boards. Another 1000 were printed on 9 September, engravers' blocks were made, and 300 copies were bound in cloth. Smith, Elder received a small amount from Sell's Advertising Agency for placing advertising in the copies that they bound in boards. This would be the most profitable of Gissing's novels to Smith, Elder, returning almost £164 to them over its lifetime.

Gissing's first wife, Nell Harrison, a prostitute, died from alcoholism and syphilis at the end of February 1888. Her death inspired Gissing to 'bear testimony against the accursed social order that brings about things of this kind'.[10] On 19 March Gissing began writing *The Nether World*, a novel in which he would realistically display the living hell of London's poor. He was in Paris when Smith, Elder made him an offer of £150 for *The Nether World*. The receipt is dated 9 October 1888 and unlike previous handwritten receipts this one is printed but with the phrase 'at home and abroad, including the United States of America' added in writing. Later receipts would have 'at home and abroad' printed, and amendments such as 'including the United States of America' written in before the title, recognizing the importance of foreign copyright and anticipating that a copyright bill then being debated in the United States Congress would be passed.

The usual 500 copies of the three-volume edition were printed at a cost of £85.18s.11d. and 450 copies bound. Three hundred and seventy-two were sold and seventy-seven remaindered. Harper Brothers paid £15 for the rights to reprint the novel in their Franklin Square Library in America in 1889, where it sold for 45 cents, or approximately two shillings. This was the first Gissing three-volume novel on which Smith, Elder lost money, the sale of 372 library and trade copies leaving them with a substantial net loss of £44.18s.10d. on sales of £286.17s.6d. They recovered only a little over one pound in 1890 and the final remainder sale of £4.5s.2d. left them with an overall loss of the library edition of £39.12s.4d. On 3 December 1889, Smith, Elder printed 750 copies of the crown octavo edition, binding 600 copies. They also printed a four-page introduction to the novel that was added to the printing of a 1500-copy colonial edition. The crown octavo edition had meagre sales in 1889 and 1890 and then only occasional sales until 1903 when Boots purchased the remaining fourteen at nine pence.

The printing for the foolscap issue is recorded for 18 June 1890. They again sold advertising to Sell's and printed and bound it into 2350 copies in

---

10 *Diary*, p. 23.

boards, binding another 300 copies in red cloth and selling another 500 to Petherick. A little over half of the cloth-bound copies were sold. Printing, engraving, binding, and commission were barely offset by sales, returning only £6.1s.4d. at the end of 1890. Sales continued to be slow, but by the summer of 1903 only twenty-five copies of the 1890 printing remained and an additional 500 more copies were printed on 21 August. Despite the slow sales, over the thirteen years from its publication to 1903, the foolscap issue returned a profit and had annual sales of over ten pounds for seven of its fifteen years.

On Gissing's return from Greece after selling *The Emancipated* to Bentley, he struggled with and abandoned three other novels. On 6 September Gissing wrote to Bertz that marriage on Gissing's income was impossible as:

Educated English girls *will* not face poverty in marriage, & to them anything under £400 a year is serious poverty. ...there is no *real* hope of my ever marrying any one of a better kind, no real hope whatever! I say it with the gravest conviction.[11]

The letter outlined what would become central to *New Grub Street*, the inability of Reardon to support his middle-class wife on his literary earnings. It also anticipated Gissing's future. Alone and frustrated, Gissing wrote in his diary on 16 September 1890 that he felt unable to work properly unless he was married. The next day he began writing 'Victor Yule', the novel that was to become *New Grub Street*. A week later he met Edith Underwood, a twenty-three year old working class woman, at a music hall. On the first of October he began again on the novel and was seeing Edith regularly for morning walks and evening visits at his flat. By the end of the week he was writing to his sister that he would possibly marry by the end of the year. The next day he sold some of his books for £6.5s.0d., an event that would appear in *New Grub Street* as a sign of Reardon's poverty and despair.[12] He and Edith were married in February, after Gissing had sold *New Grub Street*. Unfortunately, Edith was not to be a compliant working girl who would be grateful for Gissing for his intellect and attention. By 1894 Edith was showing signs of the violent insanity that would force Gissing to leave her in 1897.

Smith, Elder accepted the novel in January 1891, finding it 'very clever & original', but fearing that 'the prevailing melancholy' of the novel would not make it popular.[13] They offered £150. Gissing wrote back accepting and asking for ten pounds for the entire copyright for *Thyrza*. He received the cheque for *New Grub Street* the next day and the cheque for *Thyrza* a day later.[14] The

---

11 *Letters*, IV, 235.
12 *Diary*, pp. 226–7.
13 *Letters*, IV, 254.
14 *Diary*, p. 235.

receipt, dated 8 January, assigned the entire copyright, 'at home and abroad' and, written in above the title, 'including the United States of America'. Gissing wrote to Bertz that in being offered the same amount as he had been offered for his last two books he felt he was making no advance in his career.

The ledger entry for 3 April 1891 shows a charge of £100.0s.5d. for composing thirty three-quarter sheets of 32-page crown octavo and costs of paper and printing 500 copies. The novel was published on 7 April. The total number of 514 deposit, author, review and commercial sale copies necessitated another printing on 15 May of 250 additional copies, adding £24.11s.9d. to the production costs. A total of 525 copies were bound and £60.7s.3d. was spent on advertising but total sales never went beyond 447. Reprinting rights were sold to Tauchnitz for thirty pounds and translation rights were sold for eight pounds to Adele Berger in Austria.[15] The three-volume edition was not successful and Smith, Elder lost £16.12s.4d. on sales of £362.15s.0d. Although it was certainly talked about and even debated in the pages of *The Author*, the journal of the Society of Authors, with Walter Besant defending it and Andrew Lang condemning it (and Gissing thinking that neither of them understood the novel at all), even the most favourable reviews described it as morbid, gloomy, and as a 'long, desolate tragedy'. Perhaps Smith, Elder should have heeded L. F. Austin's review in the *Illustrated London News*: 'There is power in every line. … But will Mr Mudie's subscribers relish the process?'[16]

Even though Gissing was happy that a 'second edition' of *New Grub Street* was printed the book did not sell as well as or as profitably as *Demos*, which had an initial printing of 750 copies and sold 477 copies, a difference of thirty more copies, and earned Smith, Elder almost forty-six pounds. The difference between the two was partly in the cheaper printing costs: printing 750 copies of *New Grub Street* in two printings cost £124.12s.2d. opposed to the single 750-copy printing of *Demos* at £109.11s.3d., and mostly, of course, because Gissing was paid another fifty pounds above what he received for *Demos*. The printing of the six-shilling edition only six months after the second printing of the three-volume edition was also certain to kill further sales with the libraries. Finally, the appearance of the six-shilling edition of *Thyrza*, sent to the printers less than a month (9 June) after the second printing of *New Grub Street*, also competed with the new novel. On 25 June 1891 the colonial edition of 1500 copies was sold to Petherick and 750 copies of the domestic edition were

---

15 According to the editors of the *Letters*, it was published in serial form as 'Ein Mann des Tages' in the newspaper *Pester Lloyd* in Budapest from 29 December to 30 April (*Letters* V, 10). They did not see the ledger or translation book entry.

16 *Illustrated London News*, 2 May 1891, p. 571.

printed but fewer than 500 were sold: over the six-shilling edition's entire life to 1904 it only earned £7.18s.5d. The foolscap issue enjoyed much better sales when it appeared in 1892, with steady sales that averaged 165 copies a year.

New Grub Street would be the last Gissing book Smith, Elder would publish. The break came because of the strained relations between Gissing and Payn, and Gissing's feeling that he was worth more than Smith, Elder were offering him. In March 1891, while working on the manuscript of his next book, *Born in Exile*, Gissing wrote to Bertz that he felt he was right to remain with Smith as 'He has a solid commercial interest in my books, & he advertizes them well. I shall never again willingly leave him'.[17] Gissing was encouraged by the reviews of *New Grub Street* and wrote to Bertz on 15 May that:

'New Grub Street' seems to be more like a literary success than any other of my books. [...] Not only am I well reviewed, but positive articles are devoted to the book. [...] We shall see whether all this has any financial results – to the publishers. Dash it all! I ought to get more than £150 for my next book.[18]

On 20 July 1891 he sent the manuscript to Smith, Elder asking £250 for the English and American copyright. Because of the disappointing sales of *New Grub Street*, Payn refused to pay £250. Gissing wrote to Payn on 7 August 1891:

I must not argue the point of price, for I know nothing of the conditions which determine it, but it seems to me a most astonishing thing that a book from my hands at the present day should be worth only fifty pounds more than 'Demos' some years ago. By reserving the American copyright I gain nothing, for it is not in my power to conduct the business necessary for disposing of that right [...] after this, it will no doubt be better for me to put my affairs in the hands of Watt, or some such man. I should then reap the odds & ends of profit which I must now perforce neglect. I am not set on making money, but I must not forget that only with the help of money can one's artistic powers be developed.

On 9 August Gissing wrote in his diary that he had a letter from Payn returning the manuscript:

Saying that if I like to send it back in a month's time, he will then finish it, but could not advise Smith to give more than £150. Adds that my 'pessimism' is the cause of my failure. Forthwith wrote to A. P. Watt, the literary agent, asking if he would do business for me.[19]

Gissing never sent another manuscript to Smith, Elder and, although he would never forgive them for *Thyrza*, he certainly held them in less contempt

---

17 *Letters*, IV, 275–6.
18 Ibid., 294.
19 *Diary*, p. 253.

as publishers than he did Bentley. Nor did Smith, Elder completely shun Gissing. In January 1895 they asked him to contribute to a proposed series of 3s.6d. novels. Gissing wrote to William Morris Colles, his new agent, that 'Of *going back* to S&E., there is no question; I should merely sell a volume to them for a special cheap series. I should never dream of letting them become, again, my regular publishers.' as he preferred to keep his major works with Lawrence & Bullen.[20] At the end of 1899 he told James B. Pinker, who was then his agent that he would have remained with Smith, Elder 'had it been possible to live on what they paid me'.[21]

The one thing Gissing would always regret was selling the copyrights. On 29 September 1893 he wrote to Bertz that 'In reserving to yourself the copyright you act, of course, very wisely. I only wish I had had the courage & the foresight to refuse to sell those novels out & out to Smith & Elder. They would now have been a source of income'.[22] They would have been, especially for the sale of the film rights of *Demos* for £250 in later years. It is also possible, indeed likely, that a literary agent would have been more aggressive in selling the rights to print *New Grub Street* in the United States; it was not published in America until 1904. However, the royalties that would have come would not have been great. Sales were strongest in the first two years of an edition and profits and losses greatest during that time. From the third year of an edition on, Smith, Elder only averaged one pound on the annual sales of the six-shilling crown octavo. The foolscap issues did better and had longer lives, but even on those, from the third year on, sales only averaged ten pounds. If Gissing had been given a fifteen per cent royalty he may have made an average of £7.6s.0d. a year. On the other hand, when he did own the copyright, as with *Thyrza*, or, as with *The Emancipated*, where Bentley would have owed an additional payment to Gissing had he gone into another edition, the publishers had no incentive to sell above the copyright-earning number or to release a cheap edition.

The comparative earnings of Smith, Elder and Gissing through 1903 are illustrated in the following tables. Smith, Elder earned over a number of years about £120 more than Gissing did on copyright sales for books, and the earnings do not take their office expenses into account. If their overhead expenses were similar to John Murray's sixteen per cent estimate, Smith, Elder would have earned about £40 less than Gissing.[23]

---

20   *Letters*, IV, 285–6.
21   Ibid., 402.
22   *Letters*, V, 148.
23   Alexis Weedon, *Victorian Publishing: The Economics of Book Production for a Mass Market 1836–1916* (Aldershot, 2003), p. 63.

Smith, Elder earnings on Gissing's Book, 1886–1903[24]

Demos (1886)			Life's Morning (1888)			Nether World (1888)		
3-vol	£47	2s.		£109		3d.	(£44	18s.	10d.)
6s	(£25	4s.	7d.)	n/a	n/a	n/a	£70	6s.	7d.
2s	£125	11s.	9d.	£54	13s.	3d.	£102	3s.	3d.
Total	£147	9s.	7d.	£163	13s.	6d.	£132	17s.	6d.
Copyright	£50			£150			£100		

Thyrza (1887, 1891)			New Grub Street (1891)		
3-vol	£51	3s.	11d.	(£16	12s.	4d.)
6s	(£25	18s.	8d.)	£7	18s.	5d.
2s	£56	19s.	10d.	£112	13s.	3d.
Total	£82	5s.	1d.	£103	19s.	4d.
Copyright	£60			£150		

Was the author's life depicted in *New Grub Street* an accurate reflection of the relations between authors and publishers in the late nineteenth century? Its setting was 1882, nine years before it was published, when copyrights were commonly sold outright, literary agents almost unknown, the three-decker novel and the circulating libraries ruled, struggling authors earned little recognition and less money, and unless they gave into the commercialism that ruled the careers of Jasper Milvain or James Payn they had little chance to appeal to a broad audience that would buy enough of their books to let them, and not the publishers, dictate their terms. Less popular and lesser known authors fared worse than Gissing. The economics of the market quite simply depended on the saleability of an author.

Gissing's market value would increase, especially as he began to write novels about the middle-classes and as the three-volume novel and the power of the circulating libraries died. Gissing also began selling short stories, some of his best and most profitable work. In 1892 he would earn over £272, in 1893 £193, in 1894 and 1895 £438 and £519. His income would drop to under £200 in 1897 but rebound in the next year to £524. More importantly, experienced agents negotiated his contracts; he would be paid royalties and retain rights that would be inherited by his family after his death. He would, from the

---

24 Information from the Smith, Elder ledger and translation books now in the John Murray archives.

time he left Smith, Elder, be dealing with the commercial publishing world in the same manner as a modern author would today. Smith, Elder would continue to earn a small income from their rights to his work, and, with the development of cinema, a substantial sum for the sale of *Demos*. For a publisher each title purchased was an investment for the future. Books that continued to return even small sums would remain in print, especially if their authors, like Gissing, added some prestige to the backlist.

Gissing was an honest man and an honest craftsman, who wanted only to earn enough to have the time – leisure would be the wrong term here – to do a craftsman's job and not, like Payn, and the many other novelists of the time, write popular, successful, and ultimately forgotten novels. New Grub Street and Gissing's name remain, outliving him, Smith, Elder, and the copyrights. The art remains long after the economics have ceased to be relevant.

Lists, Inventories and Catalogues: Shifting Modes of Ordered Knowledge in the Early Modern Book Trade

DAVID L. GANTS

THE LAST ONE HUNDRED YEARS of bibliographical scholarship in the history of the English book trade have been dominated by catalogues: of books, of watermarks, of printers' ornaments and title-page borders. At the same time considerable effort has gone into the transcription and publication of primary documents such as those found in company archives and government repositories. Little research has been carried out, however, in support of the tools of quantitative analysis developed by historians and social scientists. Those bibliographical studies that have employed empirical evidence clearly demonstrate the value of such a methodology. D. F. McKenzie pored over two decades of financial records from the Cambridge University Press, enabling him to recreate a month-by-month production schedule based on composition and presswork figures.[1] Relying primarily on bibliographical evidence derived from a close physical examination of over five hundred books of varying sizes, Peter W. M. Blayney scrutinized the Nicholas Okes printing house and reconstructed the week-by-week activities of the establishment for a two-year period.[2] Overall, though, the relative paucity of quantitative-based research is due primarily to the lack of hard data upon which to work. While we know for the most part what books were published and something about the official lives of the men and women who worked in the printing houses and bookshops, we know very little about the measurable physical and material circumstances of the trade itself. As a result, we lack an essential key to understanding one of the fundamental forces that shaped the legal, economic, political, scientific, religious, and cultural growth of the modern English-speaking world.

This paper will discuss a project which seeks to create the hard bibliographical evidence required for numeric-based research – to embrace the culture of metrics. The Early English Booktrade Database (EEBD) is conceived

---

1 *The Cambridge University Press, 1696–1712* (Cambridge, 1966).
2 *The Texts of King Lear and their Origins* (Cambridge, 1982).

as the first networked electronic resource devoted to the organization and dissemination of empirical bibliographical statistics. The EEBD's goal is to measure, classify, and describe material evidence related to English printing and publishing 1475–1640 (also know as the *STC* period, after the Pollard and Redgrave *Short-Title Catalogue of Books Printed in England, Scotland & Ireland 1475–1640*). In a very real sense, the information collected by the EEBD will form an archaeology of the book, a rich collection of physical data extracted from the actual products of the printing and publishing trade, i.e. the books themselves, and out of which we can reconstruct the business practices, the labour relations, the material accounting procedures, and other heretofore obscured details of early printing houses and bookshops. This archaeological data will in turn enable us for the first time to carry out large-scale empirical analyses of all aspects of early modern print culture.

At its heart, the EEBD consists of two distinct classes of information: new material gathered from the close physical examination of every title printed during the *STC* period; and relevant data from existing resources such as the *STC* and *ESTC* that have been revised and recompiled to be used analytically in correlation with the freshly gathered evidence. New material includes:

Edition Sheet. One of the main stumbling blocks to a deeper understanding of the book trade is the lack of data detailing the productive capacity of printing houses. Most studies to date have relied upon lists of titles, an approach that does not distinguish between a 1500-page folio history and a single-sheet broadside ballad.[3] The EEBD will employ a unit of measure called the edition sheet, or the number of sheets in an exemplar volume used as a measure of the relative amount of work required to produce the complete run of that volume. By compiling edition sheet totals, the EEBD will provide a more accurate assessment of the amount of work involved in machining every book in the *STC* period.

Composition Totals. Measuring the linear amount of type used in a particular volume provides an estimate amount of composition and proofreading work involved to produce it. In conjunction with edition sheets, this information allows one to create much more sophisticated evaluations of the productive capacity of individual printing houses as well as the entire trade.

Typography. This category includes both the face and body of the types used to produce a particular volume. Such data provides long-term insights into the changing cultural fashions of the book trade, in particular the complex relationship between the subject of a book, the chosen format (folio, quarto, octavo, etc.), the size and quality of

---

3   See for example Appendix 1, *The Cambridge History of the Book in Britain, Volume IV, 1557–1695*, ed. by John Barnard and D. F. McKenzie, with the assistance of Maureen Bell (Cambridge, 2002), pp. 779–93.

paper used, the type face and body in which it was set, and the business practices of the printer who impressed it.

Paper. This fundamental building-block of the book has resisted detailed analysis due to the varied and shifting forms it takes as well as the sheer volume of paper consumed by the trade. However, research has established a strong correlation between watermarks used by the paper producer (when present) and the size and class of the sheets. The EEBD will identify the dominant watermark type and corresponding paper group used to print each title employing a classification system based upon work by leading bibliographical scholars.

Main Text Layout. The project will classify the gross design features of the main body of the text, i.e. simple header and text, text with marginal notes, ruled compartments, etc. Like typography, these data provide long-term insights into the changing cultural fashions of the book trade, such as the gradual addition of the scholarly apparatus to literary works.

Paratext. Just as books are not simply containers for texts, neither is the paratextual framework present in most books from this period merely padding. Expanding on Franklin Williams's 1962 *Index of Dedications and Commendatory Verses*, the EEBD will classify the variety of dedications, prefaces, introductions and errata as well as creating a table of personal names.

The *ESTC* has generously supplied the EEBD with a data extract of the approximately 36,000 records of titles printed 1475–1640, which will serve as the backbone of the project. Extracted data to be revised and compiled includes:

Edition-Issue-Variant. The building-block for virtually all studies of book production and circulation is the edition, i.e. a volume produced from newly set type. The first editors of the *STC* often assigned multiple record numbers to issues and minor variants of a single edition, a practice that has continued in subsequent incarnations of the resource.[4] Tests on sample pages indicate that the blurring of differences among these different classes of publication has bloated the second edition of the *STC* (and consequently the ESTC) by roughly 2000–3000 records. The EEBD will link multiple issues and variants of a single edition with a unique ID reference to enable edition-level analyses.

Multiple Editions. Equally important to an understanding of the English book trade is the ability to identify frequently printed works. In order to support large-scale market analyses as well as enable users to interpolate gaps in the historical record, the EEBD will link multiple editions of the same title with a unique ID reference. Such an apparatus will allow uses to quickly identify and extract complete information on all editions of the same work.

Shared Printing and Publishing. The *ESTC* follows the practice of the *STC* by presenting title and imprint information in a modified version of its original spelling. In order to make such data useable in digital search and display routines, the EEBD will

---

4   For a definition of these terms, see *STC*, vol. 1, p. xli.

regularize proper nouns in the imprint field using the Library of Congress Authority spellings and reference numbers.[5] Each individual record will have linked cross-references to the *ESTC* items in which the same printers or booksellers had a hand, as well as a numeric estimate of the proportional responsibility when sharing work. Additionally, the EEBD will cross-link its data with the biographical information held in the *British Book Trade Index* at the University of Birmingham.[6]

Format and Collation. The *STC* and *ESTC* include collation formulae (i.e. a precise, condensed description of how a book is physically assembled) for some of the titles, but the majority of the entries have only format designations.[7] The EEBD will add structural collation formulae to all records.

The focus of this paper is the final component of the EEBD: subject classification and analysis. On-line catalogues such as *WorldCat* and the *ESTC* employ a library-based set of subject headings designed to aid users in locating books of interest. The EEBD will instead classify volumes according to a strict taxonomy of subject groupings derived from existing historical studies and designed to support a variety of analyses, providing scholars with new ways to evaluate the business practices of printers and booksellers.

Any effort that seeks to group books according to an arbitrary taxonomy reflects to some degree the biases of those devising the groups and assigning membership. This admitted bias has been turned back on itself and multiple, overlapping information systems have been constructed, each reflecting a specific cultural perspective for the ordering of knowledge. First, a modern structure based upon literary, linguistic and historical scholarship of the past hundred years; second, an historical system that recognizes sixteenth- and seventeenth-century book trade practices and derived from published catalogues,[8] lists of 'vendible books',[9] estate inventories,[10] and the 1668–1709 Term Catalogues;[11]

---

5   'Library of Congress Authority website', < http://authorities.loc.gov/>.

6   'British Book Trade Index website', <www.bbti.bham.ac.uk>.

7   For a definition of format, see STC, vol. 1, pp. xxxix–xl. Collation is a more complicated concept, dealt with at length in Fredson Bowers's *Principles of Bibliographical Description* (Princeton, 1949).

8   See in particular the Frankfurt Fair book catalogues printed in London between 1617 and 1628 (STC 11328–11331.2).

9   In particular: *The First Part of the Catalogue of English Printed Bookes* (London, John Windet for Andrew Maunsell, 1595); *A Catalogue of Such English Bookes, as Lately Have Bene, or Now Are in Print for Publication* (London, William Jaggard, 1618); *A Catalogue of the most Vendible Books in England* (London, William London 1657–58).

10   For example, the inventories of Henry Bynneman and John Foster examined by John Barnard and Maureen Bell, *The Early Seventeenth Century Book Trade and John Foster's Inventory of 1616* (Leeds, 1994).

11   Edward Arber, *The Term Catalogues, 1668–1709 A.D.*, 3 vols. (London, 1903–6).

and third a scheme that seeks to reflect the way early modern readers organized their volumes, based on reconstructions of period libraries.[12]

Among book historians there is a rough consensus of how to group works according to contemporary standards, one that reflects to some degree a bias emerging from the echo chamber of scholarship. It is tempting to play the iconoclast, dismiss the received structure and propose a completely new system based upon a different set of assumptions. However, the utility of ongoing research increases when pursued with an awareness of its predecessors in the field, and so we have broken down the books published during the target period into categories informed by those devised by H. S. Bennett,[13] Alain Veylit,[14] and Don-John Dugas.[15] Bennett presumed that stationers responded to market pressures and arranged the publication of particular books primarily 'to satisfy the needs of contemporary readers'.[16] While also classifying books according to subject matter, Dugas recognizes that in doing so he is creating an interpretive framework 'slanted toward readers', and admits his categories 'do not necessarily reflect the printing and financial concerns of print-trade professionals'. Market forces drove the Jacobean book trade and the publisher who commissioned projects without some sense of the potential audience stood a slim chance of prospering. Nevertheless a classificatory structure based solely upon perceived readerly desires misses the important market deformations caused by the continued monopolistic exploitation of patents and the protectionist policies practised by the Stationers' Company. Dugas accommodates his project bias by further examining collaborative habits among publishers and by taking into account the popularity of the 16-page, single-sheet octavo pamphlet, which he describes as 'one of the least expensive methods of printing'.[17] Like Dugas, we include collaboration in our goals; we also distinguish between the business practices of establishments engaged primarily in the production of

---

12 Especially useful are: *Private Libraries in Renaissance England*, ed. R. J. Fehrenbach, E. S. Leedham-Green (Binghamton, NY, 1992); Sears Jayne, *Library Catalogues of the English Renaissance* (Godalming, 1983); as well as many ecclesiastical and scholastic inventories.

13 *English Books and Readers 1603 to 1640* (Cambridge, 1970). See in particular pp. 87–198. Yamada also breaks down Creede's output by generic category but he follows Bennett's model with only one minor variation.

14 'A Statistical Survey and Evaluation of the *Eighteenth-Century Short-Title Catalog*' (Dissertation, University of California Riverside, 1994). In particular Appendices 1 & 2, pp. 378–84.

15 Don-John Dugas, 'The London Book Trade in 1709', *Papers of the Bibliographical Society of America*, 95 (2001), 32–58, 157–72. See in particular pp. 43–5.

16 Bennett, *English Books and Readers*, p. 87.

17 Dugas, 'The London Book Trade in 1709', p. 44.

protected works (such as the King's Printing House) and the larger group of commercial publishers and printers. Finally, Veylit's study includes a useful word-list generated from the *ESTC* that he employed when classifying titles, a tool that proved most helpful when pursuing the difficult task of assigning individual works to a specific subject category. Linking each of these variant systems is the modern sense of how knowledge is organized into rough groupings.

After evaluating these three structures, and after considering how they might best illuminate the data we had collected, we decided upon seven main subject headings (Fig. 1):

1. Information, including works on language, business training and skills, education, husbandry, popular science and medicine.
2. Ephemera, including ballads, almanacs, catalogues and news pamphlets.
3. History, both popular and scholarly.
4. Law and Politics, including both English and law-French, and non-religious polemics.
5. Literature, including belles lettres and popular, classical and travel works.
6. Official Documents, including forms, and proclamations.
7. Religion, including sermons, Bibles, prayer books, instruction and commentary along with controversial and devotional works.

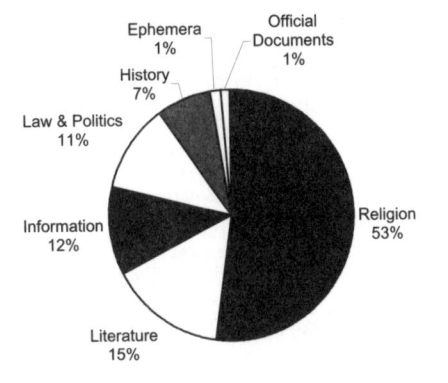

Fig. 1. Modern Classification System, All Subjects

Such an attempt to classify the diverse works circulating in early modern England must necessarily make any number of binary simplifications and arbitrary choices. It is often difficult, for example, to identify a pamphlet as either religious or political since those concepts so often shared overlapping domains. Equally slippery is the dividing line between a piece of popular verse and an encomium celebrating royal power. Because scholars like Bennett are concerned with a more narrative or impressionistic survey of the cultural landscape of Tudor and Stuart England, they made frequent illustrative digressions into numerous sub-types to flesh out their core categories. The goals of the EEBD are empirical rather than discursive, so we have attempted to create a set of modern categories limited enough to identify trends and preferences yet large enough so as to avoid blurring important distinctions.

Constructing a classificatory system that reflects the business practices of sixteenth- and seventeenth-century booksellers requires a slightly different tack. For one thing, a large number of the titles listed in catalogues and other marketing devices bear continental imprints. London presses produced mainly English-language volumes, while stationers imported large numbers of Greek and Latin titles from the continent that they then retailed through bookstalls and to a broad clientele of aristocrats and intellectuals,[18] and university presses supplemented them by printing works of divinity and classical antiquity. Reconstructions of Ben Jonson's library indicate that something in the order of eighty per cent of the books he used were printed on the continent, and Sir Edward Stanhope's book bequest to Trinity College, Cambridge in 1608 contained nearly ninety-three per cent continental imprints.[19] As well, commercial lists such as the *Term Catalogues* did not include all classes of works. Nonetheless, the surviving examples of catalogues issued by publishers and leading booksellers advertising their wares to the large number of stationers engaged in the retail trade reveal a fairly consistent approach to classification (Fig. 2):

1. Divinity, including sermons, commentary, ecclesiastical controversies, instruction, psalm paraphrases, and devotionals.
2. Physick, including medicine, chemistry, and anatomy.
3. Histories, including current and ancient subjects, romances, travel literature, and lives.
4. Humanities, including husbandry, philosophy, statecraft, language, education, shorthand, jests, music, and epigrams.

---

18 See Julian Roberts, 'The Latin Trade', *The Cambridge History of the Book in Britain*. Volume IV, 1557–1695, pp. 141–73.

19 Alain A. Wijffels, 'Sir Edward Stanhope's Bequest of Books to Trinity College, Cambridge, 1608', *Private Libraries in Renaissance England*, ed. R. J. Fehrnbach, Vol. 1 (Binghamton, 1992), 41–78.

5. Poetry and Plays.
6. Mathematics, including astrology, architecture, navigation, physics, surveying, arithmetic, carpentry, and optics.
7. Foreign Languages, including non-law Latin and French.
8. Law.
9. Miscellaneous, including state documents, political tracts, Catholic and Quaker literature, newspapers, pageants, ballads, almanacs, and 'Wonderment Tracts', all items that Arber mentions as rarely occurring in the *Term Catalogues*.

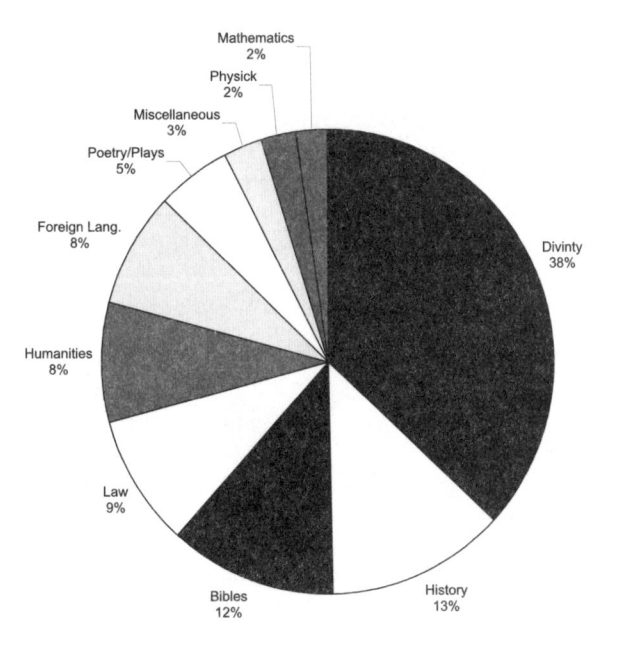

Fig. 2. Bookseller Classification System

Since the EEBD deals only with printing in the British Isles, continental imprints are excluded from the above list.

The most difficult classificatory system to construct derives from evidence detailing the way different contemporary readers viewed texts. Scholastic libraries for the most part retained the medieval learning sequence of the trivium (grammar, rhetoric, and logic), and the quadrivium (arithmetic, geometry, music, and astronomy), both of which prepared the student for philosophy and theology. Private collectors used these categories while inventing ones of their own, depending upon their particular interests: Sir Thomas Bodley famously

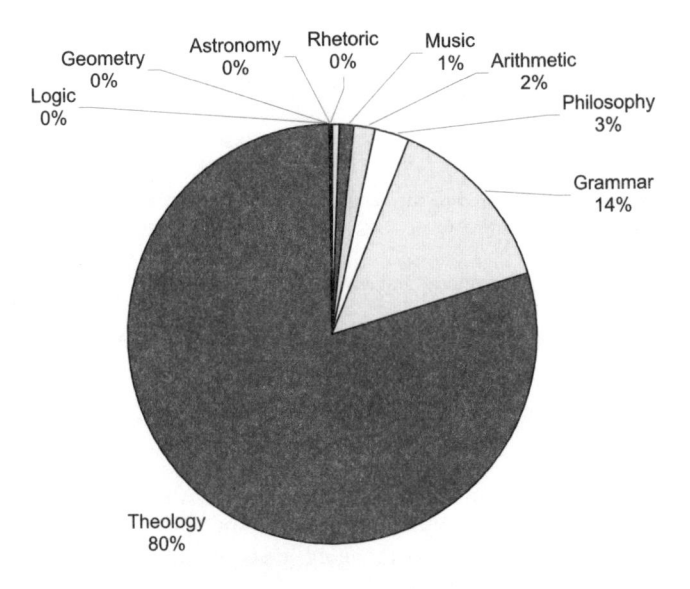

Fig. 3. Scholastic Classification System [9,114 edition sheets]

banned plays, almanacs and other such 'riffe raffe' books from his shelf; John Bateman's 1559 probate inventory includes over 500 works, over half of which were theological, with only thirty-three English titles; Sir Edward Dering's 1644 inventory of 670 books is nearly half English, including history, geography and contemporary literature.[20]

The EEBD has chosen to accommodate the public-private divide by adopting a two-level approach to grouping works (Fig. 3):

1. Scholastic
   a. Grammar
   b. Rhetoric
   c. Logic
   d. Arithmetic

---

20 Elisabeth Leedham-Green and David McKitterick, 'Ownership: Private and Public Libraries', *The Cambridge History of the Book in Britain*, Vol. 4, ed. by John Barnard and D. F. McKenzie (Cambridge, 2002), pp. 323–5.

    e. Geometry
    f. Music
    g. Astronomy
    h. Philosophy
    i. Theology

2. Secular

    a. Law.
    b. Natural Science, including medicine, chemistry, husbandry, etc.
    c. Belle Lettres, including poetry and drama.
    d. Commerce.
    e. Histories, including current and ancient subjects, romances, travel literature, and lives.
    f. Popular Theology, including inspirational and devotional texts as well as sermons.
    g. Bibles.
    h. Miscellaneous, including ephemera, popular entertainments, and informational works.

This bipartite structure will support a number of analytical approaches: an examination of the shift in emphasis between the two primary ways of organizing knowledge; an inquiry into changing levels of interest and importance

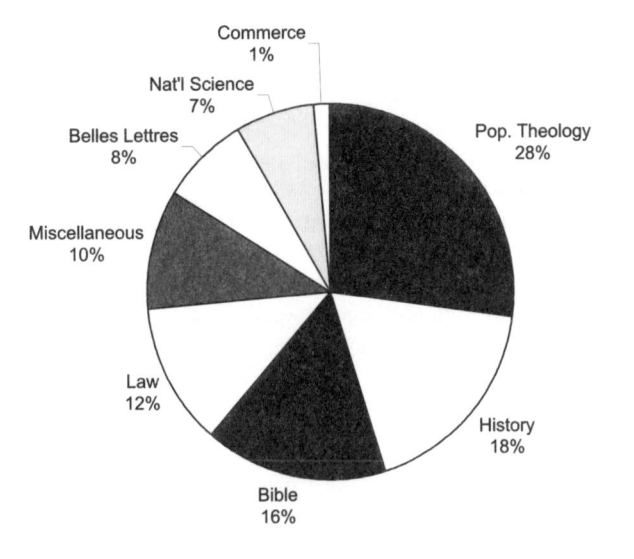

Fig. 4. Secular Classification System [28,970 edition sheets]

within one or the other primary grouping; and simultaneous interrogations of the ways that knowledge moves within and between the two groups. Of course, these classificatory models are still in flux; as the project team begins to work more deeply with books printed before the mid-Jacobean period, we will also improve and refine our categories. Nevertheless, we can use the preliminary scheme outlined above in co-ordination with the other classes of data collected to test and monitor the project's progress, and this paper will now consider a few examples.

Before proceeding, one crucial question plagues any attempt to quantify the early English book trade, and that is the many gaps in the historical record. Discussing the problems surrounding contemporary historical scholarship, Robert Hume has argued that holes in the evidentiary fabric 'are at least as troublesome as bias'.[21] D. F. McKenzie, probably the best-known pessimist among book historians, goes further. His essay contribution to Volume 4 of the *Cambridge History of the Book in Britain*[22] reads like a barrister summing up arguments for conviction as he cites a handful of lurid anecdotes that leads us to despair of ever examining in any detail the printing and publishing trade before 1700. We can say this: many books no longer exist; the number of missing books is unknowable; and different books survive at different rates. Beyond here be dragons.

Do fragile data undermine empirical studies? Perhaps we need to clarify the aims of the enterprise and the role evidence plays in it. No one would suggest that because archives like the Public Record Office or parish registers are incomplete, we should reject scholarly approaches that employ them. Literary critics, biographers and book historians all gather what they can, then use their own understanding and knowledge of the period to fill in the gaps with informed speculations and inductions – acknowledging, of course, the speculative and inductive nature of their conclusions.

Quantitative bibliographers use empirical data to construct comparisons and assess correlations rather than merely to present descriptive statistics. We compile evidence for the purpose of generating context, of mapping similarities and differences, of weighing influence. Thus while gaps may hinder our quest to provide fine-grained detail, they tend to occur across many records and to affect them all. While lost materials limit what we can say about any particular record, the impact of those breaks on comparative and correlative work is minimal. As well, large data populations ameliorate localized variations. The

21 'The Aims and Limits of Historical Scholarship', *Review of English Studies* 53 (2002), 408.

22 'Printing and Publishing 1557–1700: constraints on the London book trade', pp. 553–7.

EEBD will contain 36,000 records describing nearly a million edition sheets of presswork and billions of ens of composition. In short, while the problematic historical record limits what analyses we can reliably pursue, it by no means invalidates quantitative approaches as a whole. The sample analyses that follow come from a small, trial version of the EEBD covering the five-year period 1614–18.[23] These years were ones of relative peace at home and abroad, stable prices, and a lack of plague visitations. Without the economic disruptions that accompany wars, famine and disease, we can identify trade patterns a little more clearly.

At this point I should like to map out the similarities and differences among these three systems using exemplar works. First let me explain briefly the unit of quantification I am employing and a little about the time period I have chosen for the study. As mentioned above, we are employing as one of our output measurements the 'edition sheet', a unit that illuminates the relative amount of machining work required to produce a particular book. For example, a typical three-gathering, 48-page octavo signed A–C^8 has three edition sheets: A, B, and C. In contrast, a three-gathering, 48-page folio-in-eights, also signed A–C^8 has twelve edition sheets: four sheets in gathering A, four in B, and four in C. While not taking into account the number of actual copies printed, the edition sheet does offer a rough gauge of the number of formes machined by a house as well as an indication of capacity. Peter Blayney speculates based upon the evidence presented in McKenzie's study of the Cambridge University Press 'that while a single press could produce 300 [edition] sheets a year, the annual production of a continuously-operated printing house would in practice be more like 200 sheets per press'.[24] Edition sheets will be used to explore the tripartite classification scheme we have devised.

The tripartite subject classification can now illuminate in finer detail how London stationers managed their resources and responded to market demands. Beginning with the modern classification system (see Fig. 1), we see a confirmation of a bibliographical commonplace, that over half the trade output was devoted to religious works. A sizeable amount of literary titles were also produced, along with a diverse group of informational works, books of law and politics, and those dealing with modern and classical history. Within that large group of religious titles, the most popular subjects were those dealing with biblical and theological commentary, followed by popular religious instruction, individual and collected sermons, controversial tracts, and private devotional

23 I have written a companion piece employing the same dataset: 'A Quantitative Analysis of the London Book Trade 1614–1618', *Studies in Bibliography* 55 (2004), 185–213.
24 Blayney, *The Texts of King Lear and their origins* (Cambridge, 1982), p. 43.

books. Bibles and copies of the Book of Common Prayer also took up a substantial amount of production. In general, it appears that there was a rough 50:50 split between sacred and secular output, and within the group of religious titles, there was an audience for a diverse set of works both scholarly and popular.

Compare this with the same data displayed according to the classificatory system employed by contemporary booksellers in their catalogues (see Fig. 2). Again, divinity and copies of the Bible make up about half the output. However, the seventeenth-century knowledge system significantly shifts the balance among secular titles. Histories, which to the booksellers includes not just Walter Ralegh's incomplete *History of the World* from creation to the present or the various English Chronicles but also Samuel Purchas's enormous *Purchas His Pilgrimage* travel narrative and numerous multi-volume prose romances, doubles to 13 per cent of output. What we would call literature – poetry and plays – drops to just 3 per cent. Even more revealing, only 8 per cent of the London production is in a foreign language, underscoring the importance of titles imported from the continent.

Now contrast the above distribution with that which classifies the printing house output according to the public-private, or scholastic-secular system (see Figs. 3 and 4). Two points become clear immediately. First, the scholastic/secular production figures are imbalanced, with a quarter of the production dedicated to the former and three-quarters to the latter. As well, in the scholastic category, theological titles dominate, with a significant amount of grammar publishing as well. Such an overwhelming preference for theological titles reflects the contemporary curriculum of the institutions served by the trade. On the secular side, histories are still quite popular, as are works of popular theology. Separating the market into these two groupings helps clarify the markedly different demands of the respective readers. Scholastic audiences required a specific set of reference works, while the urban book buyers of London, York, and other English cities and towns desired a much more diverse set of titles.

The above figures demonstrate how different classification systems produce distinctive portraits of the larger market forces at work in the mid-Jacobean book trade; we can also learn a great deal about the personal dynamics of the business by using the same subject groupings to reveal who were the most active printers and what types of works they tended to produce. Looking at the most active printers in the same 1614–18 period (those whose production rate was at least 300 edition sheets per year) from the perspective of the Modern Classification system, we can see the effect that patents have on certain printers.

Examining Table 1 we see that Adam Islip's dominance of Law and Political printing reflects the exclusive rights he acquired from the Stationers' Company in 1605 to print law books, while the large amount of religious printing coming out of the King's Printing House attests to their monopoly on the printing of large- and small-format Bibles. Comparing classes of books, it is apparent that some printers dominate a field (William Stansby and history titles) while other areas are wide open (information and literary publishing). If we break down religious publishing into sub-categories, similar trends emerge.

Table 2 indicates that Edward Griffin clearly has strong business ties with publishers of a wide variety of religious subjects, as do to lesser degrees Thomas Snodham, Humphrey Lownes, and Richard Field. Other printers show a more eclectic distribution of religious output, and three classes of works – controversial, devotional, and sermons – are quite distinctly divided into those who do and those who do not print books of those subjects.

Compare the above distribution tables with one displaying the same printer output by the second Bookseller Classification as displayed in Table 3. Here the dominance of individual printers in some areas remains – Stansby and history, Griffin and divinity – while new and different leaders begin to emerge. John Legat, for example, displays strong links with publishers of 'physick' texts, and Islip, who before seemed to specialize in patented law titles, now also reveal a link in mathematics publishing. We can also see more complex pictures of the productive houses in the large amount of foreign-language titles coming from Griffin and the mathematics production of Stansby.

Finally, employing the Scholastic-Secular system (see Tables 4 and 5) rounds out the view of the printing trade. Two heretofore invisible areas of publishing, grammar and natural science, emerge as quite popular topics. Even more intriguing is the split between scholarly and popular theology. The modern and bookseller classification systems did not differentiate between these two groups, while the third system shows definite preferences among different stationers. Griffin, the leading non-patent printer of religious materials, emerges as primarily involved in scholastic theology, while Snodham deals for the most part in popular works, and other productive houses such as those run by Stansby and Felix Kingston show a balance between the two theological groupings.

Given the relatively small data population upon which the above observations are based, we quickly reach the limits of analytical significance and trustworthiness. However, the main purpose of this exercise was to test the usefulness of the EEBD provisional tripartite classification system. Even using this trial dataset we can see how grouping production according to multiple knowledge structures illuminates trends and tendencies in ways that a single-concept system does not. As the project proceeds, we anticipate augmenting and fine-tuning the subject groupings to expand possible avenues of inquiry and increase the level of sophistication of the results. Our goal is to complete the project within the next three years, and we hope to make the database and its analytical tool freely available to all scholars by the fall of 2007. Until then, we are maintaining a Web site where interested teachers and scholars can monitor our progress.[25]

---

25 'Early English Book Trade Database website', <http://purl.oclc.org/EEBD>

Table 1: Leading Printer House Output by Modern Classification

Establishment	Edition Sheets	Info	Eph.	Hist.	Law/Pol.	Lit	Official Docs	Rel
King's Printing House	6070	97	22	4	748	150	342	4707
Edward Griffin	3808	389	29	213	25	443	4	2705
Adam Islip	3752	572	--	314	2551	56	1	258
William Stansby	3581	284	24	1239	7	1015	11	1001
Thomas Snodham	2151	296	9	16	6	618	5	1201
John Legat	1970	682	--	76	--	145	4	1063
Felix Kingston	1829	118	34	--	--	142	12	1523
Humphrey Lownes	1807	178	20	--	--	314	--	1295
John Beale	1673	132	16	5	536	379	--	600
Nicholas Okes	1589	181	23	139	56	488	1	701
Richard Field	1551	241	--	210	--	310	1	789

Table 2: Leading Printer House Output by Modern Classification--Religion

Establishment	Bibles	Bk. Com. Prayer	Comment	Controversy	Devotion	Instruction	Sermon
King's Printing House	2897	700	228	740	--	68	74
Edward Griffin	14	--	1015	469	137	508	562
Adam Islip	246	--	--	6	--	--	6
William Stansby	--	--	315	277	51	127	231
Thomas Snodham	42	--	179	50	296	349	285
John Legat	--	--	587	--	21	428	27
Felix Kingston	78	--	511	72	78	476	308
Humphrey Lownes	77	--	481	145	262	173	156
John Beale	19	--	110	44	214	150	63
Nicholas Okes	4	--	124	49	151	141	232
Richard Field	40	--	202	244	100	116	87

Establishment	Divinity	Bible	Physick	Hist.	Human.	Poet/Plays	Math	For. Lang.	Law	Misc
King's Printing House	288	3526	1	4	217	--	--	1134	531	370
Edward Griffin	2563	14	50	270	335	56	15	474	--	33
Adam Islip	6	246	--	370	521	--	171	39	2398	1
William Stansby	990	--	98	1542	74	385	114	337	--	42
Thomas Snodham	1150	42	20	276	234	227	72	111	--	20
John Legat	1063	--	250	76	326	83	6	164	--	4
Felix Kingston	1445	78	--	15	55	11	29	152	--	46
Humphrey Lownes	1218	77	9	11	55	243	--	100	--	20
John Beale	576	14	--	277	130	53	52	26	--	44
Nicholas Okes	697	--	7	299	132	282	67	10	--	48
Richard Field	718	40	63	290	65	83	21	272	--	1

Table 3: Leading Printer House Output by Bookseller Classification

Establishment	Total	Gram.	Rhet.	Logic	Arith.	Geom.	Music	Astron.	Philos.	Theol.
King's Printing House	1088	33	--	8	--	--	--	--	--	968
Edward Griffin	1739	199	--	--	--	--	--	--	56	1484
Adam Islip	166	160	--	--	--	--	--	--	--	6
William Stansby	723	59	5	36	37	--	30	--	7	592
Thomas Snodham	324	12	--	--	--	--	42	--	--	229
John Legat	994	407	--	--	25	--	--	--	52	587
Felix Kingston	688	30	--	--	--	--	--	--	--	583
Humphrey Lownes	806	143	--	--	--	--	--	--	38	626
John Beale	199	--	--	--	45	--	--	--	--	154
Nicholas Okes	193	3	--	--	17	--	--	--	--	173
Richard Field	686	141	--	--	9	12	--	--	78	1

Table 4: Leading Printer House Output by Scholastic Classification

Establishment	Total	Law	Nat. Sci.	Belle Lettres	Comm.	History	Pop. Theol.	Bible	Misc.
King's Printing House	5062	531	2	60	10	8	142	3597	712
Edward Griffin	2070	--	176	73	--	293	1207	14	308
Adam Islip	3586	2431	197	--	44	370	6	246	292
William Stansby	2858	--	159	360	30	1788	409	--	113
Thomas Snodham	1827	--	175	186	68	363	930	42	64
John Legat	976	--	270	105	--	76	476	--	50
Felix Kingston	1141	--	24	72	37	15	862	78	54
Humphrey Lownes	1001	--	25	243	11	15	592	77	43
John Beale	1474	500	84	65	3	11	427	19	100
Nicholas Okes	1397	--	133	282	29	277	524	4	126
Richard Field	866	--	63	135	17	290	302	40	19

Table 5: Leading Printer House Output by Secular Classification

Index

References to illustrations are in *italic*